A Study in Monetary Macroeconomics

A Study in Monetary Macroeconomics

STEFAN HOMBURG

OXFORD
UNIVERSITY PRESS

OXFORD
UNIVERSITY PRESS

Great Clarendon Street, Oxford, OX2 6DP,
United Kingdom

Oxford University Press is a department of the University of Oxford.
It furthers the University's objective of excellence in research, scholarship,
and education by publishing worldwide. Oxford is a registered trade mark of
Oxford University Press in the UK and in certain other countries

First Edition published in 2017

Impression: 2

Published in the United States of America by Oxford University Press
198 Madison Avenue, New York, NY 10016, United States of America

British Library Cataloguing in Publication Data
Data available

Library of Congress Control Number: 2017931042

ISBN 978–0–19–880753–7

Printed and bound by
CPI Group (UK) Ltd, Croydon, CR0 4YY

Contents

List of Figures and Tables

Figures

Table

Key Symbols

A – financial assets
α – capital income share
B – bond stock
β – time preference parameter
C – private consumption
cr – currency-to-deposit ratio
D – bank deposits
D^g – real public debt
δ – depreciation rate
E – net worth
η – interest elasticity of money demand
F – borrowed funds
φ – price or wage adjustment speed
G – public consumption
I – investment
i – nominal interest rate
J – deposit cost
K – physical capital stock
L – land stock
λ – learning parameter
ltv – loan-to-value ratio
M – money stock
μ – money preference
N – working hours
P – price level
π – rate of inflation
Π – profit
Q – nominal land price
q – real land price
r – real interest rate
rr – required reserve ratio
ρ – land income share
R – bank reserves
σ – seigniorage
T – tax revenue
t – time
θ – output parameter
W – nominal wage rate
w – real wage rate
X – nonfinancial income
Y – output (GDP)
Z – dividends

Chapter 1
Introduction

The present monograph was motivated by the Great Recession, which hit the global economy in 2008–09. This remarkable event, unparalleled in the postwar era, raised two issues. The first, positive in nature, was whether one should be concerned about the future of capitalism. This question is vital not only for policymakers and wealth managers but also for everyone with a genuine interest in macroeconomics and political economy. The second point, a normative one, regarded the usefulness of unprecedented monetary and fiscal actions that were initiated during the crisis and lasted for years. When the recession set in, not a single leading macro article suggested that modern economies were in need of large and persistent doses of external stimuli—a medicine so strong that in some cases it triggered sovereign defaults. Quite the contrary, the prevailing paradigm held that monetary and fiscal policies were either ineffective or that their effectiveness was due to temporary frictions and limited to short time spans.

The tension between macro theories on the one hand and the practical actions taken on the other gave rise to a paradoxical situation. Without much recourse to mainstream thinking, policy debates were dominated by outdated models that would not find their way into scholarly journals. At the same time, macroeconomic doctrines became heavily criticized as intellectual games unsuited for grasping the real world and being largely useless for policy analysis. Current research uses dynamic general equilibrium (DGE) models. This approach disciplines theoretical reasoning: it requires the theorist to write down fully specified models that respect budget constraints and are consistent with intertemporal decision-making. Understood in this methodical sense, the DGE approach constitutes a fundamental step in the advancement of macroeconomics. No one who reads the earlier literature would seriously wish to return to static models based on ad hoc assumptions, presented as impenetrable graphs, and often violating stock-flow consistency.

However, the state of macroeconomics is definitely not good. Although it rests on DGE as a sound basis, the leading approach comes with further assumptions that are neither suggested by theoretical considerations, nor supported by evidence—nor even dictated by the DGE method itself. The most significant additional assumption, which penetrates virtually all macroeconomic reasoning, is the rational expectations (RE) hypothesis. This premise puts a straitjacket on macroeconomic research. For manageability, assuming RE suggests using sparse models and constrains the analysis to steady states and their neighborhoods. The latter limitation is particularly severe, but it was readily accepted during the Great Moderation of 1987–2007. In retrospect, RE models with scant volatility and a lack of endogenous persistence will perhaps be considered as the economics of the Great Moderation. Merely criticizing this strand is pointless, however, because *scientia horror vacui*—it takes a model to beat a model. While books that are highly critical of current macroeconomic research abound, this one aims at improvement.

The study sympathizes with Leijonhufvud's (1993) quest for a "not too rational macroeconomics" and with the approach outlined in Colander et al. (2008). Its distinctive features are clean models with a rich institutional structure encompassing credit money, external finance, borrowing constraints, net worth, real estate, and commercial banks. While such features have of course been accounted for in the literature, they do not play an essential role because the dynamics of RE models result mainly from stochastic processes whose autoregressive components govern the adjustments. Put in terms of a cost-benefit calculation, the approach offered here reduces rationality requirements in exchange for truly dynamic models that produce volatility, persistence, and propagation endogenously. During the Great Moderation, Christiano et al. (2005), as well as Smets and Wouters (2007), demonstrated that RE models equipped with many unobservable exogenous shocks produce nice in-sample fits. However, these models failed spectacularly in accounting for the Great Recession. Later research, for example by Slobodyan and Wouters (2012), showed that replacing RE with learning algorithms yields better fits. The approach followed here reduces individual information sets still further and assumes that expectations are formed from past and present observations. This modeling strategy does not at all contradict individual rationality. It is simply more modest and concedes that a universally agreed macro model from which RE equilibrium paths could be derived is not available.

Written for economists at universities, governments, and financial institutions, this book addresses an international audience. Owing to its broad scope and a balanced treatment, the text should be useful for teaching postgraduate and advanced graduate courses. However, the study is not only a survey but an exposition of new ideas. Its main objective lies in shifting the focus of macroeconomic research from analytical pyrotechnics to questions of actual economic interest. The outcome of this endeavor is not considered as the final word but as the opening of an alternative research route that narrows the gap between academic work and the concerns of policymakers and practitioners.

Starting with a simple baseline model, the text develops a comprehensive theory in a unified framework that covers almost everything of interest for monetary macroeconomics. Results are obtained from mathematical reasoning and simulations. In a sense, the text continues the venerable literature with its stronger emphasis on substantive questions. Of course, the earlier writers argued with regard to a different institutional setting and they often lacked a coherent framework; after all, it took over 200 years for economists to come to grips with DGE models. The intention here is to discuss macroeconomic issues in a timely fashion but also to maintain the focus on institutions, data, and economic relevance rather than on sterile techniques.

Chapter 2 sets out the basic framework. It considers an economy evolving indefinitely in discrete time, with producers, consumers, and a central bank as principal actors. Individuals plan over finite horizons and form expectations according to what they see. Money is conceived of as a commodity that is produced through credit creation rather than distributed by a fancy helicopter. This natural way to represent money is rarely followed in the literature and differs sharply from the usual helicopter drops because it ties money creation to credit creation. The chapter's upshot is a system of simultaneous equations determining prices, wages, and the nominal interest rate. Using this solution, individuals revise their expectations, and the economy proceeds to the next period. The chapter concludes with functional and numerical specifications for later simulations whose purpose is to analyze key economic processes and to derive meaningful results. As the numbers of variables and parameters are kept as low as possible, the simulations do not aim at yielding optimal ex post fits. Rather, the unassuming aim is to reproduce the stylized facts of macroeconomic fluctuations and trends.

Chapter 3 covers traditional topics of monetary macroeconomics. To acquaint readers with the present methods, it starts with conversant material such as superneutrality of money, the Tobin effect, and forced saving. A larger section is devoted to interactions between monetary and fiscal policies. This passage simulates the macroeconomic consequences of sovereign insolvencies and contains a comparison of Ricardian and non-Ricardian economies, a distinction that is crucial for policy analysis. Two closing sections pertain to price and wage rigidities. They emphasize that monetary policies have real effects in the presence of nominal frictions. According to the view sponsored here, models with sticky wages and prices do not compete with flexible price settings but rather complement them in that they shift attention to the short run. They also enhance model stability. The entire chapter can be considered as a preparation for the subsequent analysis, which extend the model's scope in an attempt to deal with the extraordinary events of the past years.

Chapter 4 considers economies with borrowing constraints. This assumption is motivated by the observation that monetary expansions after the Great Recession did not entail inflation in the expected manner. At the same time, nominal and real interest rates tended to decline in many advanced economies. The text offers an in-depth analysis of credit crunches, liquidity traps, and interest rates at the zero lower bound and demonstrates that borrowing constraints help reconcile theory and evidence. According to the key insight, a binding borrowing constraint detaches money creation from credit creation. Following this line of reasoning resolves empirical puzzles associated with the aftermath of the recession and facilitates a thorough analysis of unconventional monetary policies such as quantitative easing and forward guidance. Using global data on the weighted average cost of capital (WACC), the chapter also disputes the secular stagnation hypothesis, which holds that declines in interest rates reflect corresponding reductions in marginal capital productivities.

Chapter 5 focuses on producers' net worth. It joins a large strand rooted in the financial literature, which points out that under asymmetric information, producers need own equity to obtain credit. Incorporating this assumption yields scenarios with endogenous borrowing limits and shows that small variations in credit requirements have large macroeconomic consequences. A second theme concerns an unresolved problem of general equilibrium models. These determine equilibrium prices from decisions of producers and consumers who are ostensibly aware only of market prices and their own characteristics (i.e., technologies and preferences). However, consumers must also know current profits because these enter their budget constraints. As profits are determined in equilibrium, a logical circle emerges. Stock manias can be interpreted as situations where consumers overestimate profits; conversely, stock market crashes may reflect underestimations of profits. The text shows that misguided profit expectations as such do not have the expected impacts on economic activity. Changes in profit expectations affect macroeconomic variables only if they also influence credit availability. This finding reaffirms a key result from Chapter 4, according to which economic activity is driven by credit rather than money.

Chapter 6 turns to real estate as a neglected feature of actual economies. It begins with an empirical overview demonstrating the preeminent role of land as a part of nonfinancial wealth. Whereas many macroeconomic models represent nonfinancial wealth by a symbol K that is interpreted as machines and equipment (if not robots), the text makes clear that such items are of minor quantitative importance. In contemporary economies, nonfinancial wealth consists chiefly of real estate, that is, land and buildings. This is the reason so many analysts conjecture a link between house prices and the Great Recession. Changes in house prices, which are primarily changes in land prices, operate on the economy through their influence on nonfinancial wealth. Nonfinancial wealth affects consumption directly and investment indirectly since it relaxes or tightens borrowing constraints. Building on the results obtained in the previous chapters, the text studies housing manias and leverage cycles and relates its main findings to United States data. Two further topics discussed in this chapter regard the role of land as a long-run stabilizer that prevents capital overaccumulation, and an interesting feature of economies with land, referred to as quasi-Ricardian equivalence: public debt tends to crowd out private debt even if individuals are short-sighted.

Chapter 7 introduces commercial banks as creators of money and integrates them into the general equilibrium framework. The motivation to deviate from the standard approach that neglects commercial banks and entrusts all money creation to a central bank is twofold. First, apart from currency, central banks do not provide money directly but rather supply reserves that enable banks to create deposits. After the Great Recession, this transmission process staggered: increases in reserves outpaced increases in deposits. Any analysis of the monetary expansions starting in 2008 would remain incomplete and unsatisfactory unless it took account of this fact. Second, central banks normally control an overnight interbank interest rate that differs from the market interest rate on bonds. Considering an interbank market and its relationship with the bond market makes it possible to derive a term structure of interest rates. This is important because inverse term structures are good predictors for recessions. Compared with the preceding chapters, the material presented in Chapter 7 is less mature because macro models with commercial banks are uncommon. However, the findings appeared interesting enough to merit inclusion, and at best they may stimulate further advances in this under-researched area.

Chapter 8 concludes with remarks on methods. It defends key assumptions made in the main text and compares them, to the extent they deviate, with more conventional premises. A number of appendices follow that contain technical material and proofs. Appendix K provides MATLAB sample codes to make transparent the way in which the simulations were conducted.

Chapter 2

Framework

This chapter outlines the baseline framework. The exposition is kept brief and does not put every premise immediately into question. Rather, the text proceeds step by step and discusses some really restrictive assumptions only later, when they are relaxed.

The model envisages a closed economy that evolves indefinitely in discrete periods, each period indexed by $t = 1, 2, \ldots$ Variables with index t regard the present, when economic decisions are made. Variables with index $t–1$ are historically given; they are referred to as *predetermined*. Finally, variables with index $t+1$ point to the future and represent subjective uniform point expectations. For instance, the symbol P_t denotes the current price level. The preceding price level, P_{t-1}, is predetermined, a historical fact. And the future price level, P^e_{t+1}, represents a subjective expectation, where the superscript "e" prevents confusion with the actual price level prevailing one period ahead.

2.1 General Structure

Commodities

The variety of goods and services is represented by a single all-purpose commodity. This assumption characterizes most macroeconomic research and is certainly strong. Regarding monetary phenomena such as inflation, the premise is sometimes defended on the grounds that in a parallel universe—which resembles ours but actually consists of one-sector economies—nominal aggregates would presumably follow the same rules. With respect to real quantities, however, more reservation seems advisable because one-sector models rule out structural issues. For instance, if residential construction collapses after a housing boom, the model suggests idle resources that do not really exist; the capital stock in construction has become partly obsolete, and new capital must be formed in other sectors.

Output in period t is written as Y_t and represents real gross domestic product, GDP. The output is measured in commodity units per period and is used for private consumption, C_t, and gross investment, I_t. The baseline model lacks a public sector that will be added later. Recalling the timing convention mentioned above, the capital stock, K_t, is formed in period t and is used in period $t+1$. With δ denoting the depreciation rate, the capital stock evolves according to the following law of motion:

(1) $$K_t = I_t + (1-\delta)K_{t-1}.$$

Hence, the difference $I_t - \delta K_{t-1}$ gives net investment, and $Y_t - \delta K_{t-1}$ represents national income. Demand and supply in the commodity market determine the price level, P_t, measured in money units per commodity unit. The relative change in the price level is referred to as the *rate of inflation*:

$$\pi_t = \frac{P_t - P_{t-1}}{P_{t-1}} \quad \text{or} \quad \frac{P_t}{P_{t-1}} = 1 + \pi_t \ . \tag{2}$$

Current inflation, π_t, depends on the current price level, P_t, and the price level that prevailed in the preceding period, P_{t-1}.

Credit

In reality, corporations finance investment by credit and own equity. Credit comes in the form of bonds or loans, while own equity mainly takes the form of shares and retained profit. At the present level of abstraction, all of these types of financing are equivalent and there is no need to distinguish between them. Instead, investment is assumed to be entirely financed by bonds. Actual corporations are also the principal owners of nonfinancial assets (capital goods), owner-occupied housing being an important exception. These physical capital goods make up the asset side of the corporations' consolidated balance sheet, while corporate liabilities are held by households as the ultimate, but indirect, capital owners. The present model resembles this pattern that can be found in the national accounts: Producers finance capital goods by issuing bonds that are acquired by consumers.

Such a modeling strategy brings external finance and credit into the model and deviates from the usual framework where consumers hold capital goods outright and only acquire government bonds. In modern economies, corporate assets and liabilities dominate public debt by far: Typical capital–output ratios are approximately 200–300 percent and land–output ratios are of the same order of magnitude. By contrast, in most countries public debt falls short of 100 percent of output. The nominal value of bonds is denoted as B_t. Bonds issued in period t are redeemed and pay interest in period t+1. With the nominal interest rate, i_t, fixed in advance, a bond owner who invests \$1 in period t can assume to get back $\$(1 + i_t)$ in the next period. The bond market determines the nominal interest rate.

Perhaps it should be emphasized at this early stage that the nominal interest rate is conceived of as a market rate and not as a policy instrument. During the last few decades, the symbol "*i*" that appears in almost any macro text has undergone a remarkable transformation from a market price to an overnight policy rate under perfect control of the central bank. By contrast, the nominal interest rate is seen here as determined by market forces in general and expectations in particular.

Labor
A homogeneous type of labor is assumed that belongs to consumers' initial endowments and is employed by producers. The employment level, N_t, is measured in hours; the nominal wage rate, W_t, is measured in money units per hour. If wages are flexible, employment equals $\bar{N}$, an exogenous number referred to as the *natural employment level.* In the presence of price and wage rigidities, employment will generally deviate from its natural level, and unemployment can arise. Section 8.4 discusses the significance of the assumption of an exogenous labor supply.

Money
Money is modeled here as a financial asset that serves as a unit of account and bears no interest. This definition is strictly true for currency (notes and coins) and approximately true for transfer and checking accounts. Consumers use money for transaction purposes and as a store of value. In this sense, there exists a money demand that is denoted as M_t^d and understood as the *stock* of money balances consumers wish to hold at the end of the period. The stock of money balances must not be confounded with money *flows* that represent income or expenditure. Money stocks and money flows are loosely connected through the circular velocity of money, which is endogenous and volatile; cf. Laidler (1993) for a profound overview.

The text consistently avoids the terms "money market" and "money supply". While commodity markets, labor markets, and credit markets have institutional counterparts, in reality, there is no such thing as a money market (except in the language of practitioners, where it designates a short term credit market). Money is not traded in a separate market that determines its price. Rather, it is traded in *all* markets and mirrors the respective sales and purchases.

Moreover, while agents do supply commodities in actual markets, no one supplies money in the same sense of the term. In our age, money is created by banks and central banks as a by-product of credit. This suggests that the fixation on gold and commodity money in general, which has dominated macroeconomics for centuries, is no longer appropriate. Using the term "money stock" rather than "money supply" may be a matter of personal preference, but the replacement of commodity money by credit money is substantive and a core feature of the present framework. The process of money creation will be outlined in section 2.3.

2.2 Expectations

Expectation formation is crucial for rational intertemporal choice. If individuals were familiar with the true economic model, its parameters, and the nature of the stochastic processes driving its evolution, they would compute mathematical expected values. However, these overly strong informational assumptions, which constitute the heart of RE (rational expectations) analysis, are avoided here. The question of how individuals form expectations if the true economic model is unknown has a long tradition that goes back to Irving Fisher. According to this tradition, expectations result from prior beliefs reflecting long-term experience, and from current observations. If observations disprove prior beliefs—an occurrence known as cognitive dissonance in psychology—the latter are corrected to some extent.

Phillip Cagan (1956) was the first to analyze such a learning process formally, for which Mark Nerlove (1958) coined the term *adaptive expectations.* In the present context, an important application of adaptive expectations regards inflation:

(3) $$\pi_{t+1}^{e} = \pi_{t}^{e} + \lambda(\pi_{t} - \pi_{t}^{e}).$$

Expected inflation is defined as $\pi_{t+1}^{e} = (P_{t+1}^{e} - P_{t}) / P_{t}$, which parallels definition (2). It depends on the prior belief, π_{t}^{e}, and a fraction of the latter's divergence from actual inflation, π_{t}. The learning parameter $\lambda \in [0;1]$ measures the pace of the learning process. In the boundary case, $\lambda = 0$, individuals stick to their prior beliefs irrespective of what they see. In the opposite case, $\lambda = 1$, known as static expectations, individuals disregard past experience and expect current inflation to persist.

As in an RE setting, individuals use all available information. However, their information sets contain only present and past observations, and these are used to form subjective instead of mathematical expectations. Adaptive expectations make models self-referential in the sense that beliefs affect economic outcomes, which in turn affect beliefs. For instance, expected inflation influences present choices; these choices affect equilibrium prices; and the latter enter expectation formation, (3), through π_{t}.

Combined with the nominal interest rate, inflation expectations determine the expected real interest rate, r_{t+1}^{e}, which was first defined by Irving Fisher (1896):

(4) $$1 + r_{t+1}^{e} = \frac{1 + i_{t}}{1 + \pi_{t+1}^{e}}.$$

This so-called *Fisher equation* states that the expected real interest factor (one plus the real interest rate) equals the ratio of the nominal interest factor and the expected inflation factor. Unlike the nominal rate, the real interest rate is an expected variable because it depends on expected inflation. It is often written as $r_{t+1}^{e} = i_{t} - \pi_{t+1}^{e}$, the difference of the nominal interest rate and the expected inflation rate. Such an approximation deviates from the exact formula by a second-order term and works well in an environment with low inflation.

2.3 Central Bank

The baseline framework contains a one-stage banking system, an assumption common to almost all macroeconomic research. Two-stage banking systems, consisting of a central bank and many commercial banks, will be introduced in Chapter 7. Central bank activities are characterized by a balance sheet and an income statement:

$$(5) \qquad B_t^{cb} = M_t \quad \text{and} \quad \sigma_t = i_t B_t^{cb}.$$

The balance sheet on the left-hand side depicts the process of money creation: By acquiring bonds of amount B_t^{cb}, the central bank automatically creates an equal quantity of fiat money, $M_t \geq 0$. Consumers maintain transfer accounts at the central bank, and if the central bank buys a bond, it simply credits the respective account. After money has thus been created with a pen stroke, the recipient can use the resulting balance to make payments to others. Because bonds represent credit, credit creation and money creation coincide in this baseline framework.

According to the income statement on the right-hand side, central banks make a profit, σ_t, known as *seigniorage*, due to bonds being interest-bearing, while money bears no interest. Seigniorage is the value of bonds held outright times the nominal interest rate. The seigniorage is not retained but distributed at the start of the next period. For instance, if the central bank wishes to keep the money stock constant, it buys a constant amount of bonds in each period, collects the interest, and distributes the resulting seigniorage to the consumers. A back-of-the-envelope calculation shows that seigniorage is small: With a circular velocity of money, *PY*/*M*, of roughly 4 and a nominal interest rate of 5 percent, seigniorage comes to 1.25 percent of nominal GDP. In reality, this value is distorted by accounting conventions and diminished by considerable administrative costs.

The preceding description of central bank activities appears natural but diverges from the usual treatment. Since the 1990s, most macro models represent central bank activities by the scalar "*i*". They consider this variable as a policy instrument under perfect control of the central bank, but also as the principal determinant of private lending and borrowing. This misspecifies individual decision-making. Following Bernanke et al. (2004: 8), "the *short-term* policy rate has little direct effect on private sector borrowing and investment decisions. Rather, those decisions respond most sensitively to *longer-term* yields (such as the yields on mortgages and corporate bonds)". Figure 2.1 suggests that identifying short-term and long-term rates is empirically critical.

Immediately after the collapse of Lehman Brothers in autumn 2008, the federal funds rate fell to nearly zero. Figure 2.1 shows that this drastic variation had no immediate influence on long-term rates: The AAA corporate bonds rate, an interest attainable only for a few corporations with the top rating, remained largely unchanged during 2008. The same is true for the conventional mortgage rate, relevant for home buyers, and the yield of government bonds with a maturity of ten years. Naturally, the shorter the maturity of a credit contract, the closer its relationship with the federal funds rate. Nevertheless, this rate is typically irrelevant for savers and investors who have no access to central bank credit and who adapt their intertemporal choices to long-term rates. To cope with this serious problem, two strategies are employed. For the time being, the text treats the nominal interest rate as a medium-term market rate over which the central bank has no direct control. Later on, in Chapter 7, the model is augmented by a short-term target rate set by the central bank. Only this extension, which is quite uncommon in macroeconomics, enables a more realistic representation of actual monetary policies.

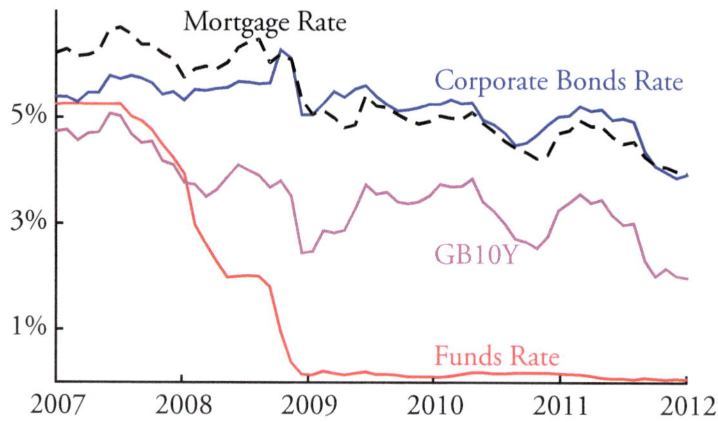

Figure 2.1: Short-term versus long-term rates. *Notes*: Monthly data, retrieved November 2015 from <https://fred.stlouisfed.org>, series FEDFUNDS, AAA, MORTGAGE30US, and WGS10YR.

A further notable departure from the mainstream concerns the specification of seigniorage: To the extent that macro models indeed include money, they define seigniorage as the total increase in the money stock, $M_t - M_{t-1}$, and assume that all newly created money is immediately distributed via the proverbial helicopter. By contrast, the present model defines seigniorage as $i_t M_t$. Especially in recent times, when the world recognized enormous jumps in central bank balance sheets due to "quantitative easing", the discrepancy between helicopter money on the one hand and credit money on the other is striking. In 2012, for instance, the balance sheet of the United States Federal Reserve System increased by $1,028 billion. In the standard framework, the Fed had immediately distributed this very amount to the public. But this is not what actually happened. Because the Federal Reserve Act prohibits helicopter distributions and prescribes seigniorage to be calculated in the spirit of (5), the Fed's remittances to the treasury accounted for only $88 billion in 2012, which amounts to only 8 percent of the increase in its balance sheet.

2.4 Producers

Assuming a unit continuum of identical producers, individual and aggregate variables can be denoted by the same symbols. Producers choose labor and capital inputs to produce output. They take market prices as given and solve two independent optimization problems in each period. The first problem, which is static, involves selecting commodity supply, Y_t^s, and labor demand, N_t^d, to maximize economic profit

(6) $$\Pi_t = P_t Y_t^s + (P_t - P_{t-1})K_{t-1}^d - \delta P_t K_{t-1}^d - W_t N_t^d - i_{t-1} B_{t-1}^s .$$

Economic profit consists of revenue from sales plus revaluation of the capital stock, K_{t-1}^d, minus current cost depreciation, wages, and interest. Interest cost is the product of the former nominal interest rate and the previously issued bonds, B_{t-1}^s. In period *t*, all variables except commodity supply and labor demand are given for producers. These two choice variables are connected through a production function that relates current labor demand and the predetermined capital stock to current output:

(7) $$Y_t = F(N_t, K_{t-1}).$$

According to the standard first-order condition, the marginal productivity of labor equals the real wage rate in a profit maximum:

(8) $$\frac{\partial F}{\partial N_t^d} = \frac{W_t}{P_t}.$$

The second optimization problem is dynamic and independent of the first. It involves determining investment and financing in order to maximize expected profit:

(9) $$\Pi_{t+1}^e = P_{t+1}^e Y_{t+1}^s + (P_{t+1}^e - P_t)K_t^d - \delta P_{t+1}^e K_t^d - W_{t+1}^e N_{t+1}^d - i_t B_t^s .$$

Maximization takes place subject to the above production function (where time indices must be shifted one period forward) and subject to the following *balance sheet*:

(10) $$P_t K_t^d = B_t^s .$$

The balance sheet represents a financing constraint that requires producers to finance the capital stock by issuing bonds, which are redeemed and pay interest one period later. Appendix A derives the first-order condition

(11) $$\frac{\partial F}{\partial K_t^d} = r_{t+1}^e + \delta ,$$

according to which the marginal productivity of capital equals the *user cost of capital*. The user cost of capital is the sum of the expected real interest rate, r_{t+1}^e, and the depreciation rate, δ, reflecting that producers must both finance investment and bear depreciation. In models where consumers own and rent out capital goods to producers, the user cost of capital is also known as capital's "real rental". But here, producers themselves own the physical capital goods and need credit from consumers to finance them.

Once the optimal capital stock has been determined, investment demand follows mechanically from (1). Equation (11) shows that capital and investment depend on the expected real interest rate and on expected employment. If employment always coincides with its natural level, $\bar{N}$, one can safely use this level as an expectation. In models with employment variations, however, this issue will need reconsideration.

If the production function is linear homogeneous, smooth, strictly increasing, and strictly quasi-concave, the optimization problems have unique solutions that are interior if the Inada conditions (see appendix A) are also satisfied. Under these assumptions, factor rewards exhaust revenue and profits vanish in equilibrium. This adding-up theorem holds for expected profits, (9), but not necessarily for the static profits defined in (6), which can take positive or negative values outside steady states. Non-zero profits are remitted to consumers, as shown section 2.5.

2.5 Consumers

Each of a unit continuum of consumers takes market prices as given. Assuming identical homothetic utility functions, consumers operate in accordance with the following aggregate budget constraint:

$$(12) \qquad P_t C_t + B_t^d + M_t^d = (1+i_{t-1})B_{t-1}^d + M_{t-1}^d + \sigma_{t-1} + W_t N_t + \Pi_t .$$

The left-hand side of the budget constraint includes the consumers' three controls. These are consumption demand, bond demand, and money demand. On the right-hand side one finds initial bond holdings (including interest), money holdings, seigniorage, wage income, and profits. To keep the model simple and to focus on first-order effects, consumers take wage income as given. Profits (which are zero in expectation) and seigniorage (which is small) enter the budget constraint to make the model consistent. The time index of the seigniorage equals the time index of the interest income; seigniorage and interest are both due at the end of the period and enter the initial endowment of the next period.

The five given items on the right-hand side of the budget constraint can be grouped into two categories, viz. financial assets on the one hand and nonfinancial income on the other. *Financial assets* and *nonfinancial income*, both expressed in units of present consumption, are henceforth denoted as

$$(13) \qquad A_t = \frac{(1+i_{t-1})B_{t-1}^d + M_{t-1}^d + \sigma_{t-1}}{P_t} \quad \text{and} \quad X_t = \frac{W_t N_t + \Pi_t}{P_t} .$$

The symbol A_t represents consumers' financial assets in real terms at the start of the period, including interest and seigniorage. These do not enter the model as a new variable but only as an abbreviation that simplifies the exposition.

Financial assets are inherited from the past and serve to finance present and future consumption. Nonfinancial income, X_t, consists of current wage and profit income. Subject to the budget constraint, (12), consumers maximize the utility function

$$U\left(C_t, A_{t+1}^e, \frac{M_t^d}{P_t}\right). \tag{14}$$

The first two arguments of the utility function depict a constrained choice between present and future consumption. Expected future consumption is not written as an infinite stream but is compressed into a single number, A_{t+1}^e, that represents expected future consumption possibilities and is defined in accordance with (13). Such a simplification of intertemporal choice makes it possible to obtain closed solutions without steady states assumptions, as discussed in section 8.2. Consumers do not care how they spend in periods t+99 and t+100 but only decide on the part of their means that they postpone for future consumption in general. Real balances enter the utility function as the third argument. This so-called money-in-the-utility (MIU) approach was introduced by Sidrauski (1967) and is widely used. It makes the model consistent with two empirical facts: First, consumers hold money willingly, though it bears no interest. Second, actual balances vary and exceed the amount necessary for transaction purposes. Section 8.3 compares the MIU approach with alternative assumptions.

Two optimality conditions emerge, which are derived in appendix B. According to the first, the intertemporal marginal rate of substitution is adjusted to the reciprocal of the expected real interest factor or, what amounts to the same thing, to the price of future in terms of present consumption:

$$\frac{\partial U / \partial A_{t+1}^e}{\partial U / \partial C_t} = \frac{1}{1 + r_{t+1}^e}. \tag{15}$$

The second optimality condition states that consumers equate their marginal rates of substitution between consumption and real balances to the *user cost of money*:

$$\frac{\partial U / \partial (M_t^d / P_t)}{\partial U / \partial C_t} = \frac{i_t}{1 + i_t}. \tag{16}$$

In a continuous-time setting, the user cost equals the nominal interest rate. With discrete time, it is somewhat lower, as the following thought experiment demonstrates: Raising nominal balances by one dollar requires a reduction in bond demand by $1/(1+i_t)$ dollars if the sum $(1+i_t)B_t^d + M_t^d + \sigma_t$, which represents future consumption, is to be kept constant. Hence, current consumption expenditure must be reduced by $1 - 1/(1+i_t)$, or $i/(1+i_t)$, dollars. Assuming utility functions to be smooth, strictly increasing, and strictly quasiconcave, the maximization program entails unique choices, and these are interior if the indifference surfaces are bounded away from the axes.

2.6 Temporary Equilibrium

The method of temporary equilibrium traces the evolution of an economy as a sequence in calendar time. Agents take state variables and prices as given, form expectations, and optimize. Their choices are equilibrated in a certain way, not necessarily by an auctioneer, and result in changes to the state variables which, in turn, determine future events. Since Hicks (1939), temporary equilibria have been widely used in macroeconomics, as documented in Grandmont's (2008) survey. Compared with general equilibrium models in the Arrow-Debreu tradition, temporary equilibrium models stress the unidirectional nature of time, the irreversibility of economic decisions, and the crucial importance of expectations.

Competitive equilibria are considered first. Subject to a given money stock, M_t, and the natural level of employment, $\bar{N}$, the state of the economy is fully determined by the initial stock K_{t-1}^d, the preceding prices P_{t-1} and i_{t-1}, and the former expected inflation rate, π_t^e. The remaining stocks follow from (5) and (10), the identity $B_{t-1}^d + B_{t-1}^{cb} \equiv B_{t-1}^s$, which states that all bonds issued in the past must have been acquired by someone, and the identity $M_{t-1}^d = M_{t-1}$.

In addition to exogenous and predetermined variables, the model contains three endogenous variables in each period: The price level, the nominal interest rate, and the nominal wage rate. Of course, output, the terminal stocks, and expected inflation are endogenous as well, but these are considered as functions. Now, a temporary equilibrium is a triple (P_t, i_t, W_t) such that market excess demands vanish and all private choices are individually optimal:

$$\text{(17)} \qquad \left.\begin{aligned} C_t + I_t &= Y_t^s \\ B_t^d + B_t^{cb} &= B_t^s \\ N_t^d &= \bar{N} \end{aligned}\right\} \Rightarrow (P_t, i_t, W_t).$$

While these equilibrium conditions form an interdependent system and determine prices jointly, it seems useful to point out the dynamics of price adjustment. An auctioneer (or a programmer who computes the temporary equilibrium) will change the price level in accordance with the excess demand in the commodity market. Similarly, the nominal interest rate is governed (inversely, in this case) by the excess demand in the bond market, and the nominal wage rate follows the excess demand in the labor market. With given initial state variables, and subject to a path of money stocks determined by the central bank, the model produces a sequence of temporary equilibria. In each period t, monetary policy may change and parameters may be affected by exogenous disturbances. Producers and consumers make plans only for the immediate future, period t+1. One period later, they realize what has happened and revise their choices accordingly.

The monetary model whose description is now complete can be seen as a formalization of the *loanable funds theory*, which was developed by Dennis

Robertson (1937) and Swedish economists notably Bertil Ohlin (1937). This theory successfully integrated credit into the monetary process and was widely accepted in the early postwar literature; see Hansen (1951), Tsiang (1956), or Patinkin (1958). However, the loanable funds approach never became part of the more rigorous models developed after the 1960s, which either represent money crudely in helicopter form or neglect it altogether. Today, the loanable funds theory has largely fallen into oblivion. Contrary to its original meaning, the term "loanable funds" is even used for theories that see interest as determined by saving and investment, without any regard to credit. The present framework does not make use of these commodity concepts. It is closer in spirit to Stiglitz and Greenwald's (2003) rediscovery of the loanable funds approach but does not focus exclusively on capital market imperfections.

The money stock, which equals central bank credit by definition, does not show up explicitly in the definition of a temporary equilibrium. It was omitted because the excess demands sum up to zero:

$$(18)\quad P_t(C_t + I_t - Y_t^s) + W_t(N_t^d - \bar{N}) + (B_t^d + B_t^{cb} - B_t^s) + (M_t^d - M_t) = 0\,.$$

Appendix C derives this equation, known as *Walras' law*, from the budget constraints. Since the derivation does not make use of equilibrium or optimum assumptions, Walras' law holds generally. Therefore, the three market clearing conditions in (17) imply that the existing money stock is held voluntarily.

Regardless of this automatism, money is a core ingredient of the model: Cashless economies satisfy an analogous version of Walras' law, with three rather than four summands. These models can only determine two of the three nominal variables considered here. Usually, cashless models leave the price level indeterminate and characterize inflation as the difference of nominal and real interest rates. From a monetary theory perspective, an approach that leaves nominal variables unexplained appears less attractive. It is also apt to produce paradoxes and problems in economic interpretation.

2.7 Setup for Simulations

Using simulations of the model and its extensions, the next chapters carve out the quantitative effects of policies and disturbances. To avoid unnecessary repetition, this section describes the functions employed in the simulations and their standard parameters. For producers, the text assumes a Cobb-Douglas production function

$$(19)\qquad F(N_t, K_{t-1}) = \theta_t N_t^{1-\alpha} K_{t-1}^{\alpha}$$

because this is easy to use and compatible with the empirical regularity that the functional income distribution between labor and capital shows no long-term trend. Thus α represents the capital income share and $1-\alpha$ the labor income share, where income is to be understood as gross income in both cases. Producers' demand and supply functions are derived in appendix A. The output parameter θ can be used to represent technological (or structural) shocks and to reflect long-term technological progress. Most of the analysis abstracts from growth and scales θ to one. The exponent α describing the functional income distribution is set to the familiar value of one-third. The rate of depreciation, δ, is set to 0.05.

Consumers' preferences are often described in terms of a logarithmic utility function with parameters β and μ, where β measures intertemporal preferences and μ measures the preference for money over bonds:

$$U = \ln C_t + \beta \ln A_{t+1}^e + \mu \ln \frac{M_t^d}{P_t}. \tag{20}$$

To describe consumers' optimizing behavior, it is convenient to define the (present value of) *real seigniorage*:

$$\sigma_t^r = \frac{\sigma_t}{(1+i_t)P_t} = \frac{i_t}{1+i_t}\frac{M_t}{P_t}. \tag{21}$$

As already noted, seigniorage is remitted to the consumers. This item does not appear on the right-hand side of the budget constraint because it is paid out only at the end of the period, as all interest income. However, consistent with definition (13), consumers regard seigniorage as part of their final financial assets, A_{t+1}^e, and take account of it during the optimization. Notably, seigniorage is not an expected variable as it only depends on the observable variables M_t, i_t, and P_t. Appendix B derives the following demand functions for the case of a logarithmic utility function:

$$C_t = \frac{A_t + X_t + \sigma_t^r}{1+\beta+\mu} \quad \text{and} \quad M_t^d = \mu \frac{P_t(A_t + X_t + \sigma_t^r)}{1+\beta+\mu}\frac{1+i_t}{i_t}. \tag{22}$$

Consumption and money demand are linear functions of consumers' *total wealth*, which consists of financial assets, nonfinancial income, and the real seigniorage. This definition of total wealth is reminiscent of Friedman's (1957) permanent income. It consists of a long-term component, financial assets, and a transitory component, nonfinancial income and seigniorage. Consumption and money demand are independent of the expected real interest rate because the substitution and income effects offset exactly. The implied zero interest elasticity of consumption (and saving) is consistent with most empirical findings; see Bernheim (2002) or Beznoska and Ochmann (2013). By contrast, money demand varies inversely with the user cost of money. Having obtained two of the three choice variables, the third one, bond demand, is inferred from the budget constraint, (12).

Logarithmic utility is a convenient functional form but has the drawback of an unreasonably high interest elasticity of money demand. Therefore, the text relies mostly on an alternative preference representation that consists of a Cobb-Douglas function nested within a CES function and is referred to as the *CDC utility function*:

$$(23)\quad U=\left[(1+\beta)\left(C_t^{\frac{1}{1+\beta}}(A_{t+1}^e)^{\frac{\beta}{1+\beta}}\right)^{\frac{1+\eta}{\eta}}+\mu^{-1/\eta}\left(\frac{M_t^d}{P_t}\right)^{\frac{1+\eta}{\eta}}\right]^{\frac{\eta}{1+\eta}},\quad \eta\leq 0.$$

In this expression, β and μ have the same meaning as above; they represent intertemporal preferences and the preference for money. The new parameter, η, equals the elasticity of money demand with respect to the user cost of money at constant consumption. To simplify, η is referred to as the *interest elasticity of money demand.* Setting $\eta=-1$ recovers the logarithmic utility. The CDC utility function is proposed because the associated demands are still linear in total wealth and are largely unresponsive to changes in the expected real interest rate, as shown in appendix B.

Standard references such as Mankiw and Summers (1986: 424), or Cooley and LeRoy (1981: 835) found values of –0.02 and –0.16, respectively, for the interest elasticity of M1 money demand. Berentsen et al. (2015: 224) took recent financial innovations into account and estimated an elasticity of –0.16 for post-1990 data. Here, an intermediate value of $\eta=-0.10$ is assumed. The money preference parameter μ is set to 0.08, implying a circular velocity, *PY*/*M*, of roughly four, a value that falls between the 2014 velocities of the United States (6.2) and the eurozone (1.8).

A reasonable steady state capital–output ratio of 3.3 is produced by selecting $\beta=4$. Finally, the learning parameter, λ, is set to 0.2, meaning that inflation expectations are corrected by one-fifth of the discrepancy between actual inflation and the prior belief. To solve the model, one substitutes consumers' and producers' optimal responses into the equilibrium conditions, (17), to determine the endogenous variables. Doing so does not require special software packages but can be accomplished with any computer language. Appendix K provides MATLAB sample codes.

Having reached this point, there are essentially two ways to proceed: Readers who are fine with the above framework can continue with Chapters 3 to 7, the theoretical part of this study. Skeptics may prefer to skip to Chapter 8, which discusses a number of methodical issues.

Chapter 3

Traditional Topics

Chapter 2 introduced a coherent and versatile framework that is now employed to review and evaluate a number of established doctrines and to discuss some controversial issues. In each case, the analysis starts from a stationary state where prices and quantities remain constant and expectations are fulfilled. This assumption is not dictated by realism but by method: Without a stationary state at the outset, variables would move in an uncontrolled manner, and these movements would interfere with the policies and disturbances under consideration. Assuming an initial stationary state avoids such interferences. However, the analysis does *not* require that the economy remain in the stationary state or in its neighborhood, nor does it make use of linear approximations. Rather, the model produces exact results that are illustrated graphically and explained in words.

3.1 Basic Lessons

Money *neutrality* means that one-shot changes in the money stock do not affect real variables such as output and employment. According to universal consensus, such a property cannot hold in the presence of nominal frictions. But what if frictions are completely absent? By tackling this question, the subsequent sections discuss issues that pertain to the longer run and provide a useful benchmark for later examinations of wage and price rigidities.

3.1.1 Quantity Theory of Money

In the history of economics, the quantity theory plays a central role. Originally proposed by astronomer Nicolaus Copernicus (1526), who observed that "money loses its value when it is issued in too great a quantity", no doctrine is better known—and none has been criticized more vigorously. In its purest form, the quantity theory states that a one-shot increase in the money stock entails an instantaneous and commensurate increase in nominal prices and wages but does not influence other variables. In particular, interest rates will remain constant. Does so simple a proposition prove true in the present framework? Experienced readers may venture a guess before proceeding. The answer is a qualified no.

To obtain the pure quantity theory, one must assume exogenous inflation expectations. The learning parameter, λ, vanishes, and individuals stick to their prior expectations irrespective of what they see. Figure 3.1 reports the consequences of this stringent supposition. As in all later graphs, rates are measured in percent whereas the initial values of all other variables are normalized at 100. The upper left panel shows the exogenous *impulse*, a 2 percent increase in the money stock. The other panels indicate the endogenous *responses* that result from individual optimizing behavior. Specifically, the price level rises instantaneously by just 2 percent, while interest and output stay unmoved. Nominal wage rates, not shown for brevity, also rise by 2 percent, and all real variables remain at their original equilibrium levels.

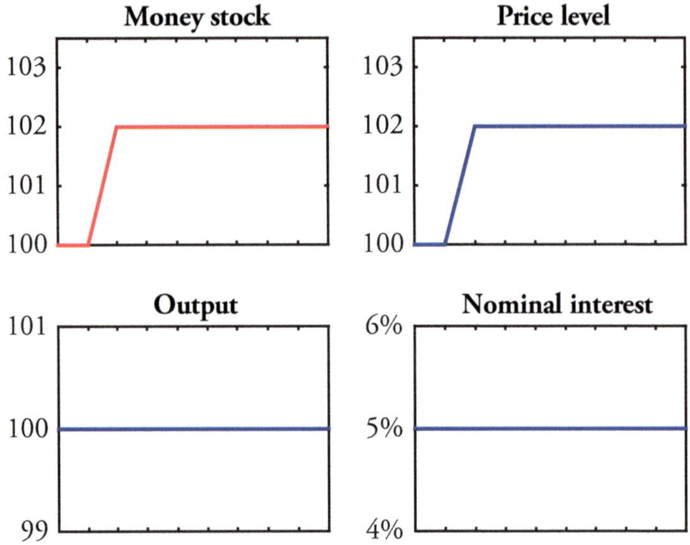

Figure 3.1: One-shot increase in the money stock, $\lambda = 0$. *Notes*: Horizontal axes represent time. Nominal interest is measured in percent. The initial values of the other variables are normalized at 100.

In which way is the monetary impulse transmitted to the economy? The literature abounds with stories of consumers holding excess money balances they wish to get rid of. In a credit economy, the true transmission process is different and merits a detailed account as a preparation for complicated scenarios. At the outset, central bank purchases in the bond market exert downward pressure on the nominal interest rate. This so-called *liquidity effect* reflects the belief that money expansions will lower interest. In an influential article without optimizing agents, Metzler (1951: 107) concluded that central banks have the power to permanently reduce interest rates via open market purchases.

However, the resulting state cannot constitute a general equilibrium. Starting from equality of supply and demand in the commodity market, lower nominal interest stimulates investment at constant expected inflation. An excess demand in the commodity market emerges that increases the price level and tends to reduce real wages; flexible nominal wage rates extinguish the latter effect. The final equilibrium is characterized by higher commodity prices and nominal wages while real variables are restored to their original equilibrium levels. Because all adjustments take place simultaneously, no liquidity effect will be visible in the data—the nominal interest rate remains unmoved. Neutrality obtains because the excess demands for commodities and labor are null homogeneous in (P_t, W_t, M_t), whereas the excess demands for bonds and money are linear homogeneous in these variables, as one can easily check. Open market purchases can be interpreted as a proposal by the central bank to hold a portfolio with a greater amount of money and a smaller amount of bonds. The private sector rejects this proposal—money demand and bond demand both increase, but their ratio remains unchanged.

Following this reasoning, there are no separate channels of monetary transmission in this economy with credit money because one and the same act of the central bank, namely, an open market purchase, has three immediate impacts: For a logical second, the purchase diminishes the nominal interest rate, increases real balances, and increases real credit. Since these impacts are intrinsically tied to each other, separate channels do not exist. John Stuart Mill (1848: 524–539) was the first eminent economist who distressed himself over the issue of whether inflation is caused by money or credit. In the present model, the correct answer reads: Inflation is caused by both, since money creation and credit creation go hand in hand.

Notably, monetary impulses are almost entirely transmitted through producers while consumers remain passive. This is because changes in expected real interest have an unequivocal impact on investment demand. By contrast, the influence on consumption is ambiguous, since the substitution effect of a rise in expected real interest is counteracted by an income effect: Higher real interest rates make present consumption more expensive but also more affordable.

The transmission works without real balance effects of the kind proposed by Pigou (1943) or Patinkin (1965), who argue that changes in money or the price level influence private spending through variations in individuals' real wealth. Borrowing useful terminology from Gurley and Shaw (1960: 73), credit money constitutes *outside money* in that it represents a financial asset of the private sector. However, this asset is created together with a corresponding private sector liability in the form of central bank bond holdings. Equation (5) makes clear that the central bank's net financial assets, $B_t^{cb} - M_t$, vanish at any time. The same holds for the private sector's net financial assets. While it is true that a rise in the price level diminishes the real value of consumers' financial assets, this loss becomes offset by a reduction in producers' liabilities. Real balances affect consumers only inasmuch as they change seigniorage, the smallest part of total wealth.

Having outlined the consequences of changes in the money stock, changes in money demand should also be mentioned. A fall in μ, the money preference parameter, induces consumers to rebalance their portfolios in favor of bonds. The surge in bond demand, or credit supply, sets into motion a process that parallels this transmission. In fact, central bank bond demand and private bond demand affect the equilibrium condition for the bond market,

$B_t^d + B_t^{cb} = B_t^s$, in precisely the same manner. Hence, decreases in money demand operate like increases in the money stock; both produce inflation.

To summarize, the quantity theory's claim that changes in the money stock induce proportional changes in prices but leave interest rates unaffected can only be sustained under the strong assumption of exogenous inflation expectations. The next subsection returns to the standard specification, $\lambda = 0.2$, and shows that this generates dynamics that appear much more interesting and relevant.

3.1.2 Fisher Effect

If inflation expectations respond to actual inflation, one-shot increases in the money stock cease to have one-shot consequences. Instead, they entail intricate adjustment processes, illustrated in Figure 3.2. An increase in the money stock of 2 percent leaves output unchanged. Likewise, it does not affect the expected real interest rate, which influences investment demand. By contrast, the monetary expansion has *persistent* effects on nominal variables which, in principle, will last forever.

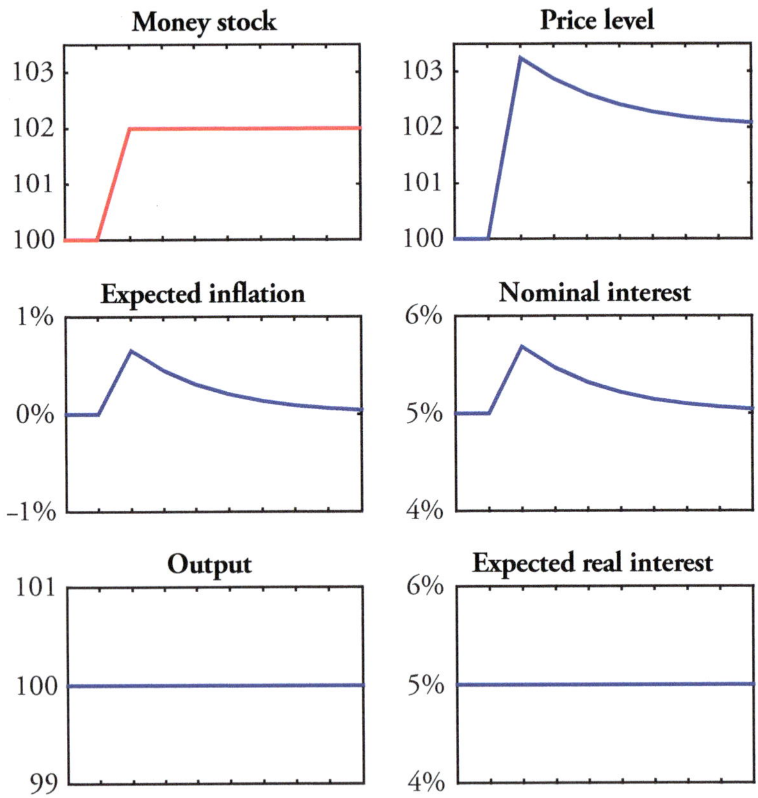

Figure 3.2: One-shot increase in the money stock, $\lambda = 0.2$. *Notes*: Horizontal axes represent time. Interest rates and expected inflation are measured in percent. The initial values of the other variables are normalized at 100.

At the outset, the transmission resembles that outlined in the preceding subsection: Central bank open market purchases diminish the nominal interest rate; this stimulates investment demand and commodity demand in general; hence, prices and wages increase, restoring real balances to their initial value. While the resulting state was an equilibrium under exogenous inflation expectations, endogenous expectations entail an additional complication because a rising price level elevates expected inflation, cf. equation (3), through its effect on actual inflation.

Rising inflation expectations initiate a subsequent process: They increase investment demand because producers expect higher revenues and revaluation gains in the following period, as equation (9) makes clear. At the original nominal interest rate, the first-order condition (11) would be violated, and credit demand would exceed credit supply. This excess demand in the credit market elevates the nominal interest rate. As the two center panels of Figure 3.2 show, the path of the nominal interest rate parallels the path of expected inflation such that the expected real interest rate stays constant. Specifically, expected inflation rises, nominal interest also, both return gradually, and the expected real interest rate remains at 5 percent. The finding that nominal interest rates respond positively to changes in expected inflation, originally attributable to Irving Fisher (1896 and 1930), is referred to as the *Fisher effect* or the expected inflation effect. The Fisher effect, which is central to contemporary macro theory, implies that monetary acceleration policies increase, rather than reduce, nominal interest rates.

An explanation of the price level path is still pending. As the upper right panel of Figure 3.2 shows, prices do not rise by 2 percent, as under exogenous expectations, but overshoot: After an initial increase of roughly 3.2 percent, deflation sets in, and the price level approaches its new neutral position. This behavior is triggered by the nominal interest rate which, as noted in section 2.3, measures the user cost of money. Rises in nominal interest diminish money demand and induce consumers to augment their bond holdings. Hence, the impact of central bank bond purchases that initiated the whole process is reinforced by a surge in private bond demand. Because both effects operate in the same direction, the price level must overshoot. During the subsequent periods, nominal interest rates return gradually, as inflation expectations recede. This stimulates money demand and entails deflation.

While the Fisher effect runs counter to the popular belief that monetary easing would lower the interest rate, it is not in fact a paradox but rather reflects established evidence. Countries afflicted with lasting inflation, such as some nations in Latin America, are mostly characterized by high nominal interest rates. At the other extreme, Switzerland, famous for its tight monetary policy and low inflation, regularly has the lowest nominal interest rates in the world. The Fisher effect also shows up in time series data. Figure 3.3 traces the paths of inflation and nominal interest rates in the United States between 1962 and 2015. Obviously, the two rates are positively correlated. Since real interest rates themselves fluctuate and inflation expectations adjust only gradually to actual inflation, the correlation is far from perfect. Nevertheless, the graph supports the notion that nominal interest rates are essentially driven by expectations: They serve as an investment brake in an inflationary environment, and as an investment promoter in the opposite scenario. Fluctuations in nominal interest rates preserve capital market equilibrium and tend to stabilize the real rate.

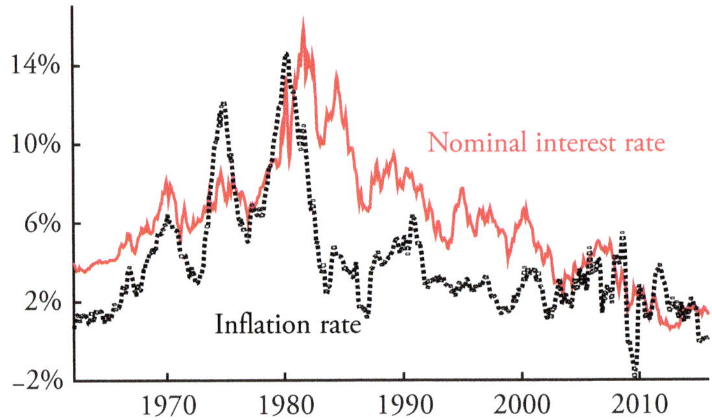

Figure 3.3: United States inflation and nominal interest rates. *Notes*: Monthly data, retrieved December 2015 from <https://fred.stlouisfed.org>. The rate of inflation is series CPIAUCS, the 5-year interest rate is series DGS5.

To sum up, a seemingly straightforward monetary operation, viz. a one-shot increase in the money stock, has persistent effects on the economy, among them mild deflation that lasts forever. The ensuing equilibrium paths of the price level, expected inflation, and nominal interest are determined by complex interactions. In this process, the learning parameter assumes the central role and dictates the adjustment speed. Only in the borderline case of a vanishing learning parameter, adjustment takes place immediately, as shown in subsection 3.1.1.

3.1.3 Erratic Expectations

Economists sometimes highlight the importance of expectations and then bury them in a steady state grave. However, another strand, exemplified by authors such as Kindleberger (1978), Minsky (1986), and Akerlof and Shiller (2009), stresses that human behavior is driven by animal spirits, implying that expectations can change sharply even in the absence of relevant news. Investors operating in stock or forex markets are familiar with such manias and depressions; they know from experience that expectations are among the most volatile variables and can change out of the blue. Black Monday, the stock market crash of 1987, is a good illustration: Following an ambiguous speech by

United States treasury secretary James Baker, global stock markets collapsed. For example, the Dow Jones Industrial Average plummeted by 22.6 percent, the largest one-day decline recorded in its history, while New Zealand stocks fell by 60 percent. Newspapers throughout the world announced a severe recession. It took some time for investors to detect that nothing had fundamentally changed. Thereafter, financial markets recovered.

A simple method to investigate how animal spirits affect inflation and the economy is to augment (3) with stochastic shocks, u_t, that disturb the adaptive expectations:

$$\pi^e_{t+1} = \pi^e_t + \lambda(\pi_t - \pi^e_t) + u_t \, . \tag{24}$$

The summand u_t represents a *white noise* process, that is, a serially uncorrelated random variable with zero mean and finite variance. Every realization of this variable is called a random shock. Shocks may result from published expert opinions that inflation is lurking around the corner, from converse opinions that the global economy faces secular stagnation and long-term deflation, from changes in purchasing manager indices, news of job openings, etc. Such shocks can also be completely unfounded.

Figure 3.4 illustrates the impact of expectation shocks. The graphs are based on the premise that the central bank takes a purely passive stance and keeps the money stock at a constant level. The upper left panel depicts the shocks, u_t that induce changes in actual inflation, expected inflation, and the nominal interest rate. Because inflation expectations are formed recursively and actual inflation is affected by changes in money demand that result from variations in the user cost of money, there is no obvious relationship between the shocks and the endogenous variables. However, the path of nominal interest rates exactly parallels the path of expected inflation rates. This pattern, which is clearly visible in the two middle panels, depicts an equilibrating process of the following kind:

- Positive expectation shocks cause producers to foresee increases in the commodity prices. This makes investment more rewarding and induces excess demands in commodity and credit markets. The nominal interest rate rises commensurately to restore the expected real interest rate to its original level.
- Conversely, negative expectation shocks diminish the nominal interest rate. The expected real interest rate remains unchanged, again, which keeps commodity and credit markets in equilibrium.

This picture contrasts with the popular conviction that high nominal interest rates are harmful to the economy. Quite the contrary, high nominal interest rates indicate, and counteract, sporadic manias, whereas low rates buffer sporadic depressions. The nominal interest rate works as an automatic stabilizer that prevents both overheating and undercooling. To the extent that adjustments take place as smoothly as here, fluctuations in nominal interest rates shield real output from the animal spirits, as the bottom panel in Figure 3.4 illustrates.

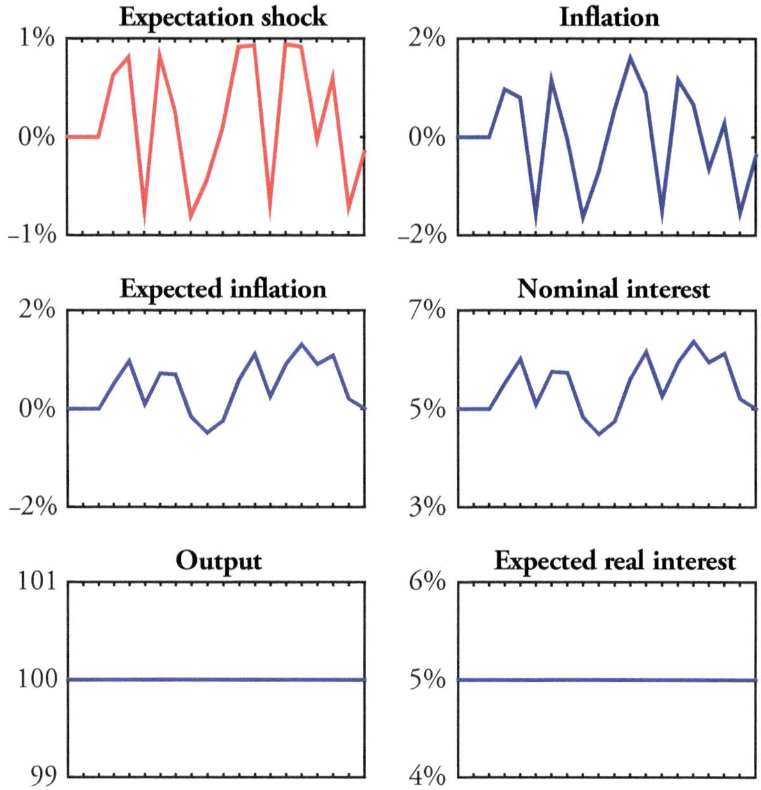

Figure 3.4: Impact of expectation shocks. *Notes*: Horizontal axes represent time. The initial value of output is normalized at 100. The other variables are measured in percent.

Theoretically, the outlined stabilizing process may go astray, as formally discussed in appendix D. This occurs if inflation expectations respond strongly to current inflation, that is, if the learning parameter, λ, is large. The above description implicitly assumes that increases in the nominal interest rate dampen investment demand because they raise the expected real interest rate.

Using the approximation $r_{t+1}^e = i_t - \pi_{t+1}^e$, the nominal interest rate has both a direct effect on the real rate (the increase in i_t itself) and an indirect effect through expected inflation that tends to work in the opposite direction: Increases in the nominal interest rate diminish money demand and elevate the price level, P_t. Hence, actual inflation rises, as does expected inflation, which reduces expected real interest. If this indirect effect dominates, a price spiral results, with the price level either diverging to infinity or collapsing to zero. A general equilibrium does not exist in these cases. Hicks (1939: 255) was the first to note problems resulting from overly elastic price expectations; see also

Grandmont (1983). These observations are valid in theory. Their empirical relevance is arguable because actual inflations and deflations go along with changes in the money stock, whereas price spirals would come in sudden bursts at a constant money stock. In reality, commodity markets are more afflicted by price stickiness than by excessive price flexibility.

3.1.4 Superneutrality

To this point, only one-shot increases in the money stock have been considered. While such measures are a suitable point of departure, it seems apt to move on to a more realistic presentation of monetary policy and to study changes in money *growth* rather than changes in *levels*. Defining the money growth rate as

$$\frac{M_t - M_{t-1}}{M_{t-1}}, \tag{25}$$

the analysis still proceeds from a stationary state with a constant money stock, that is, a money growth rate of zero. What happens if the central bank increases the money growth rate from 0 to 2 percent, effective from some period t? Figure 3.5 answers this question and outlines the equilibrium effects resulting from individual optimizing behavior.

The response of the inflation rate to an increase in the money growth rate resembles the response of the price level to a one-shot rise in the money stock: Inflation overshoots at the outset due to a decrease in money demand and asymptotically approaches money growth. In the long run, expected inflation rises gradually and coincides with actual inflation. Nominal interest rates are driven up by expected inflation and converge to roughly 7 percent.

Output stays constant, and the same is true for all other real variables except real balances. The last panel in Figure 3.5 indicates a permanent decline in real balances that stems from the rise in the user cost of money. Consumers economize on their money holdings because the opportunity costs of holding money are higher now, in the presence of higher nominal interest rates. Up to second-order effects, the reduction in real balances equals the relative increase in the user cost of money times the interest elasticity of money demand. The reduction is a level effect that has no lasting influence on the rate of inflation but induces the latter to overshoot initially.

Empirical studies generally confirm the independence of output and inflation; cf. Geweke (1986), and McCandless and Weber (1995). Haug and Dewald (2012) consider a broad sample of industrial countries over the period 1880–2001 and note that money growth and inflation are positively correlated in the long run, whereas no systematic relationship exists between money growth and real GDP growth. The preceding observations can be generalized by means of the following proposition, proven in appendix E:

Superneutrality: Money is superneutral; changes in its growth rate affect only nominal variables but have no impact on real variables other than real balances.

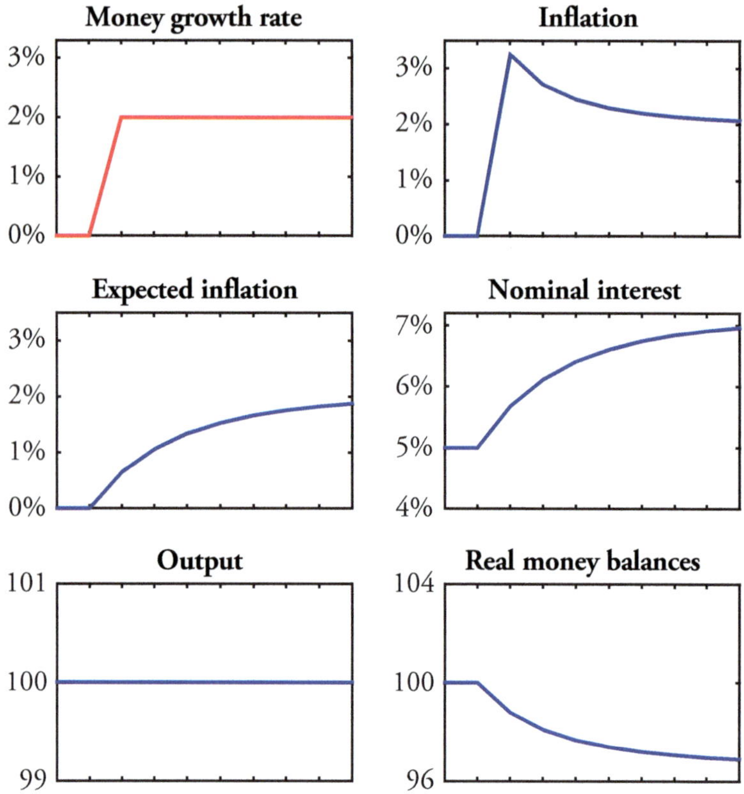

Figure 3.5: Money growth at a rate of 2 percent. *Notes*: Horizontal axes represent time. Money growth, inflation, expected inflation and nominal interest are measured in percent. The initial values of the other variables are normalized at 100.

That superneutrality holds in this setting is evident from Figure 3.5. However, the economic forces at work may be less obvious and deserve an explicit account that also points out the limits of this fundamental result. Increases in money growth affect consumers twice: First, they raise the user cost of money and induce consumers to diminish real balances. Second, the central bank produces more seigniorage. Because the entire seigniorage is distributed to consumers, the latter receive a compensation enabling them to stick to the original levels of present and future consumption. To see this formally, consider the aggregate budget constraint in real terms, as derived in appendix B:

$$C_t + \frac{A^e_{t+1}}{1+r_{t+1}} + \frac{i_t}{1+i_t}\frac{M^d_t}{P_t} = A_t + X_t + \frac{i_t}{1+i_t}\frac{M_t}{P_t}. \tag{26}$$

On the left-hand side, the budget constraint shows current consumption, the present value of future consumption, and the user cost of real balances. The right-hand side includes the seigniorage, where $\sigma_t = i_t M_t$ has been substituted. Since money is voluntarily held in equilibrium, $M_t^d = M_t$, consumers who could afford a certain pair (C_t, A_{t+1}^e) of present and future consumption before the increase in nominal interest can afford that same pair thereafter. Their only reaction is to diminish money demand. Money demand represents a choice variable, while seigniorage is exogenous for the individual. All consumers out of a continuum rightly disregard the effect of their own money demand on aggregate seigniorage.

If consumers stick to their original consumption decisions, as they do in the present model, it is clear that money must be superneutral because producers, whose decisions depend solely on real wages and expected real interest, are not at all affected by changes in monetary policy. Nominal wages move in accordance with the price level, and fluctuations in nominal interest rates absorb any changes in expected inflation, thus keeping the expected real interest rate constant. Hence, whatever the initial paths of output and employment, they will still constitute a sequence of temporary equilibria.

Superneutrality was first demonstrated by Sidrauski (1967) in a model with consumers planning over infinite horizons. It is a benchmark property that is unlikely to hold strictly in reality. Three caveats should be noted, one technical and less interesting, and the other two substantial. As argued previously, increases in seigniorage that follow increases in money growth enable consumers to stick to their original choices of present and future consumption. This behavior is also optimal for them if changes in real balances do not affect intertemporal preferences, that is, if the utility function is separable in real balances. The logarithmic and CDC utility functions used here do meet this requirement. With non-separable utility, changes in money growth can affect the equilibrium capital stock. The sign of this effect is unclear, however, since changes in intertemporal marginal rates of substitution can go in either direction. Moreover, the impact is likely to be small because money balances represent but a tiny fraction of total financial assets.

A second objection cannot be dismissed so easily. The superneutrality result rests on the premise that consumers are entitled to the full seigniorage. This supposition is so crucial and so questionable that it merits a separate treatment, which is postponed until section 3.3. The third caveat is discussed in subsection 3.1.5.

3.1.5 Forced Saving and Distributive Justice

The theory of forced saving, outlined here, is old. Hayek (1932: 124) attributes it to Thornton's and Bentham's writings around 1800. Machlup (1943) warns of the ambiguity of the term and, in fact, presents a list of 34 disparate concepts. The principle meaning of "forced saving", however, is clear. It is the presumption that changes in the money stock redistribute income between different social classes and compel the losers of this gamble to forego consumption. Defining saving as the excess of income over consumption, the losers save involuntarily if their income remains unchanged and consumption is reduced.

Models with identical consumers mask distributive issues. This common homogeneity assumption does not reflect a prejudice that distribution does not matter but is due to the empirical orientation of macroeconomics. National accounts often provide data for the household sector as a whole, which makes it difficult to test hypotheses about distributive effects. Analytically, however, it is easy to introduce a heterogeneous agent model with two types of consumers, referred to as *rentiers* and *worker-entrepreneurs*. Rentiers own all financial assets, A_t, collect the seigniorage, and behave in the accustomed way. Worker-entrepreneurs, by contrast, receive nonfinancial income, X_t, hold no financial assets, and spend their entire income on consumption. Aggregate consumption, formerly given by formula (22), becomes

$$C_t = \frac{A_t + \sigma_t^r}{1+\beta+\mu} + X_t, \tag{27}$$

where the first summand represents rentiers' consumption and the second worker-entrepreneurs' consumption. Recalling the definition of financial assets from section 2.5, the variable A_t includes money balances and bonds, both expressed in terms of present consumption. When the price level goes up, the purchasing power of financial assets deteriorates, and the rentiers suffer a loss.

In his intoxicating book, *When Money Dies—The Nightmare of Deficit Spending, Devaluation and Hyperinflation in Weimar Germany*, Fergusson (1975) clarifies what such an impassive statement can mean. It can mean that, as in 1923, the assets of a formerly well-to-do widow with young children are completely wiped out, or that people starve to death in the center of Berlin. Nonfinancial income, on the other hand, includes profits that were defined in section 2.4. Increases in the price level induce revaluation gains that benefit the recipients of nonfinancial income. This is well exemplified by German industrialist Hugo Stinnes, who borrowed vast amounts of *Reichsmarks* in the 1920s, acquired several thousand corporations and became famous as "the king of inflation".

While changes in the price level alter the income distribution, they do not affect the sum $A_t + X_t$. In a closed economy, the losses of the rentiers are exactly counterbalanced by the gains of the non-rentiers because private financial assets equal private liabilities; net financial wealth is zero. Sudden inflation forces the rentiers to cut consumption but enables worker-entrepreneurs to consume even more. Formula (27) implies a corresponding decrease in national saving that impairs superneutrality. The decrease in national saving results from the strong illustrative assumptions made here, but the general message should be obvious: If monetary policy affects the income distribution, it can enhance or diminish the real capital stock, with the direction of the impact depending on the winners' and losers' respective propensities to consume.

Before concluding, it should be noted that forced saving does not result from inflation as such but from *surprise inflation*: If the central bank accelerates the money growth rate, rentiers suffer for a while from the fall in the ex post real interest rate. Thereafter, with expectations adjusting gradually, the nominal interest rate increases correspondingly, and the original distribution is ideally restored. Nevertheless, policy changes in either direction have severe distributive consequences during the adjustment process and are questionable in this respect.

3.1.6 Welfare

Together with fire and the wheel, money presents a most important innovation. Its usefulness for efficient exchange and as a convenient store of value is without question. At a positive nominal interest rate, however, holding money balances rather than interest-bearing bonds comes at a price. Therefore, consumers increase their money holdings only up to the point where the marginal rate of substitution between consumption and real balances equals the user cost of money. Equation (16) in section 2.5 expressed this optimality condition. For an economy as a whole, by contrast, real balances are essentially costless; notes and coins can be produced at low cost, and electronic deposits almost for free. The observation that nominal interest drives a wedge between individual and social costs led a number of economists, notably Bailey (1956), to question the Pareto optimality of the associated market equilibrium.

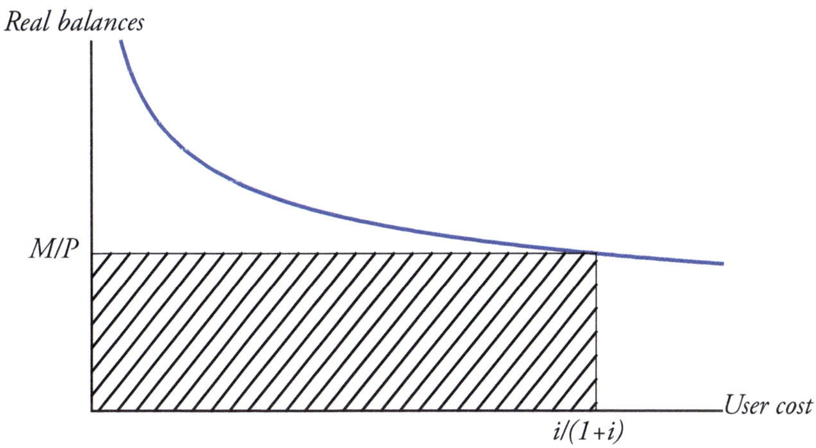

Figure 3.6: Deadweight loss of positive nominal interest. *Notes*: The solid curve is the money demand function. The hatched rectangle represents real seigniorage.

Figure 3.6 shows a typical money demand function. The graph refers to a steady state so that time indices are omitted. The area of the hatched rectangle, that is, $M/P \times i/(1+i)$, equals real seigniorage, σ^r, as defined in (21). Real seigniorage, measured in terms of consumption, constitutes an expenditure item for individual consumers and a revenue item for the central bank. The total area under the money demand function to the left of $i/(1+i)$ indicates the damage consumers suffer if they reduce balances to the level M/P; this damage is also measured in terms of present consumption.

The difference of the total area under the money demand function and the area of the rectangle represents a *deadweight loss* (DL) and is indicated by the "Harberger triangle". Formally,

$$DL = \int_{0}^{\frac{i}{1+i}} \frac{M^d}{P} d\left(\frac{i}{1+i}\right) - \sigma^r, \tag{28}$$

Section 2.7 postulated a low elasticity of money demand and a utility function that is separable in real balances. Under these premises, although money demand itself diverges for $i \to 0$, the deadweight loss remains finite and equals consumers' surplus minus seigniorage. Every positive nominal interest rate induces a deadweight loss. This observation led Friedman (1969) to suggest his famous rule that the central bank should reduce nominal interest rates to zero. More generally, the central bank should aim at reducing the nominal interest rate to the point where consumers are satiated with real balances. A true optimum is reached only if such a satiation point exists. Otherwise, the Friedman rule must be understood in the sense that monetary policy should keep nominal interest rates as low as possible, implying that deflation is generally optimal.

These findings have a simple intuition in terms of optimal tax theory. To recall this theory, consider an excise tax that is levied on some commodity with a fixed pretax price. Of course, the excise makes consumers worse off. To regain their original welfare level, consumers need a money transfer from the government known as the compensated variation (or Hicks compensation). Optimal tax theory shows that the compensating variation exceeds the tax revenue strictly if the utility function is strictly quasi-concave; see Mas-Colell et al. (1995: 85). Therefore, taxes produce a welfare loss even if the government refunds the entire revenue to the consumers. Nominal interest represents a tax on real balances. This drives a wedge between the user cost and the social cost, which are essentially zero. Refunding the entire seigniorage to the consumers does not suffice to make the latter as well off as in a steady state with zero interest. Conversely, a monetary policy that tolerates deflation and reduces the nominal interest rate improves welfare. If the seigniorage interacts with other distortionary levies, such as payroll or capital income taxes, the Friedman rule remains optimal if utility is homothetic and separable in real balances; see Chari et al. (1996). Otherwise, the optimal nominal interest rate is characterized by Ramsey's formula.

How important are the welfare effects? The easiest way to answer this question is to use formula (160) from appendix B, which gives the demand for real balances as a function of consumption, expected real interest, and the user cost of money. Owing to superneutrality, consumption and the expected real interest rate are independent of monetary policy. Therefore, substituting (160) into (28) and integrating out yields the deadweight loss as a fraction of consumption:

$$\text{(29)} \qquad \frac{DL}{C} = -\frac{\eta \mu \Theta}{1+\eta}\left(\frac{i}{1+i}\right)^{1+\eta} = 0.025\left(\frac{i}{1+i}\right)^{0.9}.$$

The numerical expression on the right-hand side accords with the model's baseline calibration. Obviously, the deadweight loss increases in the interest elasticity of money demand; it vanishes in the borderline case $\eta = 0$. Moreover, the deadweight loss also increases in the nominal interest rate and vanishes for $i \to 0$. This is the Friedman rule in a limit sense.

Substituting interest rates of 5 and 15 percent, respectively, into the formula yields deadweight losses of 0.16 and 0.40 percent of consumption. The difference of 0.24 is consistent with a rule of thumb that 10 percentage points of inflation are worth less than 1 percent of consumption. From a broad international comparison, Boel and Camera (2011: 243) infer that 10 percentage points of inflation are typically worth 0.50 percent of consumption. This figure varies considerably over the empirical studies that have been conducted, but most find relatively small values.

To conclude, seigniorage results from a tax on real balances that is often referred to as an "inflation tax". This term is incorrect because seigniorage also accrues at stable prices, provided the nominal interest rate is positive. Hence, seigniorage is a "nominal interest tax" rather than an "inflation tax". Optimal tax theory implies that a benevolent central bank should *minimize* the seigniorage via deflation. Two important caveats should be noted. First, price level stability may be superior to deflation in that it reduces information and search costs and allows individuals to anchor price expectations. Second, deflation distorts the allocation if individual prices and wages are insufficiently flexible. The bottom line is that deadweight losses present a valid case against inflation, but a consensus on the optimality of the Friedman rule has not emerged.

3.2 Arguable Lessons

The doctrines reviewed so far are widely accepted in the literature. This section presents material of a different kind. Some of the results are contested, others raise semantic issues, and yet others contradict prevailing institutions. Nevertheless, all of them seem important enough to merit consideration.

3.2.1 Endogenous Money and Interest Pegs

In section 3.1, the central bank targeted the money stock and accepted the nominal interest rate. Therefore, the money stock was exogenous while the nominal interest rate was endogenous. Is it possible to interchange the roles of the two variables, that is, to make the nominal interest rate exogenous and the money stock endogenous? This is a tough and controversial question. As Howitt (1992: 777) reports, a wide consensus existed until the 1980s to the effect that pegging (fixing) the nominal interest rate at a prescribed level was infeasible. Friedman (1968) made this point forcefully in his presidential address to the American Economic Association, and many policymakers think central banks cannot fix interest rates. However, the current mainstream represents central banks as institutions that control interest rates, and most central banks use nominal interest targets rather than money stock targets in their daily operations.

This subsection does not take sides with either position. Instead, it demonstrates that the feasibility of an interest peg depends on the *implementation* of such a policy: An interest peg combined with an endogenous money stock will generally destabilize the economy. By contrast, a policy that pegs the interest rate indirectly through deliberate adjustments in the money stock will work. To avoid any misunderstanding, the term "interest peg" refers to an absolutely fixed interest level that must not be confused with interest *rules*, which respond to observable variables.

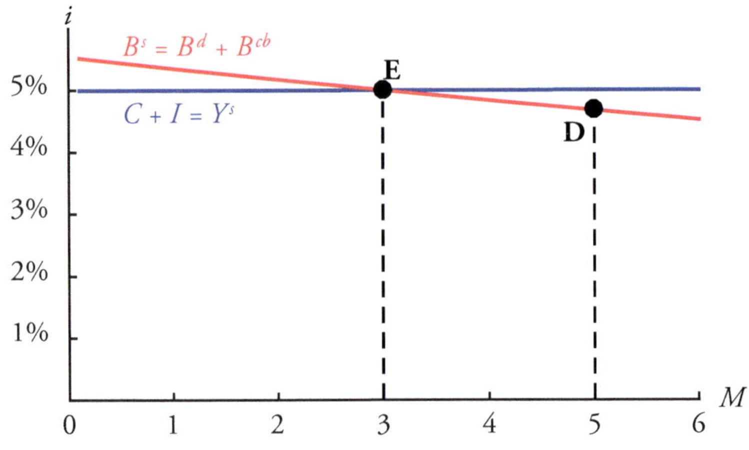

Figure 3.7: Money, interest, and market equilibria. *Note*: The money stock M=3 and the nominal interest rate i=5 percent represent the stationary equilibrium.

As a start, consider Figure 3.7, which presupposes a stationary state with zero expected inflation. The figure displays exact computations of pairs of money and interest that preserve commodity market equilibrium and bond market equilibrium. Along the line $C + I = Y^s$, commodity demand equals commodity supply. Along the line $B^s = B^d + B^{cb}$, bond supply equals bond demand. Point E represents the general equilibrium. The slopes of the curves indicate that the nominal interest rate affects both markets strongly through its influence on investment and credit demand. The money stock, which is of no relevance for producers and which affects consumers only through the seigniorage, has minor effects. Hence, to preserve equilibrium in at least one of the markets, small interest changes require enormous variations in the money stock. Keeping in mind that the nominal interest rate considered here represents a medium-term market rate, interest changes would require substantial central bank actions of the type that has become known as quantitative easing.

Point D illustrates a nominal interest peg at a level slightly below the equilibrium level of 5 percent. The central bank implements the peg through open market purchases of bonds and a corresponding increase in the money stock. To preserve equilibrium in the bond market, the money stock must be increased by no less than two-thirds, from 3 to 5. In so doing, the central bank effectively announces its readiness to buy arbitrary amounts of bonds. Point D emerges as the preliminary result. Because this point is located beneath the line $C + I = Y^s$, it corresponds to an excess demand in the commodity market. Generalizing somewhat, if the central bank tries to peg the interest rate at any level, $\bar{i}_t$, below the equilibrium level, an excess demand in the commodity market emerges, provided that inflation expectations remain unchanged:

$$C_t + I_t\left(\frac{1+\bar{i}_t}{1+\pi^e_{t+1}}\right) > Y^s_t . \tag{30}$$

The excess commodity demand is almost entirely due to an increase in investment demand, induced by a lower expected real interest rate. The real interest rate, in turn, is diminished through the interest peg at constant expected inflation. However, expected inflation will not remain constant, because the excess commodity demand triggers an instantaneous rise in the price level, P_t. The ensuing inflation does not rebalance demand and supply but *reinforces* the disequilibrium in that it raises expected inflation and depresses the real interest rate even further. Investment and prices tend to infinity. The entire reasoning can be summarized by means of a simple flow chart that starts with a pegged nominal interest rate below the equilibrium rate:

$$\bar{i}_t \Rightarrow r^e_{t+1}\downarrow \;\Rightarrow\; I_t\uparrow \;\Rightarrow\; P_t\uparrow \;\Rightarrow\; \pi_t\uparrow \;\Rightarrow\; \pi^e_{t+1}\uparrow$$

This causal chain is known in the literature as *Wicksell's cumulative process*, although it goes back to Thornton (1802); see Humphrey (1986). The initial deviation of the expected real interest rate from its equilibrium value initiates a self-reinforcing process where rising investment boosts commodity prices, inflation, and expected inflation. With the nominal interest rate pegged by hypothesis, the increase in expected inflation depresses expected real interest, which stimulates investment all the more. Wicksell (1898: 102) termed the nominal interest rate compatible with price stability the *natural rate*. To the extent that price stability entails zero expected inflation, the natural rate equals the expected *real* interest rate (a term unknown to Wicksell).

To complete the argument, two points are worth noting. First, if the central bank tries to peg the nominal interest rate *above* the natural rate, a perfectly analogous process sets in, with investment and prices plunging to zero.

Second, and more importantly, if the peg happens to coincide with the natural rate, the equilibrium becomes knife-edged (fragile) in the following sense: Any expectation shock of the kind considered in subsection 3.1.3 leads the economy astray. For instance, any negative expected inflation shock induces an indefinite fall in investment and prices if the central bank defends the interest peg. The emerging deflation fortifies deflationary fears and increases the expected real interest rate until the economy collapses.

Considered this way, the key problem behind Wicksell's cumulative process is not that the central bank pegs the interest rate at an inappropriate level. Rather, the problem is that pegs of any kind deprive the economy of its key stabilizer. As noted before, an endogenous nominal interest rate prevents both overheating and undercooling under a money target. An interest target, combined with endogenous money, impairs this automatism. Money stocks cannot stabilize the economy in the same manner as interest rates; their effects are too weak (cf. Figure 3.7), and they work in the wrong direction. Therefore, endogenous money yields knife-edge equilibria at best and cumulative processes otherwise.

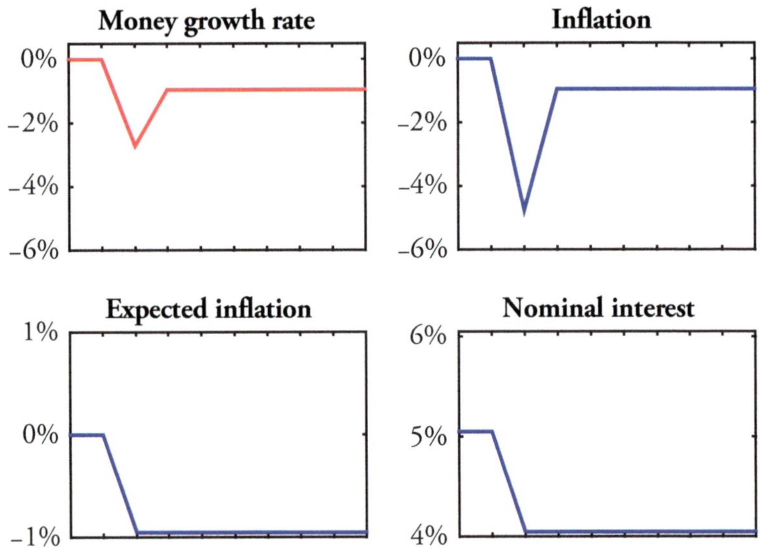

Figure 3.8: Interest peg at 4 percent. *Notes*: Horizontal axes represent time. All variables are measured in percent.

It remains to be shown that an interest peg does indeed work if the central bank keeps the money stock under control and targets the nominal interest rate indirectly through appropriate changes in the money stock. In this case, the policy must be reversed. For instance, if the central bank wishes to diminish the nominal interest rate from 5 to 4 percent, it can implement this interest target by open market sales rather than open market purchases. Such a policy, illustrated in Figure 3.8, requires a strong initial decline in money growth, associated with strong deflation. This impulse accomplishes the necessary change in expected inflation. Thereafter, the money stock is diminished at a slower pace as the adjustment in expectations is now complete. Because Figure 3.8 essentially replicates Figure 3.5 with reversed signs, some may hesitate to call this an interest peg, noting that although the policy comes with a formal interest target, the implementation takes place through variations in the money stock. However, this is a semantic issue. In practice, central banks *always* conduct their policies through open market operations or comparable credit measures, irrespective of whether they pursue money targets or interest targets.

To summarize, interest peg policies produce well-behaved outcomes if the central bank keeps the money stock under control and influences the nominal interest rate indirectly through monetary adjustments. Lower nominal interest rates require tighter monetary policies that reduce expected inflation. By contrast, policies that peg the nominal interest rate outright and let the money stock adapt endogenously eliminate a key stabilizer and are apt to result in hyperinflations or strong deflations. In the words of former Fed Governor Henry Wallich (1984: 23), "letting the market set the interest rate for a given money-growth target is a safer way of achieving an equilibrium interest rate than trying to set it directly".

3.2.2 Tobin Effect

Are central banks able to encourage investment in the long run? Many would answer this question negatively, as they believe in superneutrality. Tobin (1965: 684), however, challenged the orthodoxy with the argument that even in a stationary state, the "equilibrium interest rate and degree of capital intensity are in general affected by monetary supplies and portfolio behavior, as well as by technology and thrift". In his model, which lacks budget constraints and explicit optimization, consumers choose between capital and money balances. Their portfolio choices depend on the respective yields of these two assets. Inflationary policies diminish the return on money, discourage money holdings, depress the required return on capital, and stimulate investment. As a result, the real capital stock is an increasing function of the rate of inflation. This so-called *Tobin effect* contradicts superneutrality.

To clarify the tension between the Tobin effect and superneutrality, Figure 3.9 illustrates the flow of funds in an economy with credit money. Producers issue bonds to finance investment. Some of the bonds are acquired by consumers, others by the central bank within the context of its open market operations. Since money constitutes the offset-entry of bonds in the central bank balance sheet, the quantity of money issued by the central bank equals its bond purchases. Hence, the total amount of money and bonds in the hands of consumers coincides with the total amount of bonds issued by producers. With the central bank acting as a financial intermediary, consumers hold corporate bonds partly directly and partly indirectly.

Using Tobin's terms, thrift determines the real value of assets held by consumers. Productivity determines the real value of bonds issued by producers. The fact that bond demand equals bond supply in equilibrium, $B_t^d + B_t^{cb} = B_t^s$, is apt to suggest that central bank open market purchases come on top of private bond purchases. Such is not true, however, since central bank bond holdings always match private money balances, $B_t^{cb} = M_t^d$. Money creation crowds out private bond holdings and only affects the composition of private portfolios: If the central bank accelerates money growth, it increases the equilibrium user cost of money and induces consumers to reduce the ratio of money and bonds, M_t^d / B_t^d, whereas the sum total of the two assets remains constant in real terms. The entire adjustment process leaves the expected real interest rate unaffected.

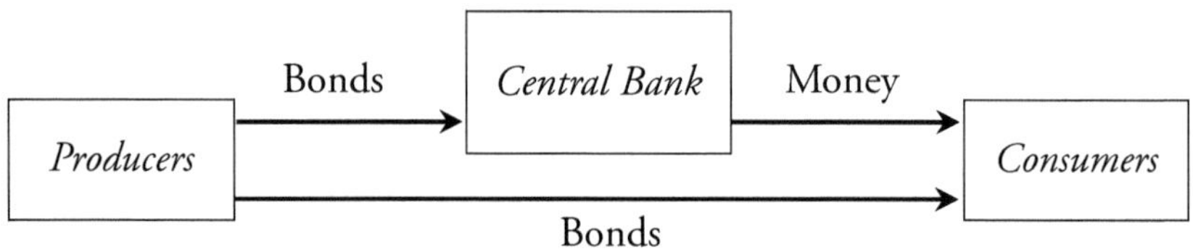

Figure 3.9: Flow of funds: Consumers hold bonds partly outright and partly through the central bank, which acts as an intermediary. Irrespective of the quantity of money, consumers' money plus bond holdings coincide with the total amount of bonds issued by the producers.

Hence, inflation cannot encourage investment in the present model, a feature supported by the evidence cited in subsection 3.1.4 about superneutrality. The forced saving argument discussed in subsection 3.1.5 demonstrated that inflation may even *diminish* investment in that it redistributes income at the expense of the savers. Contrariwise, Weiss (1980) and Drazen (1981) rationalized the Tobin effect in overlapping generations models with young savers and old pensioners. As pointed out by Abel (1987) and Gahvari (1988, 2007), inflation benefits the young savers and deprives the elderly in such a setting; see also Crettez et al. (1999), Bhattacharya et al. (2005), or Ireland (2005). The gains of the young savers reduce real interest and boost investment. This literature, however, assumes helicopter money that represents net financial wealth for the consumers. If one takes notice of actual institutions and replaces helicopter money with credit money, permanent redistributive effects of monetary policy disappear, and superneutrality is reestablished even in an overlapping generations framework; see Homburg (2015a).

3.2.3 Money Irrelevance

This subsection is intended to clarify the relationship of superneutrality on the one hand and money irrelevance on the other. To recall, superneutrality means that changes in money growth do not influence real variables except real balances, but they do affect nominal variables in the expected manner. By contrast, *irrelevance* propositions state that central bank open market operations have no impact at all. Specifically, monetary policy has no influence on the price level. The terms superneutrality and irrelevance have different meanings but are sometimes used interchangeably; for instance, Sargent and Smith (1987) deal with superneutrality but call it irrelevance.

Wallace (1981) proved an irrelevance proposition and related it to the celebrated Modigliani-Miller theorem, according to which the market value of a firm is independent of its capital structure (as shareholders can replicate the firm's leverage in their portfolios). Wallace's paper stimulated quite a debate, and not all commentators became aware of his key premise. Wallace's (1981: 269) central assumption states that money is not dominated in return by bonds. Instead, nominal interest is zero for *both* money and bonds, while deflation keeps the real returns positive. The assumption of identical returns implies that the model comprises only one financial asset. Wallace's open market purchases work as if the central bank bought \$10 notes in exchange for \$5 notes, the former being dubbed as "bonds" and the latter as "money". Since both assets are identical in every respect, except for the symbols used to represent them, no one would expect such an operation to be effectual.

It is easy to replicate the irrelevance proposition in the present framework. To do so, one simply sets the money preference parameter, μ, to zero. With money yielding no utility, the equilibrium nominal interest rate must vanish if consumers are to hold a positive amount of money balances. Money and bonds both appreciate at the real rate of interest, which implies expected deflation. Under these premises, portfolio changes induced by open market operations leave all incentives and constraints unaffected and have no impact on the equilibrium. Moreover, the price level and nominal wage rates become indeterminate. This is because only three equilibrium conditions are left: One for the commodity market, one for the labor market, and one for a money-cum-bonds credit market. By Walras' law, two of these conditions are independent; they determine the real wage rate and the real interest rate. Price level indeterminacy is a general feature of cashless economies. Such models can only determine the equilibrium rate of inflation.

In summary, it is possible to prove money irrelevance if one trivializes the economy and represents open market operations as exchanges of dollar notes of different denominations, a maneuver that cannot affect equilibrium. The ensuing indeterminacy runs counter to an established empirical regularity, the strong co-movement of money and prices. For monetary economics, irrelevance propositions are not useful.

3.2.4 Interest on Money

The present text portrays money as a financial asset that bears no interest. This assumption is realistic for currency and to a lesser extent for transfer and checking deposits. However, some economists, such as Kenneth Rogoff or Willem

Buiter, have proposed a "cash ban": If lawmakers prohibited the use of coins and notes and prescribed that all payments be made in electronic form, paying interest on money would raise no administrative difficulties. Although such proposals are still science fiction, they seem interesting enough to justify a temporary deviation from the zero interest premise and to investigate the analytical implications of interest on money.

Modeling interest on money requires two modifications of the basic model. First, the seigniorage becomes $\sigma_t = i_t B_t^{cb} - i_t^m M_t$; it equals the central bank's bond earnings minus interest paid on the outstanding money stock. The new symbol i_t^m denotes the nominal interest rate on money that is set autonomously by the central bank, whereas i_t is still conceived of as a market interest rate. Second, in the definition of consumers' financial assets, initial money holdings M_{t-1}^d must be replaced by the expression $(1+i_{t-1}^m)M_{t-1}^d$. Passing through appendix B, one checks that the first-order condition (16) becomes

(31) $$\frac{\partial U / \partial (M_t^d / P_t)}{\partial U / \partial C_t} = \frac{i_t - i_t^m}{1+i_t}.$$

At an individual optimum, the marginal rate of substitution between consumption and real balances still equals the user cost of money. However, the user cost is now represented by the (discounted) difference between the market interest rate and the rate of interest on money. With logarithmic utility, for instance, the money demand function (22) becomes

(32) $$M_t^d = \mu \frac{P_t(A_t + X_t + \sigma_t^r)}{1+\beta+\mu} \frac{1+i_t}{i_t - i_t^m},$$

and an equilibrium can obviously only exist if the central bank keeps the interest on money below the market interest rate. Under this assumption, any increase in i_t^m diminishes the user cost of money and stimulates money demand.

Changes in money demand have already been discussed at the end of subsection 3.1.1, where it turned out that an increase in money demand—then represented as an increase in the money preference parameter—has the same effects as a money stock reduction. With this suggestion, it is clear that paying interest on money resembles a restrictive monetary policy.

Figure 3.10 shows the consequences of a one-shot increase in interest on money, from 0 to 1 percent. This induces an initial deflation of roughly 5 percent and a temporary decline in the nominal interest rate. Upon completion of the adjustments, the nominal interest rate will have returned to its original level; interest on money has no permanent effect on this variable. The reason is that the nominal interest rate is determined by the expected real interest rate (which stays constant due to superneutrality) and by expected inflation (which converges to zero in the case of one-shot policy changes). The strong response of the price level follows from the fact that the central bank's decision to pay an interest on money of 1 percent reduces the user cost of money by roughly 20 percent. With the assumed interest elasticity of money demand of –0.10, money demand increases by approximately 2 percent. The initial overshooting of the price level is again due to the Fisher effect and the gradual revision of expectations.

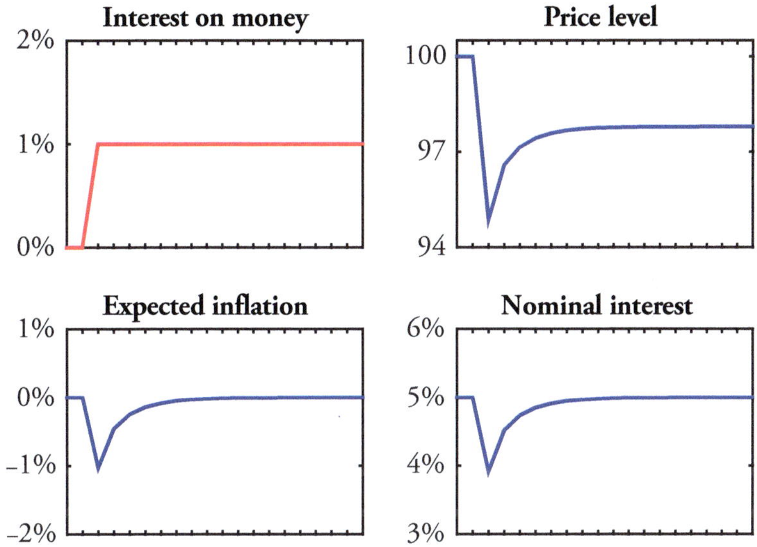

Figure 3.10: Interest on money. *Notes*: Horizontal axes represent time. The initial value of the price level is normalized at 100. The other variables are measured in percent.

As an interim result, paying interest on money diminishes the user cost and increases real balances, implying a smaller deadweight loss of positive interest rates. The additional instrument i_t^m detaches equilibrium real balances from money growth: While a central bank that uses the money stock as its only target has to accept deflation if it wishes to reduce the deadweight loss, a monetary policy consisting of target pairs (M_t, i_t^m) can reduce this loss at stable prices.

Negative interest rates on money have opposite effects. Their consideration is motivated by Silvio Gesell's celebrated *Freigeld* proposal. Gesell (1916: 182), a social reformer and heterodox economist, postulated to "deteriorate the quality of money as a commodity in order to improve it as a means of exchange". According to his fiat money scheme, currency owners were obliged to purchase stamps worth 0.1 percent weekly to keep the money valid. This amounts to a negative interest rate on currency of roughly 5 percent annually. Gesell's main objective was to boost the circular velocity, that is, to diminish the demand for money. Given this aim, his proposal makes sense. However, the present analysis suggests that an implementation of *Freigeld* would induce only temporary increases in prices and wages, combined with a permanent increase in the deadweight loss.

In sum, interest on money represents an additional instrument that allows the separation of money growth from equilibrium real balances. Positive rates resemble money stock contractions, and negative rates resemble money stock expansions. With a positive rate of interest on money slightly below the market interest rate, both seigniorage and the deadweight loss become arbitrarily small. Apart from this effect, introducing interest on money preserves the basic model properties and does not impair any of the preceding conclusions, cf. also Hornstein (2010) or Ireland (2014).

3.2.5 Digression on RE

This book represents individuals as learning agents who live in a volatile environment, try their best to make forecasts, and revise the forecasts if they recognize they are wrong. An alternative modeling strategy, to be further discussed in section 8.1, employs rational expectations, RE. Because this assumption is still frequently used in the literature, it seems useful to incorporate it into the present model for comparison.

Consider the model in the baseline specification with adaptive expectations, set out in Chapter 2. In equilibrium, money demand coincides with the money stock. Equation (160) in appendix B expresses real money demand as the product of the user cost of money, raised to the power of the elasticity of money demand, and two magnitudes that are independent of inflation. Hence, the following condition must hold in equilibrium:

$$\text{(33)} \qquad \frac{M_t}{P_t} \sim \left(\frac{i_t}{1+i_t} \right)^{\eta}.$$

Assuming zero expected inflation for the moment, $\pi^e_{t+1} = 0$, the nominal interest rate equals the expected real interest rate, which does not respond to changes in inflation because of superneutrality. Hence, P_t remains as the only free variable in the equation, and (33) yields an equilibrium price level for any given money stock. For sure, this is determined by the entire system of equilibrium conditions, as shown in section 2.6. However, since these conditions imply equality of money demand and the money stock, equation (33) must hold in any general equilibrium. In this sense, the equation characterizes a unique equilibrium price level whose stationary value may be denoted as P^*. In the absence of exogenous shocks, prices remain at this level, and expected inflation identically vanishes.

Adaptive expectations are now replaced by RE, a premise that is equivalent to perfect foresight in the absence of stochastic shocks. All other assumptions are retained. Under RE, individuals infer future variables from a forward iteration of the following kind: For each assumed price level, P_t, equation (33) defines a unique nominal interest rate and, with real interest given, a compatible expected rate of inflation. The latter implies a specific expected price level that, owing to perfect foresight, coincides with the actual price level in the next period. Schematically,

$$P_t \Rightarrow \pi^e_{t+1} \Rightarrow P^e_{t+1} = P_{t+1} \Rightarrow \pi^e_{t+2} \Rightarrow P^e_{t+2} = P_{t+2} \dots$$

Evidently, the solution under adaptive expectations, viz. $P_t = P^*$ and $\pi^e_{t+1} = 0$ for all t, is also a solution under RE: Individuals expect the price level to remain constant forever, and these expectations will prove true.

However, this RE equilibrium is not unique. In fact, *every* $P_t < P^*$ solves the problem. To see this, observe that any initial price level beneath P^* represents an equilibrium if and only if consumers accept a larger amount of real balances. Because the interest elasticity of money demand is negative, consumers will do so at a lower user cost of money. At the given real interest rate, lower user cost requires a negative expected rate of inflation that reduces the nominal rate of interest. To validate this expectation, the subsequent price level $P_{t+1} = (1 + \pi^e_{t+1})P_t$ must be smaller than P_t, which requires a further fall in expected inflation. Over time, the price level converges to zero and real balances grow unboundedly, but (33) is satisfied along the entire path.

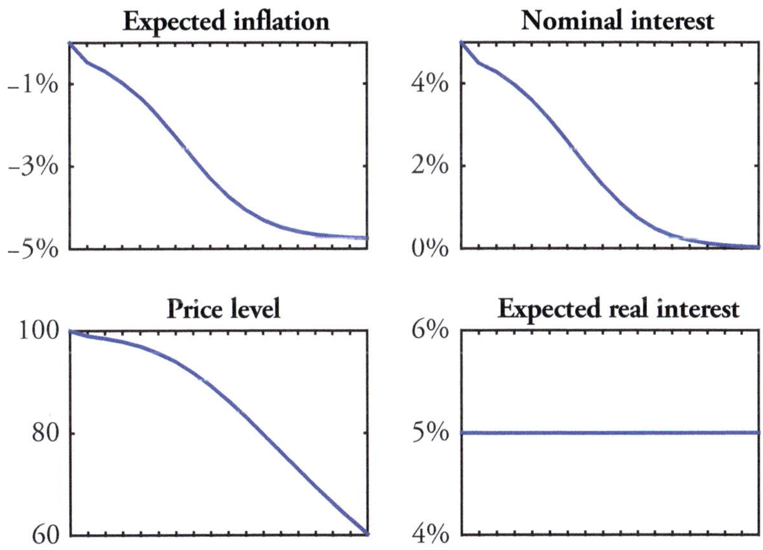

Figure 3.11: Rational expectations equilibrium. *Notes*: Horizontal axes represent time. The initial value of the price level is normalized at 100. All other variables are measured in percent.

Figure 3.11 shows exact computations of a specific RE equilibrium path that is triggered by a sudden decrease in expected inflation and the price level. The decrease itself is purely accidental. Following Azariadis (1981), it may result from changes in a *sunspot*—a variable that has no effect on fundamentals such as preferences or technologies. While the nominal interest rate is driven to zero, expected inflation approaches –5 percent, consistent with a constant expected real interest rate of 5 percent. Analogous equilibrium paths emerge for every initial price level below P^*. Therefore, nominal variables are indeterminate under RE.

To review, the simple framework used here fails to produce meaningful results if adaptive expectations are replaced by RE: Inflation, the price level, and nominal interest are all indeterminate. Classic articles such as Brock (1975), Obstfeld and Rogoff (1983), Carlstrom and Fuerst (2001), Benhabib et al. (2001), and Cochrane (2011) have shown that RE models often suffer from indeterminacy; infinite forward iterations simply do not pin down unique equilibria. While adaptive expectations link forecasts to a past that is predetermined, hence unique, RE link forecasts to an indefinite future that can take many forms. To rule out indeterminacy and sunspot equilibria, RE models require *ad hoc* boundary assumptions; see Galí (2015: 44) and Woodford (2003: 106), or restrictions on preferences. Blanchard and Kahn (1980) provide solutions for linear RE models that satisfy strong boundary conditions.

3.3 Fiscal Policy

This section augments the baseline model with a government sector. To do so is motivated by the observation that the government is typically a country's most important actor, with an expenditure sometimes reaching or exceeding 50 percent of GDP. Also, central banks do not remit seigniorage to consumers, as in the framework considered so far, but transfer it to the country's treasury. More generally, governments and central banks maintain intimate financial relationships, a fact that induced Sargent and Wallace (1981) to analyze fiscal and monetary policy in terms of a consolidated budget constraint of the two institutions. This approach is not followed here because it makes the government-central bank relationship even more opaque. Instead, the analysis separates fiscal and monetary institutions as far as possible and models interactions as explicit government decrees.

In what follows, government activities are described by three variables, viz. real public consumption, G_t, real tax revenue, T_t, and the nominal stock of public debt, B_t^g. Public consumption comprises government spending on goods and services but does not include transfer payments. Since transfers make up a large fraction of annual budgets in modern welfare states, the value of public consumption, $P_t G_t$, falls considerably short of public expenditure. Transfers are netted here against lump sum taxes, such that T_t represents the balance. Consequently, T_t captures only the income effects of taxes and transfers. While raising taxes and transfers is likely to produce disincentive effects in reality, such a policy is neutral here as long as taxes minus transfers remain unchanged. This is an important caveat but seems acceptable in a context focusing on monetary rather than public finance issues.

The government acts in accordance with a budget constraint that describes the evolution of public debt. Interest payments and public consumption increase the stock of government bonds while seigniorage and tax revenue reduce it:

(34) $$B_t^g = (1+i_{t-1})B_{t-1}^g - \sigma_{t-1} + P_t G_t - P_t T_t .$$

Specifically, debt is increased by the interest paid thereon, $i_{t-1}B_{t-1}^g$, and is diminished by the seigniorage, σ_{t-1}, which equals central bank interest revenue. The government budget constraint contains a first indication of fiscal-monetary interrelationships: If the central bank owned all public debt, interest outlays and seigniorage remittances would cancel each other out, $i_{t-1}B_{t-1}^g = \sigma_{t-1}$, so that total interest payments would only represent a transitory item in the government budget.

Because central bank profit is now collected by the government, which also levies taxes, seigniorage income must be replaced by tax payments in the consumers' budget constraints. This requires a redefinition of financial assets, indicated by a circle, which excludes seigniorage:

(35) $$\mathring{A}_t = \frac{(1+i_{t-1})B_{t-1}^d + M_{t-1}^d}{P_t} .$$

Now, consumers maximize the utility function $U(C_t, \mathring{A}_{t+1}^e, M_t^d / P_t)$, which replaces (14), subject to the modified budget constraint

(36) $$P_t C_t + B_t^d + M_t^d = (1+i_{t-1})B_{t-1}^d + M_{t-1}^d + W_t N_t + \Pi_t - P_t T_t ,$$

which replaces (12). Appendix F derives the associated behavioral responses and shows that consumption and money demand are still linear functions of consumers' total wealth. Total wealth, however, equals $\mathring{A}_t + X_t - T_t$ in the fiscal model, as opposed to $A_t + X_t + \sigma_t^r$ in the baseline model; hence, tax payments replace seigniorage. Assuming that government bonds and corporate bonds are perfect substitutes and observing that public consumption constitutes a part of total commodity demand in this one-sector economy, a temporary equilibrium is a triple (P_t, i_t, W_t) such that the following conditions hold and all private choices are individually optimal:

(37) $$\left.\begin{array}{l} C_t + I_t + G_t = Y_t^s \\ B_t^d + B_t^{cb} = B_t^s + B_t^g \\ N_t^d = \bar{N} \end{array}\right\} \Rightarrow (P_t, i_t, W_t) .$$

The terms on the right-hand side of the bond market equilibrium condition represent corporate and public liabilities whereas the terms on the left-hand side represent private and central bank claims. Of course, the equilibrium is subject to central bank decisions on the money stock as well as to government decisions on public consumption and taxes. This completes the description of the fiscal model.

3.3.1 Superneutrality Revisited

Subsection 3.1.4 introduced superneutrality of money as a useful benchmark property according to which changes in money growth have no real effects. It is natural to ask whether this property also holds in the presence of a government sector. The analysis starts with a preliminary question: Is it possible to replicate the allocation of the baseline model in the fiscal model? Of course, this requires public consumption to vanish because it crowds out private expenditure in this model class. At zero public consumption, superneutrality obtains if public debt and tax payments satisfy

$$B_{t-1}^{g} = \frac{\sigma_{t-1}}{1+i_{t-1}} \quad \text{and} \quad T_t = -\sigma_t^r . \tag{38}$$

Fiscal policies that transfer the entire real seigniorage, defined in (21), to the consumers keep the final stock of public debt at $B_t^g = \sigma_t / (1+i_t)$, as can be seen from substituting (38) and $G_t = 0$ into the budget constraint, (34). Therefore, the left-hand equation will be satisfied forever.

Under such a policy, equation (35) implies that financial assets in the fiscal and the baseline model are identical: At unchanged values of central bank bond holdings and producers' bond issues, the equilibrium condition for the bond market in (37) entails that private bond holdings, B_{t-1}^d, increase by an amount of public debt that equals $\sigma_{t-1} / (1+i_{t-1})$. Multiplying by the nominal interest factor shows that private bond demand including interest rises by σ_{t-1}. This offsets the lack of seigniorage in the redefined financial assets. In conjunction with transfers $T_t = -\sigma_t^r$, consumers' total wealth is the same as in the baseline model. Intuitively, the government acts on behalf of the consumers—it collects the seigniorage and remits the entire amount. Therefore, monetary policy is superneutral.

In the more interesting case of positive public consumption, monetary policy is still superneutral if the government keeps public debt at the level defined in (38) and collects taxes of the amount

$$T_t = G_t - \sigma_t^r . \tag{39}$$

Fiscal policies of this type specify real public consumption, G_t, and levy taxes that equal public consumption minus real seigniorage. Public debt is kept close to zero and any increase in seigniorage is transferred to the consumers via tax rebates. Notably, monetary policy affects nominal tax payments in three ways, through its effects on prices, the nominal interest rate, and the money stock. Notwithstanding this interaction, the separate effects cancel each other out; monetary policy is still superneutral.

In almost all countries, public debt exceeds seigniorage. In this case, superneutrality does not hold in general. Actually, it becomes difficult to *define* this property. This point is crucial as it underlines anew the close interrelationships between fiscal and monetary policies. A seemingly sensible definition of superneutrality would require that changes in money growth have no real effects if fiscal policy is kept constant in real terms. However, with three policy instruments—public consumption, taxes, and public debt—a government that accepts interest and seigniorage as given and acts in accordance with its budget constraint cannot keep all three instruments constant, except in the special cases outlined. Changes in monetary policy will commonly force the government to adjust at least one of its three choice variables, and this adjustment is bound to produce real effects.

As an illustration, consider a government that chooses a given level of public consumption and adjusts tax revenue to preserve budget balance. If the central bank accelerates money growth, such a policy produces a permanent increase in real output. The reason is simple: With a balanced budget, public debt remains constant in nominal terms so that the *public debt ratio*, $B_t^g / (P_t Y_t)$, converges to zero. Consequently, the expected real interest rate declines, which spurs capital formation and output.

To summarize, monetary policy is superneutral in an economy with a fiscal sector if the government keeps public debt close to zero, sets a given path for real public consumption, and forwards all seigniorage remittances to the consumers through transfers or tax reductions. Combined, these reservations are strong. If the government issues large amounts of public debt, or if it takes an opportunistic stance and uses seigniorage to increase public consumption, superneutrality ceases to hold because seigniorage represents a close link between the government and the central bank. As a result, fiscal and monetary policy cannot be strictly separated.

3.3.2 Ricardian Equivalence

Public debt changes the model critically. In the absence of a government sector, the private sector's net financial wealth was always zero. Specifically, consumers were net creditors, producers were net debtors, and since the central bank maintained a neutral financial position, consumers and producers together held no net financial wealth. This is different in the fiscal model because public debt epitomizes a liability for the government and a corresponding financial asset for the consumers. The premise that consumers regard government bonds as part of their wealth destabilizes the model and produces unexpected results.

Figure 3.12 illustrates a somewhat eerie scenario that starts with a balanced budget and a public debt ratio of 25 percent. After a while, the government increases public consumption by 10 percent but leaves taxes unchanged. The public debt ratio increases as a result, as shown in the bottom right panel. Nominal and expected real interest rates also rise, while output and the capital stock decline. The stunning element is the behavior of private consumption. Notwithstanding that output and capital fall steadily, consumers feel as prosperous as ever because government bonds—perceived as net wealth—replace corporate bonds in the portfolios. As a result, private consumption does not decline until the party ends abruptly: With a real capital stock diminished through persistent disinvestment, producers eventually become unable to satisfy public and private consumption demand, and a general equilibrium ceases to exist. The inexistence of equilibrium is a consequence of the resource constraint, $C_t + I_t + G_t = F(\bar{N}, K_{t-1})$, which indicates that excessive total consumption, $C_t + G_t$, can be financed only temporarily by disinvestment. Thereafter, the economy collapses. Of course, investors and governments do not usually wait for the crash to come but anticipate it. The result is a *sovereign default* that diminishes private consumption and restores equilibrium.

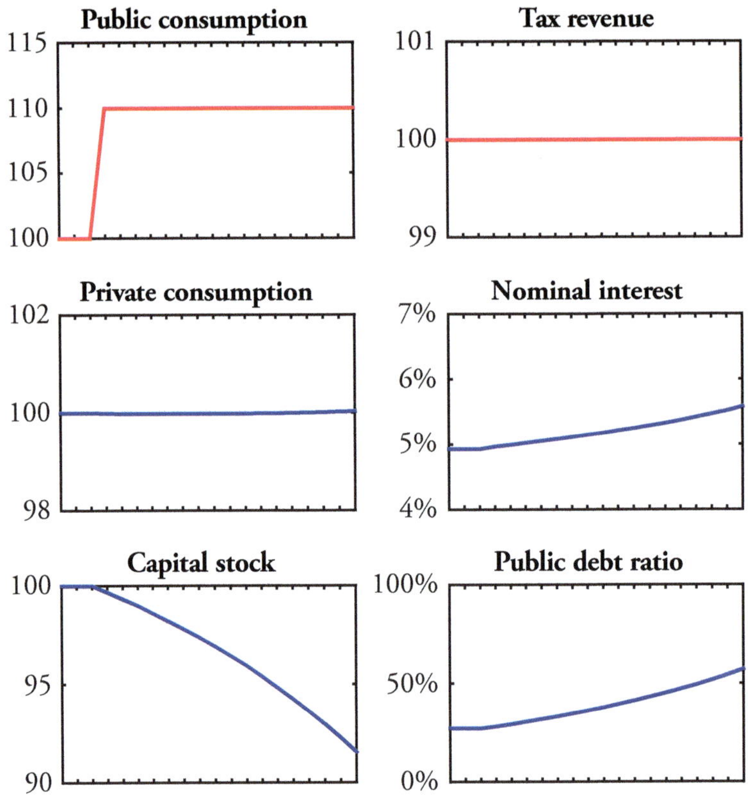

Figure 3.12: Unsustainable fiscal policy. *Notes*: Horizontal axes represent time. Nominal interest and the public debt ratio are measured in percent. The initial values of the other variables are normalized at 100.

Figure 3.13 shows how this works. The simulation assumes that the government applies a 50 percent haircut to its debt, keeps public consumption constant, and increases taxes after the default to preserve budget balance. The haircut, indicated by the arrow in the bottom right panel, reduces the public debt ratio and extinguishes a considerable part of consumers' perceived wealth. This impact, reinforced by the tax hike, brings down private consumption. After a sharp initial reduction, private consumption recovers together with the real capital stock but does not regain its previous level under debt financing.

Hence, combining a haircut with subsequent austerity works in a technical sense but deprives many individuals of their retirement provisions. Although sovereign defaults cause much pain and turmoil, they are by no means a rare occurrence. In their book *This Time is Different*, Reinhart and Rogoff (2009) document hundreds of government bankruptcies. The authors also indicate that there is no general rule determining the exact date of default; this date depends on investors' willingness to buy government bonds and on the government's willingness to serve its debt.

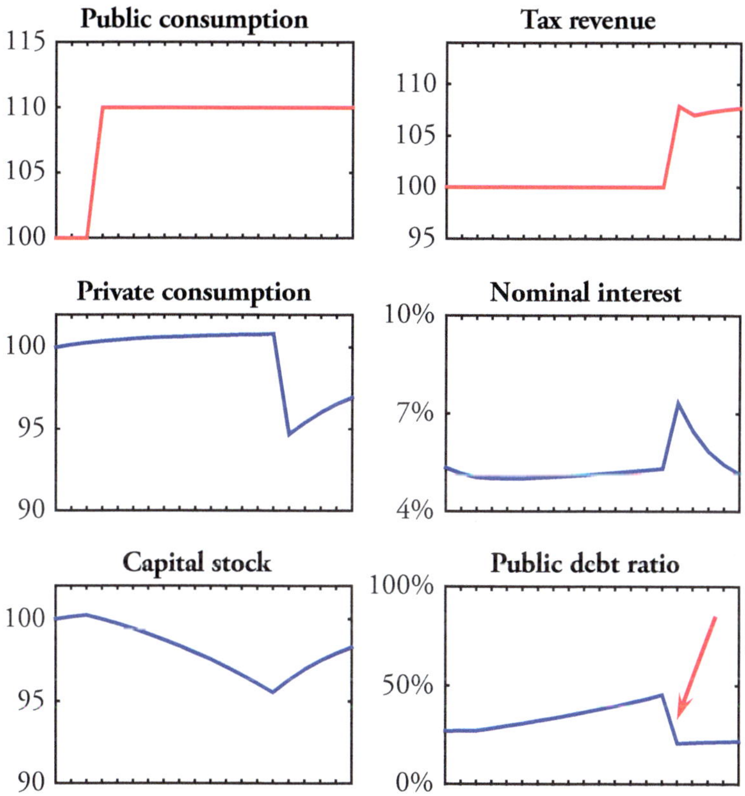

Figure 3.13: Sovereign default. *Notes*: Horizontal axes represent time. Nominal interest and the public debt ratio are measured in percent. The initial values of the other variables are normalized at 100.

This line of reasoning suggests that the method of financing is crucial: Debt financing keeps consumers happy but is a dangerous policy—it leads to default. Tax financing limits total consumption and constitutes a rock-solid fiscal policy. A comprehensive literature, however, initiated by Barro (1974) and surveyed by Bernheim (1987) and Ricciuti (2003), challenges this view and argues that debt and taxes are equivalent ways to finance public expenditure, a hypothesis known as Ricardian equivalence. As O'Driscoll (1977) points out, the term is a misnomer because Ricardo—who was both an eminent economist and an able investor—denied the equivalence of debt and tax financing. O'Driscoll's objection is correct but disregarded here because Ricardian equivalence has become an established technical term. In the fiscal model considered so far, Ricardian equivalence does not hold. Yet it is easy to incorporate this property. Consider public debt in real terms,

$$D_t^g = \frac{(1+i_{t-1})B_{t-1}^g - \sigma_{t-1}}{P_t}, \tag{40}$$

whose definition parallels the definition of consumers' financial assets. Real public debt equals debt inherited from the past plus interest payments minus seigniorage, divided by the price level. In a Ricardian economy, consumers perceive public debt as their own liability because they assume it will provoke higher taxes in the future. On this condition, consumers' *perceived financial wealth* equals financial assets minus public debt, and consumers maximize

$$U(C_t, \mathring{A}_{t+1}^e - D_{t+1}^g, \frac{M_t^d}{P_t}). \tag{41}$$

The public debt term in the second argument of the utility function represents the only difference between a Ricardian and a non-Ricardian model. At the same time, equilibrium conditions and consumers' budget constraints are not at all affected by this change in assumptions: Even consumers who disregard public debt as net wealth have to pay for government bonds and collect interest thereon.

Ricardian equivalence: If consumers maximize (41) subject to (36), changes in tax payments do not have any real effects; debt and tax financing are equivalent.

Appendix F outlines the proof and shows that with a logarithmic utility function, consumer optimization yields

$$C_t = \frac{\mathring{A}_t + X_t + \sigma_t^r - G_t - D_t^g}{1+\beta+\mu}. \tag{42}$$

This formula has two remarkable features. First, it contains the real seigniorage in the same way as the baseline model. Although the seigniorage is not explicitly transferred to consumers, the latter take it fully into account because it reduces public debt. Second, taxes do not appear in the consumption function; they reduce consumers' disposable income but also diminish public debt. The burden on the private sector is fully described by only two variables, viz. public consumption and initial public debt. Taxes do not change this burden but merely affect the time profile of the payments.

Figure 3.14 illustrates a fiscal policy that starts with a balanced budget and a constant public debt ratio. At a certain point in time, the government reduces real taxes but leaves public consumption unchanged. Consumers who act in accordance with (42) resist the temptation to increase consumption. Instead, they use the additional income exclusively for the acquisition of government bonds. As it happens, the emerging rise in bond demand equals the increase in public debt that follows from the tax reduction at unchanged public expenditure. The public debt ratio is of no concern since debt is always backed by private bond demand. In each subsequent period, the variables $\mathring{A}_t$ and D_t^g rise by an equal amount such that consumption remains constant along the entire equilibrium path.

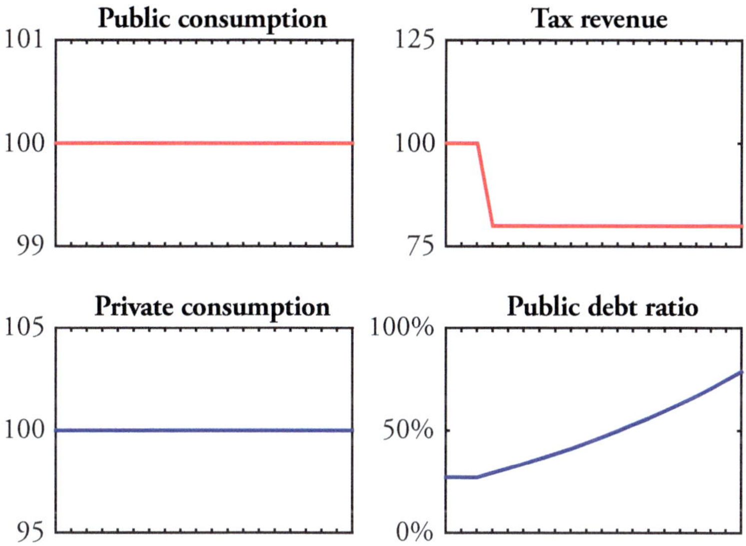

Figure 3.14: Ricardian equivalence. *Notes*: Horizontal axes represent time. The public debt ratio is measured in percent. The initial values of the other variables are normalized at 100.

To summarize, if consumers perceive public debt as their own liability, debt financing and tax financing are equivalent. Incidentally, monetary policy is superneutral in this case, as the presence of real seigniorage in (42) indicates. The central bank can determine any money stock path—and the government can choose any path of tax payments—without affecting the economy's real equilibrium. Notably, Ricardian equivalence and superneutrality of money do not presuppose that consumers plan over infinite horizons. To make optimal choices, consumers only need to know the observable policy variables. With this in mind, D_{t+1}^g depends only on the current levels of public debt, seigniorage, and the nominal interest rate, as well as on the expected price level whose later realization plays no role under superneutrality.

There is no consensus in the literature as to whether models should be Ricardian or non-Ricardian. While most contemporary papers entail Ricardian equivalence, this is not due to an assumed usefulness of this property but more a by-product of the premise that consumers make RE plans over infinite horizons. Ricardian models predict that public debt has no effects unless frictions are added. In this sense, deploring public debt would be pointless in a Ricardian world.

Another strand goes back to Amilcare Puviani's (1903) theory of *fiscal illusions*, a work that was improved by Buchanan and Wagner (1977) and can be seen as a cornerstone of modern behavioral public finance. According to Puviani, ordinary people are unable to see through the veil of fiscal institutions and do not recognize the basic equivalence of different forms of taxation, public debt, and money creation. As a result, governments can address resistance to taxation by an appropriate mix of instruments—a strategy that would make no sense in a world with ultra-rational consumers. Puviani noticed that revenue-maximizing governments favor indirect over direct taxes (since the former are less noticeable), debt financing over tax financing (to shift the burden from current voters to future generations), and inflation over stable prices (to increase seigniorage). His observations lead directly to the next section, which returns to the non-Ricardian model.

3.3.3 Leviathan

The term leviathan, borrowed from Brennan and Buchanan (1980) and the public choice literature, designates a government that maximizes public consumption. This subsection discusses fiscal and monetary policy with such an objective in mind. It starts with deriving the government budget constraint in real terms. Dividing the budget constraint, (36), by the price level and using (40), the definition of real public debt, yields $B_t^g / P_t = D_t^g + G_t - T_t$. This expression can be simplified further if one shifts (40) one period forward, uses definitions (4) and (21) of real interest and real seigniorage, respectively, and rearranges terms: $B_t^g / P_t = D_{t+1}^g / (1 + r_{t+1}^e) + \sigma_t^r$. The government budget constraint in real terms follows from equalizing the two preceding equations:

$$(43) \qquad G_t = \underbrace{\frac{D_{t+1}^g}{1 + r_{t+1}^e} + T_t}_{\text{fiscal instruments}} + \underbrace{\sigma_t^r - D_t^g}_{\text{monetary instruments}} .$$

This identity states that public consumption equals final public debt plus tax revenue plus real seigniorage minus initial public debt. The revenue terms on the right-hand side represent four distinct policy instruments. Which of these instruments are available for the leviathan depends on the policy regime.

In a regime of *monetary dominance*, the central bank is truly independent and sets the money stock autonomously. The government must accept this choice and can only use taxes and final public debt. In its determination of tax revenue, a reasonable government will not seize consumers' total wealth since this would reduce the capital stock to zero and exclude future taxes. Rather, it will maximize a discounted sum of future taxes. Irrespective of its concrete objective, the government could confine itself to levying taxes and would not need public debt as an additional source of revenue if there were no obstacles to taxation. Put differently, debt finance only becomes attractive if the power to tax is exogenously restricted. Such restrictions can take many forms. The government may fear tax evasion or an open revolt, or there may be constitutional or legal obstacles to over-tighten the tax screw. Under such circumstances, fiscal illusions become important: While taxes must be resolutely enforced, debt financing is purely voluntary; bond buyers think they get something in exchange for their payments. As a result, debt financing enables the leviathan to increase public consumption beyond tax revenue.

In a regime of *fiscal dominance*, two monetary instruments are also available to the government. Although central banks are formally independent in many countries, governments unquestionably have the upper hand. They can use moral suasion, select suitable central bank officers, and, ultimately, remove central bank independence by changing the law. A regime of fiscal dominance enables the government to raise real seigniorage, the third term in its budget constraint, by ordering an increase in money growth. Such a measure has two possible rationales. First, seigniorage taxes are technically distinct from ordinary taxes. Specifically, they make it possible to charge basic needs (which are often taxed at reduced rates) and the subsistence level (which is normally exempt under the income tax). The seigniorage tax also hits activities in the shadow economy. Drug dealers, for instance, who are unlikely to file income tax returns but make extensive use of banknotes, bear the full burden of seigniorage.

A second possible rationale is, again, fiscal illusion. Regarding taxes, individuals put all the blame on the government. However, they are less aware of the user cost of money and not so sure about its causes. In 1804, Jeremy Bentham, cited from Hayek (1932: 124), was the first economist to describe the tax character of money creation: "The effect of forced frugality is also produced by the creating of paper money by government, or the suffering of the creation of paper money by individuals. In this case, the effect is produced by a species of indirect taxation, which has hitherto passed almost unnoticed."

This version of the forced saving doctrine recognizes that inflation, which redistributed wealth between different social classes in the model in subsection 3.1.5, now redirects wealth from the private sector to the government. Bentham's astute observation calls into question the metaphor of central bank "money injections" and its connotation that increases in the money stock come as a gift to consumers. Quite the contrary, increases in the money stock belong on the expenditure side of consumers' budget constraints, not on the revenue side. The need to permanently replenish money balances in an inflationary environment reduces consumers' purchasing power and enables the government to extract additional means via a method that is subtle and hardly perceptible to most individuals.

Cagan (1956: 80) conducted a partial equilibrium analysis of seigniorage maximization. In his continuous-time framework, the user cost of money coincides with the nominal interest rate, and steady state real seigniorage amounts to iM/P. If the government maximizes seigniorage through its influence on money growth and the nominal interest rate, it must ensure that the money stock equals money demand, which is a decreasing function of the nominal interest rate. Differentiating $i\,M^d/P$ with respect to nominal interest yields the first-order condition $M^d/P + i(dM^d/di)/P = 0$, which can be rewritten as

$$\frac{dM^d}{di}\frac{i}{M^d} = -1\,. \tag{44}$$

Therefore, a seigniorage maximizer will push inflation and nominal interest to the point where the elasticity of money demand equals unity; a rule reminiscent of the behavior of a revenue-maximizing monopolist. To make the result meaningful, Cagan assumed a money demand function of the form $M^d/P = \exp(k\,i)$, where $k < 0$ represents the constant semi-elasticity of money demand (actually, he assumed an exogenous real interest rate and put inflation rather than the nominal interest rate into the exponent). Since the associated elasticity of money demand, $k\,i$, increases in nominal interest, (44) yields the inverse semi-elasticity rule, $i = -1/k$.

However, this result does not carry over to a general equilibrium framework where matters are more complicated. Specifically, inflation triggers not only a substitution effect of the kind considered by Cagan, but also an income effect in that it diminishes consumers' real wealth. Therefore, increases in seigniorage have the same detrimental effect on the capital stock as increases in taxes. To elaborate this point, assume zero public debt for the moment and let T^* indicate the maximum tax revenue that can be extracted in a steady state. Obviously, seigniorage financing is only useful in the presence of an exogenous restriction $\bar{T} < T^*$ that makes it impossible for the government to reach the desired revenue maximum via ordinary taxes. Under this premise, optimal seigniorage is given by $\sigma_t^r = T^* - \bar{T}$. As this expression decreases in $\bar{T}$, seigniorage financing becomes particularly attractive if the government faces technical difficulties with or strong resistance to ordinary taxes, both of which diminish the exogenous limit. Hence, the essence of seigniorage financing is not that it allows total revenue to be pushed beyond T^* but that it enables the government to circumvent the limit $\bar{T}$.

As indicated in Chapter 2, seigniorage constitutes but a minor fraction of public revenue in many contemporary economies, typically beneath 1 percent of GDP. In high-inflation countries, the figure may be higher but is unlikely to exceed 10 percent; see Kimbrough (2006: 1975) and the references cited therein. Fischer (1982: 302) reports that during the 1960s and 1970s, seigniorage exceeded 3 percent of GDP in European countries such as Greece, Italy, and Portugal. He also notes that in countries with high inflation, national currencies tend to become substituted by foreign currencies ("dollarization") with the effect that the national government loses its seigniorage to a foreign government. The danger of currency substitution places a further restriction on seigniorage maximization.

Returning to (43), initial real public debt represents the fourth and final instrument in a regime of fiscal dominance. Definition (40) shows that this magnitude comprises three predetermined variables (i_{t-1}, σ_{t-1}, B^g_{t-1}) as well as the current price level. With effective control over the money stock in the fiscal regime, the government can diminish its real debt by increasing P_t. Inflating the debt away wipes out parts of private wealth and makes it possible for the government to increase public consumption at given levels of final public debt, taxes, and seigniorage. Initial public debt can be written in an alternative form if one shifts the time index in the definition of the expected real interest rate one period back:

(45) $$D^g_t = (1+r_t)\left(\frac{B^g_{t-1}}{P_{t-1}} + \sigma^r_{t-1}\right).$$

The variable r_t has not been defined as yet. It is referred to as the ex post real interest rate. Unlike the expected real interest rate, which is an ex ante magnitude, the ex post real rate depends on the nominal interest rate that had been agreed upon in the past, the previous price level, and the current price level. While monetary policy cannot generally affect the expected real rate, as discussed so often, it can easily diminish the ex post real rate by surprise inflation. If the price level were to go to infinity, r_t would approach minus 100 percent.

However, a one-shot increase in the money stock does not contribute much to preserving government solvency. As Figure 3.2 suggested, such a measure is liable to produce unexpected inflation followed by unexpected deflation. Hence, the initial depreciation of real public debt would be followed by a corresponding appreciation. To obtain a favorable permanent effect, the government must instead increase the money growth rate. This avoids subsequent deflation and has a lasting effect on real seigniorage revenue. Of course, the government can also repeat this policy, ordering a further rise in the money growth rate. Such an *acceleration policy* triggers recurring declines in consumers' total wealth and the public debt ratio. Each round, however, raises inflation permanently and is apt to result in hyperinflation and currency substitution. This happened in Zimbabwe, for instance, a country that printed its final banknote in 2008, with a face value of 100 trillion dollars.

3.3.4 Debt Monetization

Since the Great Recession of 2008–09, several governments have amassed large amounts of debt. In some countries, debt sustainability has become questionable, and other countries have already defaulted, Greece being the most prominent example. The threat of future insolvencies has stimulated a discussion about debt monetization, a policy that converts interest-bearing bonds into interest-free money and is also referred to as monetary financing. Turner (2016), for instance, vigorously advocates such measures. The argument seems intriguing: Governments can become insolvent—central banks cannot—hence, debt monetization effectively impedes sovereign default.

Before analyzing the case for such a policy, some caveats should be noted. Debt monetization is only feasible in a fiscal regime. In particular, governments that issue debt denominated in a foreign currency cannot make use of such a policy. Debt monetization is also impossible under a gold standard or for members of a currency union with an independent central bank. The latter case is not so clear-cut, however. If many union members run into over-indebtedness and favor debt monetization, they may succeed in transforming the original regime of monetary dominance into a regime of fiscal dominance. A final caveat pertains to central bank insolvency. From a legal perspective, a central bank cannot become insolvent in the sense of an inability to meet financial obligations. Lawmakers can also prevent balance-sheet insolvency by creating "adjustment items" after a financial loss. In economic terms, however, a central bank can lose its capability to produce seigniorage. Such is possible in conjunction with bad debt losses or after currency substitution.

Debt monetization involves purchases of government bonds by the central bank. Of course, central banks always buy such bonds in the course of their open market operations; in this sense, debt monetization is ubiquitous. Under monetary dominance, however, a central bank will not buy more bonds only because the government has issued more bonds, and this is the crux of the matter. With fiscal dominance, by contrast, the government can instruct the central bank to buy the entire amount of public debt, irrespective of the size of that amount. Hence, in its purest form, debt monetization is represented by the equation

$$B_t^{cb} \equiv B_t^g . \tag{46}$$

With a view to capital market equilibrium, $B_t^d + B_t^{cb} = B_t^s + B_t^g$, it is largely irrelevant whether the central bank buys government or corporate bonds; these are not earmarked. It is also immaterial whether the central bank buys government bonds in the secondary market or acquires them directly from the government. Under debt monetization, every increase in public consumption expenditure, $\Delta(P_t G_t)$, that is financed by additional public debt, ΔB_t^g, induces a commensurate increase in central bank bond holdings, ΔB_t^{cb}, and the money stock, ΔM_t. As a result, this policy is analytically equivalent to an institutional arrangement where government consumption is directly financed by the money press, $\Delta(P_t G_t) = \Delta M_t$, as in settings with helicopter money.

In Figure 3.12, the government increased public consumption in the presence of a given tax revenue and a given money stock. This policy was shown to be unsustainable; the ensuing rise in public debt made default inevitable. Figure 3.15 illustrates an otherwise identical scenario where the money stock follows (46).

The policy path is evidently sustainable. The money stock rises exponentially, as does the price level, with an asymptotically stable rate of inflation of nearly 5 percent. As inflation expectations adjust, the nominal interest rate also rises by 5 percent due to the Fisher effect. Public debt increases permanently but at the same rate as the price level; the public debt ratio remains roughly stable. As an interim result, a fiscal policy that is unsustainable in a regime of monetary dominance can be sustainable under debt monetization.

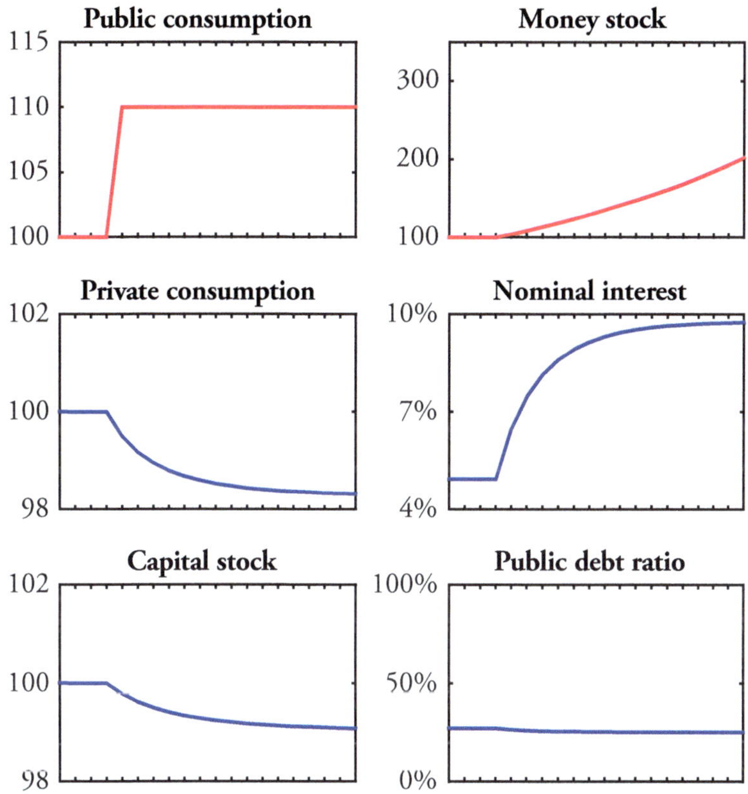

Figure 3.15: Debt monetization. *Notes*: Horizontal axes represent time. Nominal interest and the public debt ratio are measured in percent. The initial values of the other variables are normalized at 100.

This finding may at first be suspected as a miracle (if not fake) but it has a natural explanation. The decrease in private consumption, shown in the middle left panel of Figure 3.15, is key to the process and distinguishes the present policy from the unsustainable policy depicted in Figure 3.12, where private consumption remained almost unchanged after an increase in public consumption, so that capital and output fell in each subsequent period.

An economic collapse is avoided here because additional public consumption diminishes private consumption. The adjustment is brought about by inflation: The rise in the price level forces consumers—who desire a certain amount of real balances—to increase nominal balances in every period and to reduce consumption expenditure accordingly. Therefore, debt monetization is very similar to taxation; it produces seigniorage that adds to government revenue and places a burden on consumers. The allocation depicted in Figure 3.15 could be reproduced with a scheme that abstains from public debt and its monetization but finances the increase in public consumption exclusively through higher taxes.

To conclude, one can consider debt monetization as a delusive policy, or as a decision of last resort. In any case, such a policy does not represent a free lunch but substitutes seigniorage for ordinary taxes. Debt monetization affects consumers in the same way as taxation, and it has similar limits: One should not infer from the preceding example that debt monetization would make *any* fiscal policy sustainable.

3.4 Wage Rigidities

The previous sections assumed flexible prices and wages that were determined jointly with the interest rate through the equilibrium conditions (17) from section 2.6. Such a setting simplifies the model and focuses the analysis on the medium term. For a short-run analysis, however, perfect price and wage flexibility is an arguable premise. In reality, prices and wages are not determined in auction markets but take some time to adjust. Nominal wage rates, for instance, are typically agreed upon for one year. The following paragraphs take account of such rigidities and suppose that prices and wages are either fixed or at least sticky. Before moving on, it should be noted that the assumed degree of price flexibility is not a matter of principle or something suitable to identifying "schools" that are at loggerheads. Rather, the proper choice of price adjustment speed depends on the time horizon under consideration.

The analysis starts with a fixed nominal wage rate and outlines the changes that are necessary to keep the model consistent. Basically, wage rates and employment swap roles: While a competitive model determined wage rates, W_t, at the natural employment level, $\bar{N}$, the present model determines actual employment, N_t, at a given wage rate, $\bar{W}$. Hence, employment becomes endogenous, nominal wage rates become exogenous, and the equilibrium conditions (17) are replaced by

$$\left.\begin{array}{l} C_t + I_t = Y_t^s \\ B_t^d + B_t^{cb} = B_t^s \end{array}\right\} \Rightarrow (P_t, i_t). \tag{47}$$

In addition, actual employment is demand-determined, $N_t \equiv N_t^d$. At a high nominal wage rate, employment will fall short of the natural level, $\bar{N}$, and vice versa. The natural level itself generally differs from full employment because unemployment may result from search and matching processes, welfare benefits and other frictions outside the model's scope. The unemployment rate that prevails if employment coincides with the natural level is known as the *natural rate of unemployment*. Note that this is not the only method to model rigid wages. The number $\bar{N}$ can also be interpreted as maximum employment, so that actual employment equals $N_t = \min\{N_t^d; \bar{N}\}$. Both approaches are equivalent as long as the real wage rate exceeds its competitive equilibrium level.

Consumers optimize in the same way as before because wage income enters their budget constraints, (12), as a given variable. Therefore, this part of the model does not require modification. For producers, however, profit maximization becomes a bit more difficult. As stated by the first-order condition (11), the marginal productivity of capital equals the user cost of capital at an individual optimum, $\partial F(N_{t+1}^d, K_t^d) / \partial K_t^d = r_{t+1}^e + \delta$. Since a production function with constant returns to scale has positive cross-derivatives, the marginal productivity of capital increases in employment; more employees make a given capital stock more useful. As a result, producers who decide in period t on the capital stock to be used in period $t+1$ must forecast employment. This issue shows up in any coherent model with constant returns to scale but is often obscured by a perfect foresight assumption. The problem cannot be circumvented by introducing nominal wage rate forecasts. Under constant returns to scale, a pair (w_{t+1}^e, r_{t+1}^e) defines only the optimal factor intensity but leaves the capital stock indeterminate unless the future employment level is known. However, a simple recursion makes it possible to replace expected employment by *expected output*, which allows a more natural exposition. Subject to a given output expectation, the optimal capital stock is uniquely defined by the first-order condition

(48) $$\frac{\partial F[F^{-1}(Y_{t+1}^e, K_t^d), K_t^d]}{\partial K_t^d} = r_{t+1}^e + \delta ,$$

where F^{-1} represents the partial inverse of the production function with respect to labor demand. Capital and investment demand become dependent on expected output, which can be interpreted as a forecast of the business climate. As with expected inflation, expected output is assumed to result from a prior belief, Y_t^e, that is corrected by a fraction of the forecast error:

(49) $$Y_{t+1}^e = Y_t^e + \lambda_Y (Y_t - Y_t^e) .$$

The learning parameter λ_Y is set to 0.2 in the following simulations. In short, the fixed wage model differs from the competitive model in just two respects. First, wages and employment change roles, giving rise to the new set of equilibrium conditions, (47). Second, investment decisions depend on output expectations; see (48), that are formed adaptively according to (49).

3.4.1 Employment Trap

After these preparations, it is easy to simulate the impact of an exogenous and permanent increase in the nominal wage rate. Every economist is acquainted with such experiments from elementary courses that discuss the issue in static partial equilibrium models. A dynamic general equilibrium framework entails richer results and proves its power by revealing some subtle and unexpected consequences. In Figure 3.16, employment equals the natural level at the outset. The initial impulse, a 5 percent increase in the nominal wage rate, triggers a decline in employment, a rise in prices, and a temporary increase in the real wage rate. Because monetary policy is purely passive in this scenario and does not try to counteract the impulse, the exact return of the real wage rate to its original equilibrium level seems amazing. A step-by-step outline of the forces at work helps to understand the conundrum.

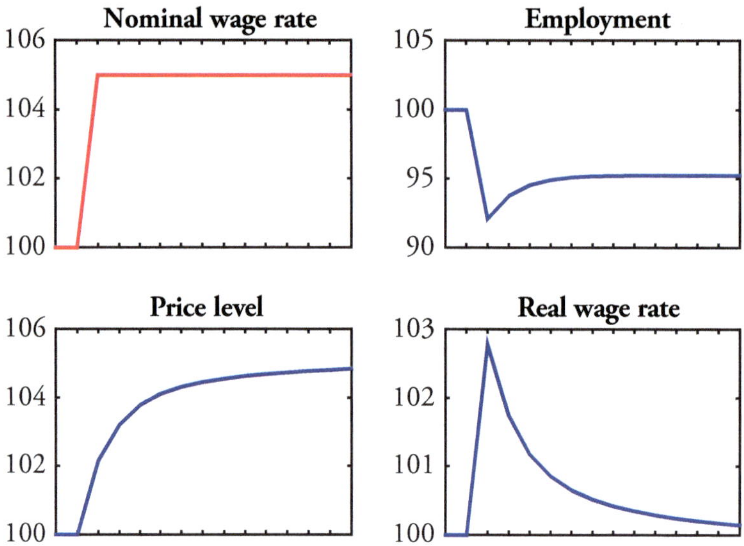

Figure 3.16: Fixed nominal wage rate. *Notes*: Horizontal axes represent time. The initial values of all variables are normalized at 100.

First, the plunge in employment—which accords with partial equilibrium thinking and needs no further comment—depresses consumers' income and money demand. Together with an unchanged money stock, the decrease in money demand induces an increase in the equilibrium price level. Rising prices, in turn, diminish the real wage rate. The latter effect explains why real wages rise by 2.7 percent initially, less than nominal wages that increased by 5 percent. From the labor demand function in appendix A, (133), one can easily calculate that the elasticity of labor demand with respect to the real wage rate amounts to –3 under the present calibration. Hence, the 2.7 percent increase in real wages is consistent with an initial fall in employment of roughly 8 percent, as shown in the upper right panel.

The subsequent adjustment is characterized by gradual declines in the capital stock, which result from consumers' decisions to diminish both present and future consumption. Importantly, because labor demand depends on real wage rates and the capital stock—see equations (7) and (8)—the gradual decline in capital reinforces the initial impact of the wage increase. In the new steady state, output, employment, and the capital stock are all reduced in the same proportion; the price level has risen inversely; and real wage and interest rates are the same as at the outset. The increase in the price level is not due to a *cost-push effect*, where producers pass on higher wages to their customers, but is induced by a *demand-pull effect* that results from the linearity of money demand in nominal wealth, $P_t(A_t + X_t + \sigma_t^r)$; see (163) in appendix B. Intuitively, consumers who face a lower level of real economic activity and conduct a smaller number of transactions are only satisfied with their nominal money balances if commodity prices have risen in inverse proportion.

The upshot is that a seemingly trivial rise in nominal wages induces a downward spiral that affects the entire economy and results in a potential Pareto-deterioration. After the economy has fully adjusted, some consumers are unemployed while others earn the same real wage rate as before. Moreover, if one adds a tax-transfer scheme that supports the unemployed outsiders and is financed by the employed insiders, every single consumer becomes worse off, as Economides and Moutos (2014) discuss in a related model. Such an *employment trap* emerges because an increase in wage *rates* diminishes wage *income* under an elastic labor demand which, in turn, is a consequence of the assumed Cobb-Douglas technology. Incidentally, consumers' total wealth (which includes wage and capital income) falls irrespective of the labor demand elasticity; if one were to assume an inelastic labor demand, the reduction in capital income would be even sharper. With consumption, bond and money demand depending on consumers' total wealth, aggregate demand will inevitably fall after a reduction in employment.

Static models suggest a clear-cut inverse relationship between real wages and employment. In business cycle terminology, real wages are *countercyclical* (i.e., show a negative correlation with output) while employment is *procyclical* (i.e., shows a positive correlation with output). In a dynamic context, one and the same real wage rate is compatible with different employment levels: In Figure 3.16, the initial and terminal real wage rates coincide, while the employment levels differ. This suggests that, while employment moves strongly procyclically, the cyclical behavior of real wages is less pronounced, making estimation of a labor demand schedule difficult. A further important point regards the elasticity of labor demand with respect to the real wage rate. With a reasonably parameterized Cobb-Douglas production function, the static value of the elasticity amounts to –3, as indicated above. Dynamically, by contrast, labor demand becomes *infinitely* elastic in the long run; employment falls while the real wage rate remains unchanged.

Can monetary policy get the economy out of an employment trap and bring about a Pareto-improvement? In the present setting with a fixed nominal wage rate, the answer is, of course, yes. A money stock increase of 5 percent will reverse the above changes in employment and the real wage rate. During the adjustment process, employment returns to the natural level and all real variables are restored to their original equilibrium values. Notwithstanding a transitory increase in prices, followed by a decrease, monetary expansion is not even inflationary: Reconsidering Figure 3.16, prices and nominal wages have already risen by 5 percent *before* a monetary expansion sets in. The only persistent effect of the expansion is to boost output and the other real variables.

To summarize the theoretical point, monetary policy is non-neutral in the presence of fixed nominal wage rates. While excessive wages have the expected static consequences of reducing employment somewhat, their dynamic effects are much more pronounced, since they shrink the entire economy. On the condition that nominal wages do not respond at all, monetary policy is in a position to lead the economy out of such an employment trap; a simple increase in the money stock reverses the previous contraction and elevates all real variables to their original equilibrium values. The proportional shrinkage of the entire economy is driven by two core assumptions, namely, the linear homogeneity of nominal variables in the money stock and the linear homogeneity of the production functions. Both assumptions are entirely standard.

What is not so standard is the assumption of a completely rigid nominal wage rate that does not respond to changes in unemployment. Such a behavior may be dismissed as irrational. However, real labor markets do not work in a simplistic perfect competition manner since they are exempt from competition law, often unionized, and subject to government interferences such as minimum wages or closed shop enforcements. Therefore, modeling labor markets is not so much a matter of rationality but of factual observation.

As an empirical motivation, consider labor market performance in three Mediterranean economies between 2007 and 2014: In France, unemployment rose from 8.0 to 10.2 percent while nominal wage rates increased by 14 percent; in Italy, unemployment more than doubled from 6.1 to 12.7 percent while nominal wage rates increased by 20 percent; and in Spain, unemployment rose even more sharply from 8.2 to 22.1 percent while nominal wage rates increased by 16 percent.

Concurrently, eurozone prices (measured by the GDP deflator) showed a cumulative increase of only 8 percent, indicating that the surges in nominal wages did not mirror inflation. Although the initial responses may reflect a composition effect, according to which the average wage rate is also influenced by the composition of labor demand—see Solon et al. (1994)—the figures suggest that wage rates have become largely detached from labor market conditions in Mediterranean Europe. Their movements are inconsistent with notions such as downward wage rigidity or short-term stickiness and are more compatible with a view that sees wage rates as politicized variables.

3.4.2 Phillips Curve

The premise of completely fixed nominal wage rates is now replaced by endogenous wage formation. Changes in nominal wages are described by the *wage inflation rate*,

(50) $$\pi_t^W = \frac{W_t - W_{t-1}}{W_{t-1}} \quad \text{or} \quad \frac{W_t}{W_{t-1}} = 1 + \pi_t^W,$$

whose definition parallels the definition of the inflation rate, equation (2). In a first specification, wages are set with a view to the *employment gap*, the relative deviation of actual employment from the natural employment level:

(51) $$\hat{N}_t = \frac{N_t - \bar{N}}{\bar{N}}, \text{ where } N_t \equiv N_t^d.$$

With actual employment determined by labor demand, the employment gap, which can be positive or negative, measures the excess demand in the labor market. A simple description of wage setting, known as the *Phillips curve*, assumes that wage inflation reflects labor market conditions. With $\varphi^W > 0$ denoting an exogenous adjustment speed, nominal wages increase in response to an excess labor demand and decrease in response to an excess supply in the labor market:

(52) $$\pi_t^W = \varphi^W \hat{N}_t.$$

In the case of a labor market equilibrium, the employment gap vanishes, and nominal wages remain unchanged. Wages set in this manner are referred to as *sticky* because adjustment takes time. Stickiness arbitrates between the polar assumptions of instantaneous adjustment on the one hand and total rigidity on the other. Fisher (1926) and Phillips (1958) inferred equation (52) from long-term observations. Both detected a persistent inverse relationship between wage inflation and the unemployment rate. In the present notation, this translates to a positive relationship between wage inflation and the employment gap.

Assuming that wages are set in accordance with the Phillips curve, equation (52), all individual responses derived so far continue to apply. The system of equilibrium conditions, however, takes the following form:

(53) $$\left.\begin{aligned} C_t + I_t &= Y_t^s \\ B_t^d + B_t^{cb} &= B_t^s \\ \pi_t^W &= \varphi^W \hat{N}_t \end{aligned}\right\} \Rightarrow (P_t, i_t, W_t).$$

The last equation determines wage inflation, which implies a specific nominal wage rate via the right-hand equation in (50). Compared with the original system from section 2.6, the equilibrium conditions for the commodity and bond markets are identical but the condition for labor market equilibrium is replaced by the Phillips curve. While commodity prices and the nominal interest rate still adjust instantaneously, nominal wages are sticky such that the labor market does not clear at every moment.

To illustrate the consequences of sticky wages, Figure 3.17 assumes an increase of 1 percent in the money demand parameter, μ. This diminishes the equilibrium price level and initially boosts the real wage rate because the nominal wage rate reacts slowly. However, the resulting fall in employment gives rise to gradual reductions in the nominal wage rate. This process eventually returns the economy to its initial equilibrium. Hence, if wages are sticky rather than absolutely fixed, the employment gap disappears automatically, and the economy returns to its original equilibrium. In this respect, sticky wage models and fixed wage models differ fundamentally.

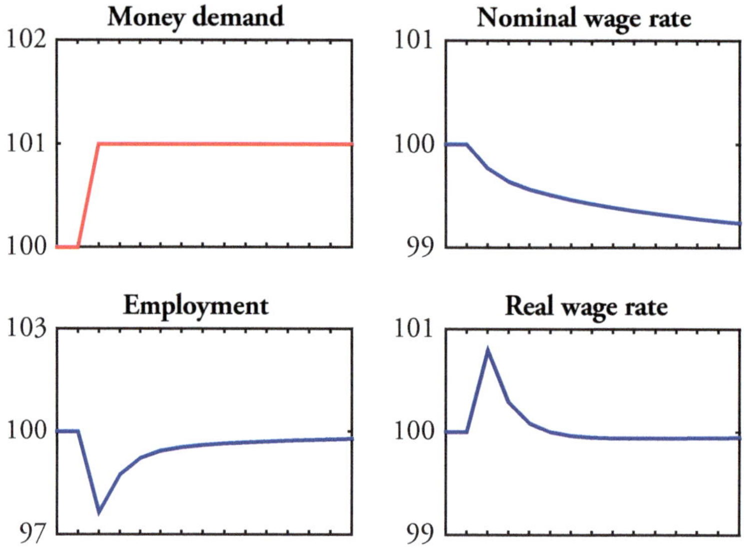

Figure 3.17: Sticky wages. *Notes*: Horizontal axes represent time. The initial values of all variables are normalized at 100.

Figure 3.18 shows that an increase in the money stock is non-neutral in the short run. Contrary to the case of perfect wage adjustment—which was illustrated in Figure 3.2—the ensuing inflation reduces the real wage rate and entails an increase in output, owing to the positive reaction of labor demand. As a side effect that dampens inflation, the subsequent rise in income stimulates money demand; the price level does not overshoot. Therefore, the Fisher effect and the rise in nominal interest become weaker.

Nominal and real interest rates are also affected through a second channel in this scenario, known as the *expected output effect*: The real expansion improves the output expectations via (49) and stimulates capital and investment demand. In equilibrium, investment demand fills the gap between commodity supply and consumption demand, the former being determined by the real wage rate and the latter resulting from the increase in total wealth. With equilibrium investment thus determined, a stronger expected output effect, that is, a stronger increase in investment demand, entails a lower reduction in the expected real interest rate. This force runs counter to the accustomed Fisher effect.

Compared with the flexible wage setting, the most important consequences of sticky wages can be summed up as follows. First, monetary policy leaves output and employment still unchanged in the long run. Second, changes in the money stock have real effects during the transition to a new equilibrium. Third, one-shot increases in the money stock are likely to raise the nominal interest rate even in the short run, but this Fisher effect becomes weaker because it is counteracted by an expected output effect.

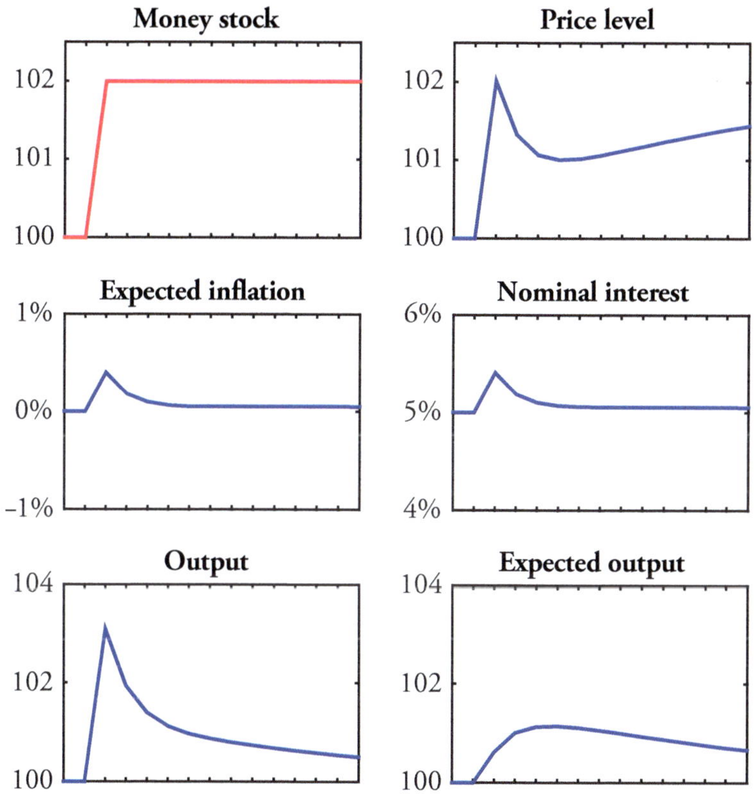

Figure 3.18: One-shot increase in the money stock. *Notes*: Horizontal axes represent time. Nominal interest and expected inflation are measured in percent. The initial values of the other variables are normalized at 100.

3.4.3 Policy Implications

The previous finding that money has temporary real effects in the presence of sticky wages raises the question of whether monetary policy can be used to diminish unemployment. This fundamental issue has many facets, four of which are discussed here. First, central banks can stabilize the economy in the presence of an exogenous change, provided they are able to react faster than wage setters. For instance, after an increase in money demand as considered in Figure 3.17, monetary policy can restore employment and output if it responds promptly and carefully. To what extent such stabilization policies are feasible is largely an institutional and political issue.

Second, if one augments the model by downward wage rigidity, as suggested by Phillips (1958: 295) himself, the case for active monetary policy becomes more compelling. Downward rigidity means that wage inflation follows $\pi_t^W = \max\{\varphi^W \hat{N}_t; 0\}$. Hence, nominal wages will rise during an employment boom but will otherwise stay constant. The premise is motivated by observations that wage setters often abstain from nominal wage reductions even in the presence of high unemployment. Bewley (1999) as well as Falk and Fehr (1999) explain such behavior by pointing out that wage cuts may reduce workers' efforts. In an incomplete contract setting, managers may thus find it optimal to abstain from wage rate cuts. The following reasoning envisions an economy with a constant money stock and a money demand parameter that is subject to white noise shocks: Assuming a Phillips curve, prices and nominal wages would oscillate around their initial equilibrium values. Downward rigidity, however, cuts off wage reductions, so that average employment will settle below the natural level. A more expansive stance of monetary policy diminishes the need for nominal wage reductions and contributes to restoring average employment at the natural level. In the presence of inflation, moderate money demand shocks do not require a fall in nominal wages but only a smaller increase. In this sense, downward wage rigidity gives rise to a tradeoff between unemployment and inflation.

Third, the Phillips curve suggests that monetary policy can even permanently reduce the unemployment rate below its natural level. To see this, assume a positive money growth rate, associated with increases in equilibrium prices and wages. According to (52), nominal wage rates will indeed rise but they will also *lag behind* the price level because their rise presupposes an unemployment rate below the natural rate. Hence, unemployment will settle below the natural level. In the 1960s and 1970s, this finding and Phillips' results induced many economists and policymakers to believe in a permanent inflation-unemployment tradeoff. However, practical attempts to exploit the seeming tradeoff resulted in *stagflation*—inflation and unemployment rose concurrently. The reason is that the original Phillips curve makes sense only in an environment with stable prices. Formula $\pi_t^W = \varphi^W \hat{N}_t$ expresses the objective to attain the natural employment level through tentative variations in nominal wage rates. If wage setters notice that their attempts fail systematically because prices hurry ahead in an inflationary environment, they will learn from this experience and set wages in accordance with the following rule, suggested by Friedman (1968) and Phelps (1968), which is known as the *expectations-augmented Phillips curve*

(54) $$\pi_t^W = \pi_t^e + \varphi^W \hat{N}_t .$$

Nominal wages are now set with a view to expected inflation, corrected by the employment gap. Under price stability, there is no difference between the original and the expectations-augmented Phillips curve. In the case of a positive inflation rate, however, the new rule ensures that employment converges to the natural level. Hence, there is no permanent tradeoff between inflation and unemployment; the long-run Phillips curve becomes vertical in the inflation–unemployment space. At the same time, changes in money growth still have temporary real effects, implying a downward-sloping short-run Phillips curve. For instance, if the central bank accelerates money growth, individuals underestimate inflation at first, as shown in subsection 3.1.2. Employment increases temporarily until inflation expectations have adapted. In the new equilibrium, employment is restored to its natural level, but inflation is higher. Such a policy does not appear particularly attractive because to reverse it, the central bank needs to restrict money growth. The restriction will increase unemployment in the same manner as the preceding expansion diminished it. Over the entire cycle, the policy represents a zero-sum game.

Fourth, the last observations lead directly to the *acceleration theorem*, which states that permanent accelerations in money growth have permanent real effects. In fact, if the central bank increased the money growth rate (not the money stock) in each period, expected inflation would always lag behind actual inflation, and employment would always exceed the natural level. For this reason, the unemployment rate associated with the natural employment level is also known as the *non-accelerating inflation rate of unemployment*, or *NAIRU*. The acceleration theorem has sometimes been seen as a sweeping criticism of the adaptive expectations hypothesis but the critique is not compelling: individuals switch to a first-order learning process if they notice that static expectations prove systematically wrong. Under monetary acceleration, they would likely use a second-order learning process that took account of changes in the inflation rate. In addition to this, monetary acceleration is an unsustainable policy anyway, which ultimately results in hyperinflation.

The move from the original to an expectations-augmented Phillips curve—and possible generalizations to higher-order learning—point to an insight of wider relevance that is known as the *Lucas critique*. This states that policies attempting to exploit statistical relationships such as the inflation–unemployment tradeoff are doomed to fail to the extent that they change the expectations underlying the relationships. According to Lucas (1976: 21), policy measures affect the structure of an economy "if they are known in advance". Of course, this leaves open the question of how *unreliable* policy announcements influence the economy. The deeper point of the Lucas critique is that it suggests avoiding models with superior information on the side of the government. Before the 1970s, it was common to assume that governments are better informed than anyone else, and many results were due to this alleged asymmetry.

3.5 Price Rigidities

In a market economy, commodity prices adjust regularly to equate demand and supply—this is what makes it a market economy. The speed of price adjustments, however, is open to debate. All model variants considered so far assumed that commodity prices moved as quickly as interest rates, implying that the commodity market cleared at every instant. This section, by contrast, supposes *sticky prices* that react with a delay if demand and supply differ. Specifically, actual output in period *t*, henceforth denoted as Y_t, can temporarily deviate from the profit maximizing commodity supply, Y_t^s. The relative deviation of actual output from supply is referred to as the *output gap*:

$$\text{(55)} \qquad \hat{Y}_t = \frac{Y_t - Y_t^s}{Y_t^s} \quad , \text{ where } \; Y_t \equiv C_t + I_t .$$

Negative output gaps indicate a shortfall of commodity demand, and vice versa. If the output gap vanishes, commodity demand and supply coincide. Naturally, individual price setters tend to increase commodity prices in the presence of excess demand, and tend to decrease them in the presence of excess supply. This suggests a price adjustment process of the form $\pi_t = \varphi^P \hat{Y}_t$, where $\varphi^P > 0$ represents the speed of adjustment. Such an assumption, however, is not realistic in an inflationary environment. If price setters have become accustomed to a constant inflation rate of, say, 10 percent, they will not leave individual prices unchanged in the case of a zero output gap but will increase them by just 10 percent in order to keep pace with the general inflation. Taken together, these hypotheses imply that prices are set in accordance with the output gap, corrected for expected inflation:

$$\text{(56)} \qquad \pi_t = \pi_t^e + \varphi^P \hat{Y}_t .$$

This equation resembles the expectations-augmented Phillips curve, (54), considered in subsection 3.4.3. In the literature, the formula is itself referred to as an expectations-augmented Phillips curve, for example by Romer (2012: 261), notwithstanding that it relates to the commodity market while the original Phillips curve relates to the labor market. To make the terminology even more bewildering, a third variant of the Phillips curve, suggested by Samuelson and Solow (1960), connects commodity price inflation with the employment gap. The empirical relevance of this third type, which relates prices in one market to quantities in another, is disputed; see Hall (2011) and Gordon (2013).

The Phillips curves for the labor and commodity markets rest on the same idea. Following equation (56), commodity price setters enter period *t* with an expected inflation prior, π_t^e. They increase commodity prices in accordance with this prior, but they also adjust them with a view to the current output gap. Inflation expectations for the following period are formed simultaneously. Because the latter influence demand, especially investment demand, they also affect current inflation. In sum, equation (56) specifies actual inflation as a function of predetermined inflation expectations, a given price adjustment speed, and the output gap. The current price level follows from the identity (2).

Before moving to the full model, it seems appropriate to briefly assess the sticky price premise. Such an endeavor encounters two difficulties. First, price adjustment speeds vary substantially across commodities. In an empirical study for the United States, 1995–7, Bils and Klenow (2004) evaluated the frequency of price changes for 350 categories of goods and services. They found remarkably high price adjustment speeds for goods such as gasoline, fresh vegetables, dresses, and suits, and very low speeds for commodities such as dry cleaning, newspapers, and haircuts. One-sector models aggregate this diversity into a single figure and conceal shifts in relative prices that result from different adjustment speeds.

Second, and more fundamentally, empirical observations do not provide conclusive information about price stickiness in the sense of *obstacles* to price adjustment. To illustrate this key point, imagine an economy with an auctioneer that stands ready to adjust all prices instantaneously and at zero cost. Even under this extreme assumption, which is most favorable to perfect price flexibility, an external observer will detect no price changes at all if the economy happens to be located in a stationary state. Therefore, small variances in observed prices do not justify the conclusion that market participants find price adjustments costly or cumbersome. Constant prices can simply indicate market equilibria that are currently undisturbed by exogenous shocks. Conversely, commodity prices move swiftly in an inflationary environment; during hyperinflation even nominal wage rates are reviewed every week.

The Great Recession of 2008–09 provides a natural experiment to evaluate price adjustment processes because it induced large variations in the data. Figure 3.19 reports United States real GDP, inflation, and wage inflation from 2007–10. GDP data are available only at quarterly frequency, while inflation and wage inflation are monthly data. The figures suggest some stylized facts that can also be found in corresponding eurozone data: After the recession set in during 2008, inflation receded quickly and even turned negative, implying an absolute decrease in the price level. And soon after the recession had been overcome in summer 2009, inflation rebounded. By contrast, wage inflation receded only slightly. This is consistent with the evidence that the unemployment rate took several years to return to its pre-crisis level; dropping below 5 percent as late as 2016. Excess commodity stocks, by contrast, which motivated measures such as the "cash for clunkers" program, evaporated shortly after 2009.

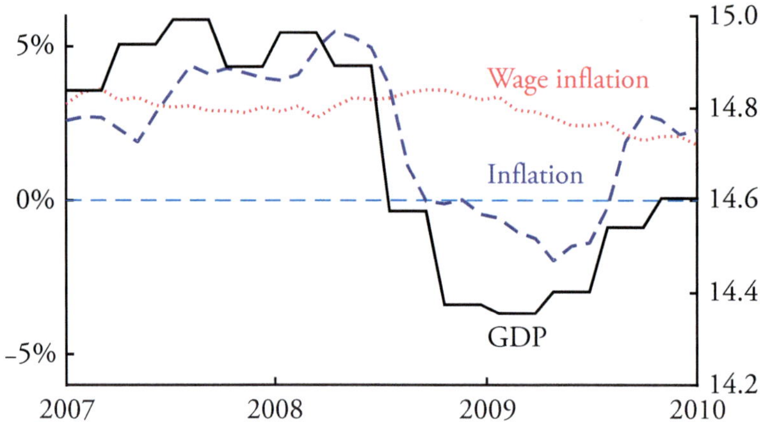

Figure 3.19: Great Recession. *Notes*: United States data, retrieved March 2016 from <https://fred.stlouisfed.org>. Real GDP in trillion dollars (right-hand scale) is series GDPC1, inflation (left-hand scale) is series CPIAUCSL_PC1, wage inflation (left-hand scale) is series CES0500000003_PC1.

In summary, inflation tended to be procyclical and responded to changes in commodity market conditions while nominal wage rates were characterized by a higher degree of inertia. With commodity prices moving faster than wages, it seems pointless to consider economies characterized by price stickiness on the one hand and perfect labor market competition on the other. Therefore, the following model retains the sticky wages assumption:

$$\left.\begin{aligned} \pi_t &= \pi_t^e + \varphi^P \hat{Y}_t \\ B_t^d + B_t^{cb} &= B_t^s \\ \pi_t^W &= \pi_t^e + \varphi^W \hat{N}_t \end{aligned}\right\} \Rightarrow (P_t, i_t, W_t). \tag{57}$$

Evidently, the nominal interest rate is left as the only price variable that changes instantaneously. Compared with equation (17), the equilibrium conditions for the commodity and labor market have been replaced by the two Phillips curves. Together with the specifications of actual employment, $N_t \equiv N_t^d$, and actual output, $Y_t \equiv C_t + I_t$, the new system determines the three price variables in the usual manner. Consumers select consumption demand, bond demand, and money demand optimally in the same way as in the baseline framework. Producers choose capital and labor demand optimally in accordance with (48) and (136) respectively. However, because output can differ from commodity supply, producers will diminish output and commodity prices in the case of deficient demand. In the opposite case, producers will serve excess demand, but will also charge higher prices, as expressed by the Phillips curve. Substituting commodity supply by actual output in the profit definition, (6), makes the model consistent and completes its description.

3.5.1 Liquidity Effect

When central banks aim at stimulating economic activity, they provide liquidity through open market purchases. This measure is believed to diminish interest and to boost investment. The short-run nexus between monetary expansions and reductions in nominal and real interest rates is known as the *liquidity effect*; see Friedman (1969: 365). Liquidity effects are ubiquitous in static textbook models that lack expectations and a distinction between nominal and real interest rates. For instance, shifting an LM-curve to the right lowers interest and raises investment. The empirical evidence for liquidity effects, however, is at best mixed; see Reichenstein (1987), Strongin (1995), or Bernanke and Mihov (1998). This is all the more notable since these studies pertained to the relationship between money stock variations and the short-term funds rate. With respect to medium-term interest rates that are relevant for investors and savers, the existence of a liquidity effect is still more doubtful. From a theoretical point of view, Christiano and Eichenbaum (1992) discuss the challenge to produce liquidity effects within a dynamic general equilibrium framework. While none of the models considered so far support the view that monetary expansions lower interest rates, the sticky price assumption makes it possible to reconcile popular wisdom and rigorous derivation.

Figure 3.20 sheds light on the "liquidity puzzle". To visualize liquidity effects as clearly as possible, the illustration presumes fixed prices and wages. An increase in the money stock of 1 percent reduces the nominal and expected real interest rate from 5.00 to 4.98 percent. Nominal and real rates coincide because prices, inflation, and expected inflation do not change at all. Thereafter, both rates return to their initial equilibrium values, whereas output, investment, and consumption stay at higher levels.

Section 3.1 showed that a flexible price framework leaves no room for liquidity effects. After a monetary expansion, exogenous inflation expectations left real balances and nominal interest rates unaffected, while adaptive expectations diminished real balances and raised (rather than reduced) the nominal interest rate. In this respect, sticky prices open a novel transmission mechanism that stems from an initial *increase* in real balances: With fixed commodity prices, central bank open market purchases in period t are bound to increase M_t / P_t and to diminish B_t^d / P_t. Consumers keep the resulting portfolio—which contains a greater amount of money and a smaller amount of bonds—only at a lower interest rate. Contrary to the flexible price model, the central bank is now in a position to enforce a different portfolio composition, and this is the driving force behind the liquidity effect.

The two bottom panels in Figure 3.20 suggest that consumption reacts only moderately, while investment is more volatile compared with output.

The relative size of the three amplitudes is a typical feature of business cycles: Investment shows the highest volatility, consumption the lowest, and output takes an intermediate position. The high elasticity of investment demand is also key to the liquidity puzzle; it explains why nearly imperceptible changes in interest rates trigger large variations in investment demand.

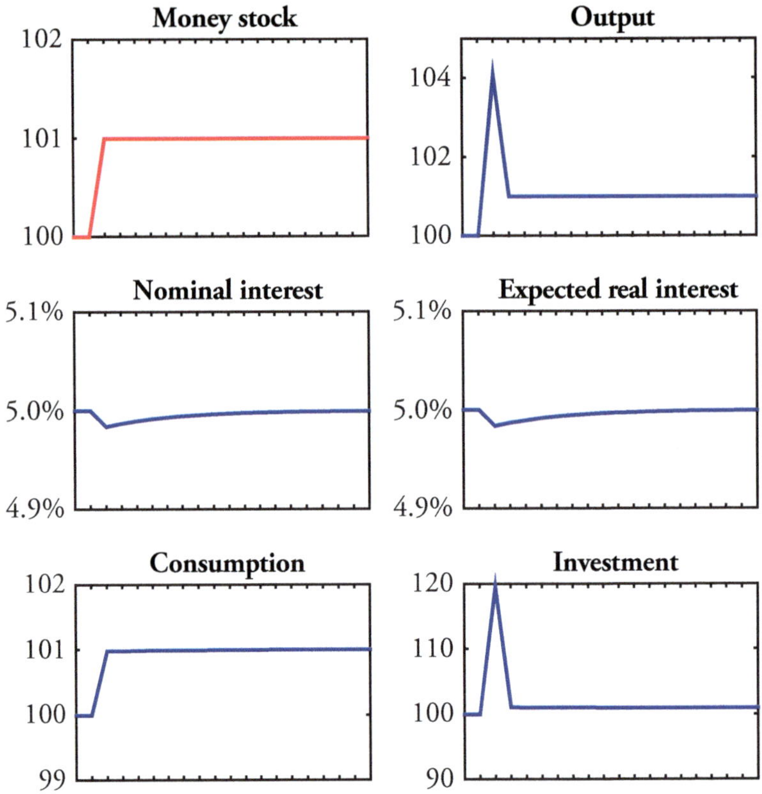

Figure 3.20: Liquidity effect, $\varphi^W, \varphi^P = 0$. *Notes*: Horizontal axes represent time. Nominal interest and expected real interest are measured in percent. The initial values of the other variables are normalized at 100.

The strong reaction of investment is not peculiar to sticky price models. It is characteristic of all models that derive investment explicitly from capital demand and entail a *stock-flow effect* of the following kind: In a stationary state, investment equals a tiny fraction of the capital stock, $I = \delta K$, a fact which follows directly from definition (1). With an assumed depreciation rate of 5 percent, an increase in the optimal capital stock of only 1 percent boosts investment demand by 20 percent. As a concrete example, consider trucks with a durability of 20 years. If the owners use a total of 20,000 such trucks, they will order 1,000 new trucks annually as replacements. If the desired stock falls to 19,500 trucks during a recession—a marginal decrease of 2.5 percent—annual truck orders will plunge from 1,000 to 500, or by no less than one half. The latter response exaggerates the underlying change in fundamentals (but will likely find its way into the newspapers, adding itself to other horror stories).

Therefore, small changes in interest produce large changes in investment even if the capital stock is relatively interest inelastic. This is the first part of the explanation for why liquidity effects are difficult to discern. The second part relates to the expected output effect mentioned previously. Because output expectations are formed contemporaneously, any output increase makes investors more optimistic or, technically, hikes up the marginal productivity of capital and the expected real interest rate; see (48). As nominal and expected real interest rates coincide under fixed commodity prices, the expected output effect counteracts the liquidity effect; their net impact is indeterminate.

All these considerations, however, rest on the extreme premise of fixed commodity prices. Assuming sticky prices instead, the adjustment processes discussed so far are superseded by the familiar Fisher effect: Increases in commodity prices, however small, elevate expected inflation. Since the money increase considered here diminished nominal interest by a trifling 0.02 percent, but will ultimately elevate the price level by 1 percent, the Fisher effect becomes the dominant force. Hence, monetary expansions may entail minimal temporary reductions in expected real interest but will almost invariably raise the nominal interest rate. These conclusions accord with the empirical literature but contradict textbook presentations that rest on fixed prices and shape common thought. At the same time, the results are by no means at variance with propositions that monetary impulses have short-run real effects; such impulses are actually non-neutral until prices and wages have fully adjusted. The crucial point is that monetary policy efficacy does not work through flashy changes in interest rates. Quite the contrary, equilibrium interest movements will be less pronounced, the stronger output reacts.

3.5.2 Deterministic Business Cycles

A classic insight states that monetary impulses influence the economy with "long and variable lags". According to a wide consensus among macroeconomists that was reached in the 1990s, the lags extend beyond our forecasting horizon, which makes fine-tuning impossible; see Parkin (1998). The sticky price model introduced above can be used to demonstrate that the proverbial time lags do not result from the intricacies of money creation per se but reflect general equilibrium outcomes.

Figure 3.21 illustrates a monetary impulse that sets into motion a deterministic business cycle with endogenous turning points. Initially, output, employment, and prices respond strongly to the impulse. Then, a mild recession sets in during which output and employment plunge below their original levels. The price level overshoots and undershoots its terminal equilibrium level, so that periods of inflation and deflation alternate. Even after 60 periods, the time span shown in the figure, there is perceptible variance in the data.

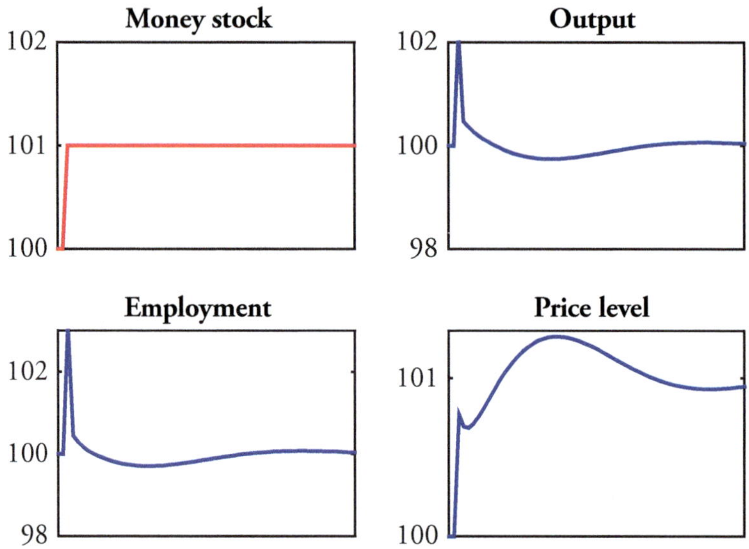

Figure 3.21: Monetary impulse, $\varphi^W, \varphi^P > 0$. *Notes*: Horizontal axes represent time. The initial values of the variables are normalized at 100.

Section 3.1.2 discussed that one-shot monetary policies generate persistent *nominal* effects in a flexible price economy. With price and wage rigidities, such policies also have persistent *real* effects, notwithstanding that money is still neutral in the long run. Prices and wages—set in accordance with the two Phillips curves—lag behind after a monetary acceleration, such that output and employment increase. Conversely, if inflation has reached an uncomfortably high plateau and the central bank wishes to disinflate, the required monetary deceleration will come with a social cost in the form of a temporary recession because price setters diminish inflation only in the presence of a negative output gap.

Perhaps the most prominent example of such an occurrence is the *Volcker reflation* of the 1980s. It is named after then Fed chairman Paul Volcker who implemented a distinctly restrictive monetary policy in order to terminate a decade of escalating inflation. His course was successful in that it diminished the inflation rate from 11.3 percent in 1979 to 3.2 percent in 1983. Concurrently, however, civilian unemployment surged from 5.9 to 9.6 percent and still exceeded 6 percent by 1988. The 1980s were characterized by high real interest rates, perhaps because inflation expectations had become anchored at a high level in the preceding decade.

Unlike stochastic business cycles that merely reflect *assumed* shocks, the above deterministic cycle results from the internal operations of the model. The persistence of a one-shot impulse is due to adaptive expectations that provide a long-run memory and slow down adjustment processes that would take place immediately under perfect foresight or RE; see Grandmont (1985) for a related model. Hence, the high degrees of *inertia* (inflation inertia and output inertia) can be traced back to adaptive expectations on the one hand and the two Phillips curves on the other, which admit only gradual price and wage adjustments. The entire model accords well with three undisputed business cycle features, namely:

- *Persistence*: One-shot impulses propagate over time and generate persistent changes in nominal and real variables.
- *Comovement*: Macroeconomic aggregates such as output, employment, consumption, and investment show high contemporaneous correlations. Movements in single sectors do not cancel out (as in thermodynamics) but reinforce each other.
- *Relative volatilities*: Consumption is less and investment more volatile than output and employment, as indicated in subsection 3.5.1.

3.5.3 The Limit Economy

The sticky price model developed here is not a competitor to the flexible price model. Rather, the reactions to monetary disturbances of the sticky price model include the reactions of the flexible price as a special case. To see this, observe that the equilibrium conditions (17) and (57) determine two triples (P_t, i_t, W_t) that solve the respective system of equations. Considering a sequence of sticky price economies for which price adjustment speeds grow without bound $(\varphi^P, \varphi^W \rightarrow \infty)$, it becomes clear from (57) that the output and employment gaps converge to zero. This is because if these gaps were bounded away from zero, price inflation and wage inflation would become infinite, contradicting the existence of a solution. Because vanishing output and employment gaps define the equilibrium of a flexible price economy, the latter represents the *limit* of a sequence of sticky price economies.

Considered in this way, superneutrality of money represents a limit property whose closeness to reality depends on the prevailing degree of price flexibility. Conversely, real effects of monetary policy are more pronounced in an environment with sluggish price adjustment. Because price adjustment speeds are inversely related to the period length, sticky price models suggest themselves for business cycle analyses. The strength of flexible price models lies in their conceptual simplicity, which makes them preferable for medium-term scenarios. Models with absolutely fixed prices appear useful in neither case because prices do adjust to some extent even at quarterly frequencies, the shortest period for which many macroeconomic aggregates are available.

Chapter 4

Constrained Credit

Sometimes, prices hike out of the blue—an event known as non-anticipated inflation. The aftermath of the Great Recession of 2008–09 brought forth an opposite experience that could be dubbed "non-anticipated price stability". After the United States, Japan, and Europe had started monetary expansions on a scale no one had ever seen, many economists believed that inflation would accelerate soon. This was also the prediction of standard macro models. Yet, actual inflation remained low and some countries even experienced moderate deflation. Such a development contradicts all models studied so far and represents what John Cochrane called the Michelson-Morley moment of monetary economics.

This chapter takes a step toward reconciling theory and evidence. It augments the basic framework with a borrowing constraint, an upper limit to bond issues. This single change in assumptions crucially alters the model's behavior and entails the testable implication that money has no influence on prices. As a preparation, section 4.1 reviews some stylized facts and shows in detail why received theories are unable to explain the co-existence of stable prices, exceptionally low interest rates, low unemployment, and ineffective monetary policy. Thereafter, section 4.2 devises and illustrates the new approach. Section 4.3 outlines tentative conclusions for monetary and fiscal policy, section 4.4 contains a comparative evaluation of the key assumption, and section 4.5 concludes.

4.1 Liquidity Traps

A liquidity trap is commonly understood as a situation where interest is low and monetary policy does not produce inflation. In many textbook presentations, liquidity traps are *malign* in the sense that they entail evil outcomes such as depression and mass unemployment. The following discussion takes account of this possibility but focuses on *benign* liquidity traps. These are characterized by stable prices, low unemployment, low interest rates, and monetary policy ineffectiveness; thus, the real economic outcomes are by no means harmful. Because such situations have gained little attention in the literature, an important first step is to demonstrate that their typical features do not define an empty set. Beforehand, however, it should be noted that benign liquidity traps are far from omnipresent. Since the Great Recession, many countries have experienced double-digit inflation that can be explained conventionally. High and persistent unemployment rates are also still plaguing large parts of the world. Therefore, the following observations pertain to only a part of the global economy, a subset that includes countries such as Canada, Germany, Japan, Switzerland, the United Kingdom, and the United States.

Table 4.1 presents a snapshot of the four largest economies in this subset: Germany, Japan, the United Kingdom, and the United States. The snapshot was taken in May 2016, more than six years after the recession. It documents strikingly low long-term nominal interest rates ranging between –0.1 and 1.8 percent, nearly stable price levels, and unemployment rates that are all near or below their pre-crisis levels. Between 2010 and 2015, average real growth rates ranged from 1.5 to 2.0 percent in these countries. For highly industrialized nations, such a performance is not exactly stellar but also not worrisome; in any case, it does not indicate serious economic trouble. Combined with the fact that the relevant central banks undertook super-expansionary policies for over half a decade, the figures neatly illustrate the essence of a benign liquidity trap.

Country	Interest rate	Inflation rate	Unemployment rate
Germany	0.1%	0.1%	4.2%
Japan	–0.1%	–0.5%	3.2%
United Kingdom	1.5%	0.3%	4.8%
United States	1.8%	1.0%	4.5%

Table 4.1: Economic indicators, May 2016. *Source*: Retrieved 6 November 2016 from <http//:stats.oecd.org>, series long-term interest rates; consumer price indices (all items); harmonized unemployment rates (total, all persons).

Of the four economies under consideration, Japan—which was long considered an exceptional case—is the most interesting because its liquidity trap started in the 1990s. Japan was the first country to introduce quantitative easing, or QE, in the sense of unprecedented monetary expansions. As an attempt to boost inflation, Japan's central bank intensified its measures over the years, but to no avail. Even *Abenomics*, a further amplification of fiscal and monetary actions initiated by Prime Minister Shinzo Abe in 2013, did not generate visible increases in the price level—three years later, Japan's inflation rate was still stuck below zero.

In 2014, just before his retirement as chairman of the board of the Federal Reserve System, Ben Bernanke passed the following judgment on the monetary expansions he had advocated for years: "Well, the problem with QE is it works in practice, but it doesn't work in theory"; see Wessel (2014: 12). Regarding practice, many economists are convinced that QE tended to reduce interest rates and to increase asset prices. But the measure obviously failed to boost the price level. In this respect, it was also a practical failure. Regarding theory, the following subsection shows why the evidence referred to above presents a major challenge to the orthodoxy.

The Puzzle

A natural question to ask is which of the monetary models reviewed so far is able to reproduce the following four stylized facts that define a benign liquidity trap:

- Zero inflation,
- low unemployment,
- low nominal and real interest rates,
- inability of monetary policy to generate inflation.

The flexible price model introduced in Chapter 2 is compatible with zero inflation and low unemployment. Depending on the parameterization, this model can also deliver low interest rates. However, expansionary monetary policies will inevitably increase prices, nominal wages, and nominal interest rates, contradicting the fourth fact.

A model with sticky wages and flexible prices, as studied in section 3.4, also responds to monetary expansions with inflation. If nominal wage rates are excessive, it delivers low unemployment only if the inflationary impact of monetary policy, which reduces the real wage rate, is strong enough. Conversely, the model would predict high unemployment in the presence of stable prices. If prices and wages are both sticky, monetary policy has short-run real effects that delay—but do not inhibit—inflation and wage inflation. In the medium run—say, over a couple of quarters—the economic outcomes resemble those of the flexible price model, and nominal interest rates will rise. Surely, inflation would fail to appear if prices were completely fixed for years. But then, monetary expansions would induce an ever-increasing output gap, with producers ready to supply more than the profit maximizing amount at unchanged prices. Such an assumption contradicts the experience that positive output gaps spur inflation.

Zero Lower Bound

Summed up, neither of the model versions considered so far is able to account for the four stylized facts. This suggests discussing a further variant that is commonly referred to as a saving glut or secular stagnation. The term "saving glut" refers to a desired level of future consumption so high that producers cannot absorb the resulting bond demand, while "secular stagnation" designates a decline in capital productivity. Assuming a stationary state, the connecting element of these scenarios is a *negative* expected real interest rate, $r^e_{t+1} < 0$. Of course, negative real interest rates are of no concern in abstract cashless economies, where they indicate that the relative price of future consumption in terms of present consumption is less than one—a result as exciting as an equilibrium where the price of apples in terms of oranges is less than one. In a monetary economy, by contrast, negative real rates preclude the existence of equilibrium if expected inflation vanishes.

To see this, recall the relationship $r^e_{t+1} = i_t - \pi^e_{t+1}$ between the nominal and the expected real interest rate. With zero expected inflation, the two interest rates coincide. Hence, a negative expected real rate implies that the nominal rate must also fall into negative territory, $i_t < 0$. However, negative nominal interest is impossible if individuals prefer money balances to bonds, as they do under usual specifications of the utility function. In practice, slightly negative nominal rates are possible because cash cannot be stored free of charge but this caveat is commonly neglected in formal models. Hence, the presence of money as an alternative store of value places a *zero lower bound*, or ZLB, on the nominal interest rate.

Analyzing the consequences of this restriction does not require a new model. Rather, a suitable parameterization of the baseline model devised in Chapter 2 suffices: For instance, selecting a large time preference parameter, β, induces a saving glut—credit supply is high. Likewise, permanent reductions in the output parameter, θ, or a declining population, induce secular stagnation—capital and credit demand are low. In both cases, the equilibrium real interest rate can become negative, precluding the existence of a solution if expected inflation is zero.

What are the empirical implications of saving gluts or secular stagnation? To keep matters simple, consider an economy with stable prices, zero expected inflation and an equilibrium real interest rate of –2 percent. The condition $i_t > 0$ and the identity $r^e_{t+1} = i_t$ prevent the real rate from reaching this equilibrium level. Consequently, credit supply exceeds credit demand. In the commodity market, investment demand does not suffice to close the gap between commodity supply and consumption. This has two further consequences: First, prices fall owing to an excess commodity supply. Second, producers who recognize themselves as unable to sell the desired output will diminish labor demand, depressing nominal wages. A general price-wage deflation emerges.

Crucially, such a deflation does not restore equilibrium but feeds a downward spiral of deflationary expectations, which induces the expected real interest rate to depart all the more from its negative equilibrium level. Earlier authors, most notably Pigou (1943), proposed an escape route. According to his argument, deflation increases the value of real balances, which will eventually stimulate consumption demand. This reasoning may be correct for an economy on the gold standard or with helicopter money. It does not apply, however, to an economy with credit money because deflation increases consumers' real balances and producers' real liabilities toward the central bank correspondingly, leaving the private sector's net financial wealth at zero.

To summarize, saving gluts and secular stagnation entail low interest, mass unemployment, and a downward spiral of price-wage deflation. In blogs and the media, they are probably the most popular narrative of situations characterized by low interest rates and monetary policy ineffectiveness. At the same time, these malign liquidity traps contradict two of the above stylized facts, namely low unemployment and stable price levels. They are also not appropriate as recession theories because long-term interest rates remained far from the ZLB during and after the Great Recession, as Figure 2.1 demonstrated. In the United States and Europe, long-term interest rates declined only after 2012, or roughly three years past the end of the recession.

4.2 Borrowing Constraint

Drawing on Homburg (2015b), this section proposes an alternative approach to liquidity traps. To focus on medium-term effects, it starts with the flexible price framework presented in Chapter 2, the essence of which is reproduced here for convenience:

$$\left.\begin{aligned} C_t + I_t &= Y_t^s \\ B_t^d + B_t^{cb} &= B_t^s \\ N_t^d &= \bar{N} \end{aligned}\right\} \Rightarrow (P_t, i_t, W_t). \tag{58}$$

The model comprises three equilibrium conditions for the commodity market, the bond market, and the labor market that determine prices, interest, and wages. While the central bank selects the money stock, consumers optimize in the same way as outlined before. The only difference between the original and the new model regards producers who maximize expected profits now subject to an additional *borrowing constraint*:

$$B_t^s \leq \bar{B}_t . \tag{59}$$

In this inequality, the number $\bar{B}_t$ represents an exogenous borrowing limit. If the limit binds, producers cannot obtain as much credit as they wish but become rationed in the credit market. The principal interpretation of (59) states that only a certain amount of bonds qualifies for issuance. Together with the balance sheet (10), which reads $P_t K_t^d = B_t^s$, the borrowing constraint places a restriction upon investment at any given price level. Of course, the constraint could also be written in real terms as $B_t^s / P_t \leq \bar{B}_t / P_t$ without changing the results.

Denoting bond issues in the unconstrained equilibrium as B_t^*, the borrowing constraint is binding if $B_t^* > \bar{B}_t$; otherwise it is ineffective. The following simulation starts from a stationary state and illustrates the impact of a sudden credit crunch: After the first period, a binding borrowing limit diminishes nominal credit by 2 percent.

The upper left panel in Figure 4.1 displays the impulse, a 2 percent reduction in the borrowing limit. This forces producers to shrink their balance sheets and to diminish capital and investment demand. As a result, commodity demand declines, which induces a fall in the general price level. However, commodity prices do not fall into an abyss but only fall by 2 percent. Combining the balance sheet and the borrowing constraint, which yields $P_t K_t^d = \bar{B}_t$, it is immediately clear that producers can maintain the *original* capital stock if prices decrease by the same factor. To preserve labor market equilibrium, nominal wages are also reduced by 2 percent, leaving real wages at their previous level. Hence, producers have no incentive to revise commodity supply—output, consumption, and employment remain unchanged. The upshot is that a nominal friction in the form of a borrowing limit has no real effects on the economy as long as prices and wages are sufficiently flexible. This distinguishes borrowing limits from nominal frictions such as sticky prices and wages that are bound to generate real effects.

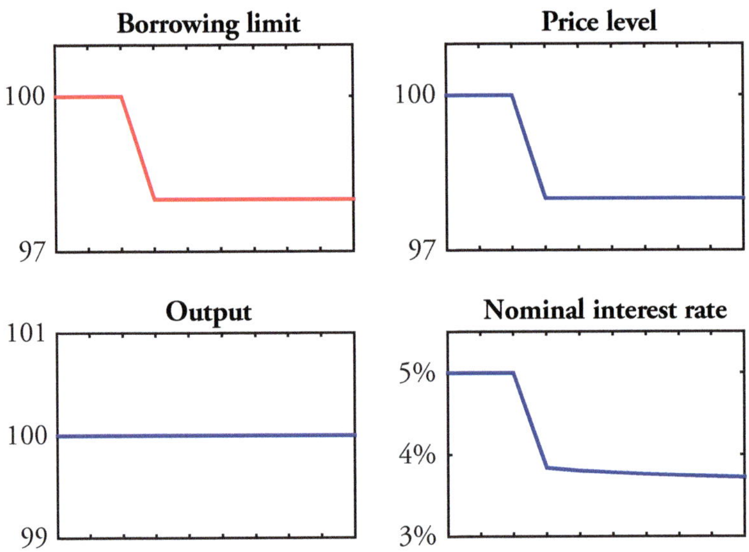

Figure 4.1: Credit crunch. *Notes*: Horizontal axes represent time. Nominal interest is measured in percent. The initial values of the other variables are normalized at 100.

While the credit crunch proves neutral with respect to output and employment, it changes nominal and real interest rates permanently. In particular, the nominal interest rate falls from 5.0 to 3.7 percent, as indicated in the bottom right panel. This liquidity effect is more difficult to explain and calls for rethinking. Compared with the original stationary state, the constrained equilibrium is characterized by lower bond issues and lower prices, while bond issues are constant in real terms. At the same time, no change in the money stock has been assumed. Therefore, consumers hold portfolios with a *constant* real amount of bonds, B_t^d / P_t, and a *higher* amount of real balances, M_t^d / P_t. Because consumers hold such a portfolio only at a lower user cost of money, the equilibrium nominal interest rate must fall.

Unlike prices and wages, however, the nominal interest rate does not immediately reach its new equilibrium level but declines for a while. This is because falling commodity prices induce deflation expectations. After a new stationary state has been reached, expected inflation vanishes so that nominal and real interest rates coincide. At a lower nominal interest rate, the expected real interest rate falls permanently as well. This implication may appear strange because conventional models pin down the real rate by the marginal productivity of capital, corrected for depreciation. However, the coincidence of the marginal productivity and the user cost of capital, a cornerstone of macroeconomic thinking, does *not* hold under a borrowing constraint, and this is the model's key feature. As demonstrated in appendix G, any equilibrium with a binding borrowing constraint—referred to as a *constrained equilibrium*, for short—is characterized by the inequality

$$\frac{\partial F}{\partial K_t^d} > r_{t+1}^e + \delta . \tag{60}$$

According to the preceding reasoning, the economy responds to the emergence of a borrowing limit by falling prices that shrink the producers' balance sheets, relax the borrowing constraint, and enable producers to maintain their original investment plans. Thus, the real capital stock remains unchanged. However, producers are still constrained in the new equilibrium precisely because the expected real interest rate is *lower* now, whereas the marginal productivity of capital is the same as at the outset.

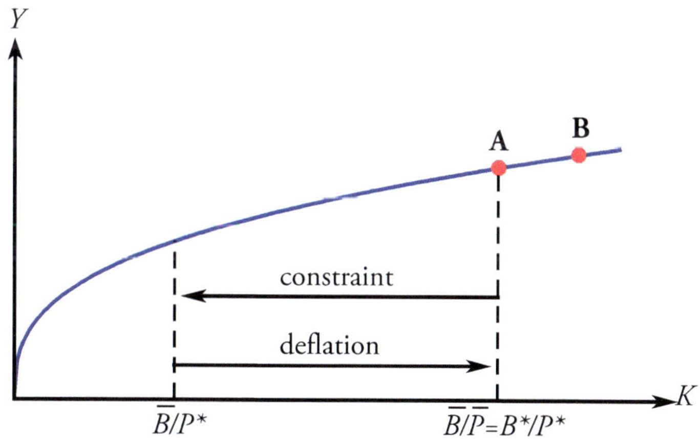

Figure 4.2: Adjustments after a credit crunch. *Note*: The solid curve is the production function.

Figure 4.2 illustrates how this works. It shows the production function and the original capital stock, denoted as B^*/P^*. The borrowing constraint entails a balance sheet reduction (left-pointing arrow), followed by deflation (right-pointing arrow). Deflation helps restore the original capital stock. Thus, point A represents both the original and the new equilibrium capital stock. Since nominal and real interest rates are lower in the constrained equilibrium—inducing consumers to hold a greater amount of real balances—producers would like to increase the capital stock to a higher level, such as indicated by point B.

However, point B is unattainable, and it will remain so if the borrowing constraint were to relax: This would reverse the adjustment process and trigger an increase in the price level. Therefore, inflation is not a monetary phenomenon in the presence of a borrowing constraint; it may result from pure credit relaxation at a given money stock. A further crucial feature of a constrained equilibrium is that observed real interest rates misrepresent the marginal productivity of capital.

In a stationary state with zero expected inflation, inequality (60) assumes a simple form. Specifically, the marginal productivity exceeds the user cost of capital by the *shadow price* of the borrowing constraint, ξ, which is derived in appendix G:

(61) $$\frac{\partial F}{\partial K^d} \aleph i \quad \delta \quad \xi .$$

The shadow price indicates the change in profit that results from a marginal relaxation of the constraint. It is strictly positive in the presence of a binding constraint and vanishes otherwise. In Figure 4.2, the shadow price equals the difference of the slopes of the production function between points A and B.

The preceding model represents a benign liquidity trap in its purest form. Its predictions concur with the stylized facts outlined earlier in this chapter: Prices are stable, unemployment is as low as in the absence of a borrowing limit, and nominal and real interest rates are depressed. Moreover, the following section demonstrates that monetary policy is unable to generate inflation, matching the fourth fact. Price stability and low unemployment are easy to derive, whereas the dynamics of nominal and real interest rates appear less straightforward. The next proposition, proven in appendix G, summarizes and generalizes the main findings.

Credit crunch: Assume a stationary state with unconstrained credit of the amount B^*. Introducing a borrowing limit $\overline{B} \in (0; B^*)$ leaves output, employment, capital and consumption unaffected, diminishes prices and wages by $\overline{B} / B^*$, and decreases interest. Moreover, the marginal productivity exceeds the user cost of capital.

Sticky Prices and Wages

Because the foregoing text assumed flexible prices and wages in order to grasp medium-term effects, it appears useful to complement it with a short-term analysis of the effects of a borrowing constraint. For this purpose, the model with sticky wages and prices from section 3.5 is well suited. To recall, the model derived the price level, the nominal interest rate and the nominal wage rate from the following three equilibrium conditions:

(62) $$\left.\begin{aligned} \pi_t &= \pi_t^e + \varphi^P \hat{Y}_t \\ B_t^d + B_t^{cb} &= B_t^s \\ \pi_t^W &= \pi_t^e + \varphi^W \hat{N}_t \end{aligned}\right\} \Rightarrow (P_t, i_t, W_t).$$

Prices and wages determined by the two Phillips curves—adjust slowly, whereas the nominal interest rate always equilibrates the bond market.

Augmenting this model with the borrowing constraint $B_t^s \leq \overline{B}$ generates the results illustrated in Figure 4.3. Under sticky prices and wages, the constraint is no longer neutral. After the onset of a credit crunch of 2 percent, prices initially fall by *less* than 2 percent, causing a temporary recession. As is familiar from section 3.5.2 on deterministic cycles, output then exceeds its medium-term level for a while and eventually converges to its original position. All other results resemble those of the flexible price model. Eventually, prices and nominal wage rates move in proportion to credit, while nominal as well as real interest rates become permanently depressed.

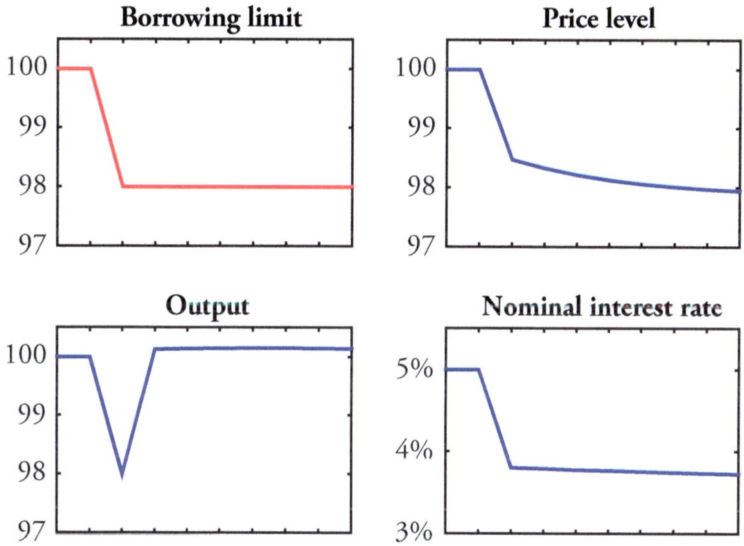

Figure 4.3: Credit crunch with sticky prices and wages. *Notes*: Horizontal axes represent time. Nominal interest is measured in percent. The initial values of the other variables are normalized at 100.

4.3 Policy Implications

Under a binding borrowing constraint, monetary expansions diminish interest rates and leave the general price level unaffected. These testable hypotheses, which constitute the key implications of the present approach, turn upside down the standard results derived in Chapter 3, where monetary expansions were found to *increase* both nominal interest and inflation.

Quantitative Easing

The new findings are illustrated in Figure 4.4, which assumes a stationary state with flexible prices and wages and a borrowing limit that happens to equal the unconstrained bond issues, $\overline{B} = B^*$. In this limiting case, the borrowing constraint has no visible effects. A first round of QE initiated by the central bank drives the economy into a benign liquidity trap.

Prices and output remain unchanged but the nominal interest rate falls from 5 to 3.7 percent. A second dose of QE, also shown in Figure 4.4, still leaves prices and output unchanged and further depresses the nominal interest rate from 3.7 to 2.8 percent. Unlike in the absence of a borrowing constraint, monetary expansions entail strong and lasting *liquidity effects*—they depress the nominal as well as the real rate of interest. Such persistent liquidity effects are a distinguishing feature of models with constrained credit.

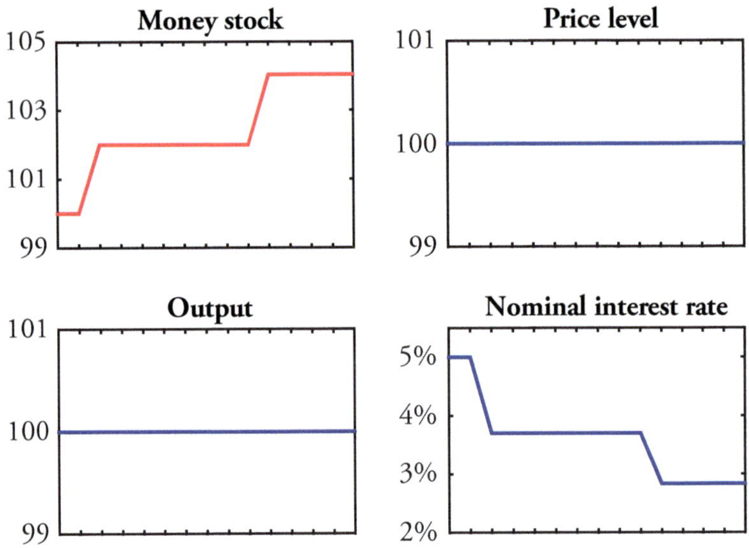

Figure 4.4: Quantitative easing. *Notes*: Horizontal axes represent time. Nominal interest is measured in percent. The initial values of the other variables are normalized at 100.

Importantly, the constancy of the price level is not due to an imposed stickiness here. Prices were assumed perfectly flexible, and that they remain at the original level is due to a lack of excess demand or supply in the commodity market. With sticky prices, the results of this model would be the same.

Equilibria with constrained credit can result either from drops in the borrowing limit (credit crunch), or from rises in the money stock (quantitative easing). The first instance relates to a nominal friction that becomes tighter, while the second involves deliberate central bank decisions to engage in large-scale open market purchases; hence, liquidity traps may well be policy induced. The two possible causes are not independent of each other but are interrelated in the following way: In a stationary state, the unconstrained credit amount, B^*, is a linear function of the money stock, M, owing to money neutrality. Since the borrowing limit and the money stock are both exogenous, the common characteristic of constrained equilibria is a borrowing limit that is too tight relative to the money stock.

In the absence of a binding borrowing constraint, increases in the money stock cause proportional increases in total credit, B^*; money creation and credit creation go hand in hand. This scenario yields the standard results reported in Chapter 3. If the borrowing limit binds, however, increases in the money stock cease to influence total credit. While the central bank balance sheet implies $M = B^{cb}$, such that money creation is still accomplished through credit creation, increases in central bank bond purchases entail corresponding reductions in consumer bond purchases. The sum of the two sources of credit remains constant and equals the given limit, $B^d + B^{cb} = \overline{B}$. This equation may suggest that the borrowing limit places an upper bound on money creation, rendering further expansions impossible until consumers' bond purchases have been driven to zero. Such an inference, however, is invalid: If the central bank were to continue the expansion, consumer bond purchases would eventually become negative.

A further empirical implication of the borrowing constraint concerns the impact of monetary expansions on equilibrium real balances. In the unconstrained scenarios, one-shot increases in the money stock had no impact on real balances, while permanent money growth diminished them. Under a binding borrowing constraint, increases in the money stock will raise real balances instead. This is obvious because expansionary policies of any kind do not generate inflation; any rise in M leaves P unaffected and elevates M/P.

After the Great Recession, several central banks, notably those of the United States and the eurozone, engaged in QE with the explicit objective of raising inflation rates. The present analysis offers a possible explanation why these policies did not in fact produce inflation. It suggests that the emerging liquidity traps—characterized by low interest rates and nearly stable prices—were induced by the central banks themselves, rather than by credit crunches that should have entailed deflation. To the extent that this is true, central banks have impaired their ability to influence the economy. This possibility represents a clear downside of QE. At the same time, the case for policy responses to changes in money demand becomes weaker in a constrained equilibrium: While money demand variations have real effects in a standard framework with sticky prices and wages, they are as ineffective as money stock variations if the borrowing constraint binds.

Forward Guidance

After the failures of QE to raise inflation, some central banks turned to a different strategy known as expectations management or forward guidance. Because this matter is highly disputed, some preliminary remarks seem appropriate. Most RE models portray monetary policy as announcements of rules or sequences of policy variables. In such a setting, individuals listen to the announcements, believe them, and optimize accordingly. Critics of this approach point out that many market participants do not pay attention to central bank proclamations but optimize in an insular environment and react only to what they see. Market participants may also disregard central bank notices because they do not trust them. Central banks, of course, consider themselves trustworthy actors that are able to influence the economy not only through choices of current instruments but also via announcements of their future course. Accepting this view for a moment, the central bank strategy of forward guidance originates in the first-order condition (11), rewritten here as

$$\frac{\partial F}{\partial K_t^d} = r_{t+1}^e + \delta . \tag{63}$$

This condition relates the marginal productivity to the user cost of capital. It implies an inverse relationship between investment and the expected real interest rate. If the economy has approached the ZLB, the central bank can no longer stimulate investment through reductions in the nominal interest rate. However, it can still reduce the expected real interest rate, $r_{t+1}^e = i_t - \pi_{t+1}^e$, to the extent that it convinces investors of higher future inflation. This would reduce the user cost of capital and make investment more attractive.

Assuming, for the sake of argument, that investors really believed in central bank announcements of higher inflation, notwithstanding the experience that for years these banks did not deliver the promised results, a deeper problem with forward guidance concerns the underlying premise, (63): As emphasized in the preceding section, a constrained equilibrium with overabundant money and a congruent ZLB is characterized by the inequality

$$\frac{\partial F}{\partial K_t^d} > r_{t+1}^e + \delta , \tag{64}$$

which states that the expected real interest rate is irrelevant for investment decisions. Hence, central bank announcements may succeed in reducing expected real interest. Nevertheless, they are incapable of boosting investment since the latter is not restricted by credit cost but by credit availability. As long as the borrowing constraint remains operative, reductions in credit cost fail to stimulate investment and have no effect on the price level. The real-world experience with forward guidance policies after 2013 supports the findings; these policies failed to lift price levels.

Financial Repression

As is well known, public debt in many countries surged sharply during and after the Great Recession of 2008–09. Sovereign interest payments, by contrast, remained limited because interest rates fell concurrently. Many observers have attributed the reductions in interest to central bank interventions and have interpreted them as the outcome of a deliberate strategy, referred to as *financial repression*, which aims to expropriate savers and favors governments. Carmen

Reinhart (2012: 41), for instance, has no doubt that aggressive monetary expansions are a critical factor in explaining low interest rates.

While financial repression is a widely accepted narrative in the applied literature and the political sphere, theorists often hesitate to accept such a hypothesis. Recalling the key results of Chapter 3, the reason for this reservation should be clear: In the absence of borrowing constraints, central banks can influence market interest rates through inflation, but they have no control over expected real interest rates. Whereas surprise inflation depresses the ex post real rate, benefitting the government and other debtors for a while, this temporary advantage is reversed when the central bank turns to a restrictive stance in order to lower inflation. Hence, in a scenario with unconstrained borrowing, the financial repression hypothesis is all but convincing.

From this perspective, constrained credit yields a theoretical foundation for the allegation that monetary policies may have a redistributive rationale. As shown above, the existence of a binding borrowing limit puts the central bank in a position to control both nominal and real interest rates. Specifically, QE will depress interest rates, making savers worse off and governments better off. Such a policy works as long as the borrowing limit remains operative.

Stealth Crowding-out

In Japan, *Abenomics* was not restricted to QE but also included government spending (as well as some unspecified growth strategies). After the global decline in nominal and real interest rates, several economists, including Summers (2014) and von Weizsäcker (2014), suggested deficit spending as the right measure. According to Summers, it would be "madness not to be engaged in substantially stimulative fiscal policies" at essentially zero interest. The next paragraphs analyze deficit spending in the presence of a borrowing constraint, using the fiscal model introduced in section 3.3. To recall, this model amends the basic framework with public consumption, taxes, and public debt. Its general equilibrium is described by the following system of equations:

$$(65) \qquad \left.\begin{array}{l} C_t + I_t + G_t = Y_t^s \\ B_t^d + B_t^{cb} = B_t^s + B_t^g \\ N_t^d = \bar{N} \end{array}\right\} \Rightarrow (P_t, i_t, W_t).$$

Supplementing the fiscal model with a borrowing constraint, $B_t^s \leq \bar{B}_t$, allows one to investigate the consequences of simultaneous monetary and fiscal expansions in a constrained equilibrium. Importantly, such a setting presupposes that the borrowing constraint applies only to producers while the government has unrestricted access to credit. Possible rationales for this assumption are that investors consider sovereign bonds to be safe or that the latter benefit from regulatory preferences.

Figure 4.5 shows an initial stationary state with a balanced government budget and a binding borrowing constraint. Throughout, the central bank pursues QE by maintaining a money growth rate of 2 percent. This drives down the nominal interest rate in the expected manner. After a while, the government initiates a temporary increase in public consumption of 10 percent at unchanged tax revenue. Evidently, deficit spending does not affect the nominal interest rate but generates minimal inflation, which disappears after budget balance has been restored. The public debt ratio increases, whereas the capital stock is diminished. If the government returns to a balanced budget policy, inflation recedes; otherwise, sovereign insolvency would result.

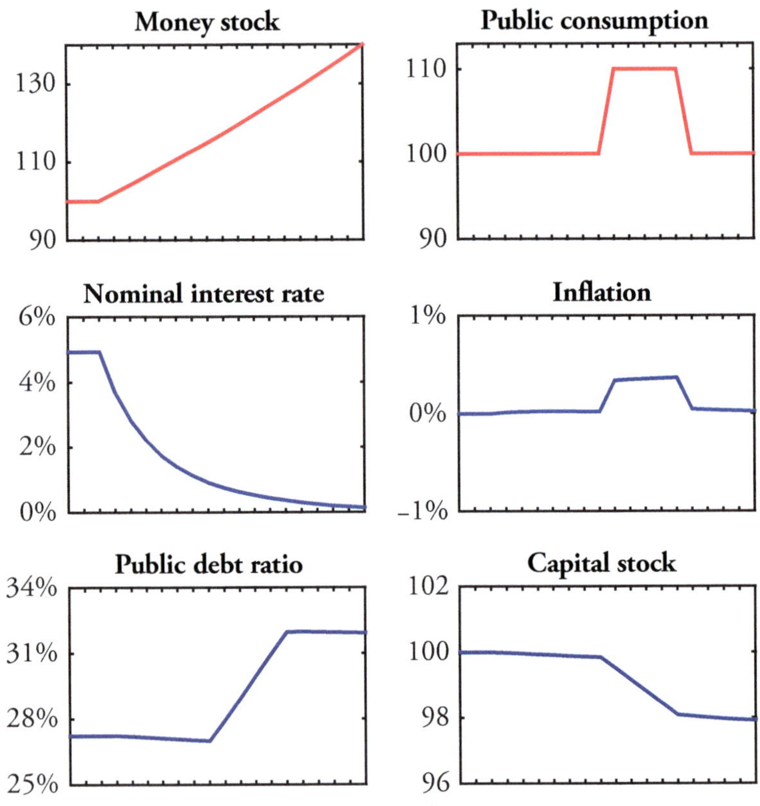

Figure 4.5: QE *cum* deficit spending. *Notes*: Horizontal axes represent time. Nominal interest, inflation and the public debt ratio are measured in percent. The initial values of the other variables are normalized at 100.

The most surprising result of this scenario is that deficit spending entails inflation, while monetary expansions do not. Understanding the mechanism requires recalling that the fiscal model is non-Ricardian; consumers do not simply offset changes in public debt by reducing current consumption. Nevertheless, the impact of deficit spending on prices would normally be contained, except for an indirect effect through changes in the nominal interest rate:

Although public consumption represents a part of commodity demand, increases in the former will not affect the latter because the rise in public debt crowds out an equal amount of private investment through higher interest. According to the traditional crowding-out argument, slight increases in interest preserve bond market equilibrium and ensure that aggregate demand, the sum $C+I+G$, is independent of the level of public consumption. Public consumption affects only the composition of demand, implying that commodity prices remain unchanged.

Clearly, the traditional crowding-out argument is no longer applicable in a constrained equilibrium. If the marginal productivity of capital exceeds the user cost, changes in real interest do not affect investment. Therefore, deficit spending actually increases ex ante commodity demand in this exceptional case, such that the price level is bound to rise. The ensuing inflation tightens the constraint $\overline{B}_t = P_t K_t^d$ and diminishes investment. A downward spiral of lower investment, lower output, and subsequent increases in prices follows. This novel mechanism is referred to as *stealth crowding-out* because it is invisible. An observer trying to determine whether deficit spending has crowded out investment through higher interest rates would find no supporting evidence.

To summarize, this section has shown that binding borrowing constraints have profound consequences for economic policy. First and foremost, QE will neither stimulate output nor trigger inflation; such a policy is even apt to push an unconstrained economy into a liquidity trap, making further policy moves inoperative. Second, forward guidance also leaves output and inflation unaffected. Like QE, forward guidance reduces interest but this has only redistributive consequences; financial repression becomes possible. Third, deficit spending crowds out private investment stealthily through higher prices rather than higher interest rates. All these results have as their common root the inequality (64): When the marginal productivity exceeds the user cost of capital, investment is not constrained by credit cost but by credit availability, a point made forcefully by Geanakoplos (2009). Conventional conclusions founded on the premise that lower interest stimulates investment will fail to hold. Indirectly, the findings also suggest a way to escape constrained equilibria. Bearing in mind that liquidity traps are characterized by an overabundance of money relative to the borrowing limit, reducing the money stock would suffice.

4.4 Evaluation

In microeconomics and corporate finance, the analysis of borrowing constraints has a long tradition that goes back to Stiglitz (1969), Barro (1976), Sinn (1980), and Stiglitz and Weiss (1981). One of the main insights of this literature is that credit markets do not necessarily equate demand and supply in the usual manner. Adverse selection, moral hazard, and other forms of market incompleteness may entail equilibria with credit rationing, where market interest falls short of the return on capital. In macroeconomics, the use of borrowing constraints originated in the *equity premium puzzle*. Mehra and Prescott (1985: 159) argued that the difference between equity returns and safe interest rates, referred to as the equity premium, cannot be attributed to risk aversion. For plausibly parameterized economies, they derived risk premiums beneath 0.5 percent. This figure falls considerably short of observed equity premiums of at 3 percent; see Siegel (2014: 171). Mehra and Prescott surmised that financial frictions may help resolve the puzzle.

Following this suggestion, Huggett (1993: 962) augmented a real business cycle model with a borrowing constraint and showed that credit tightening diminishes the equilibrium riskless rate. In a related paper, Aiyagari (1994) showed that borrowing constraints reduce aggregate saving in a heterogeneous agent setting because they leave savers unaffected and restrict borrowers. Similar results were derived by Constantinides et al. (2002) for economies with three overlapping generations, the youngest of which is subject to borrowing restrictions. Following this strand, Eggertsson and Krugman (2012) as well as Eggertsson and Mehrotra (2015) used borrowing constraints to develop scenarios with permanent depression and unemployment.

All the cited models are non-monetary in the following sense: They portray cashless economies with indeterminate price levels; producers are mostly absent or at least do not need credit; borrowing constraints come in real terms; and the latter affect only consumers. The present model differs in four respects from the earlier literature: It comprises money balances and a determinate price level; represents producers as entities that finance investment by bond issues; uses a nominal borrowing limit; and applies the constraint to the producers. This monetary approach is in line with recommendations by Claudio Borio (2014: 188 ff.) who argued vigorously that to understand financial crises, one must move away from RE, consider true monetary economies instead of real business cycle economies in disguise, accept that contracts are set in nominal rather than real terms, and base the model on credit, a financial concept, rather than on saving and investment, which are commodity concepts.

In fact, managers and their regulators are mainly concerned with *nominal* balance sheet items; they often do not think in real terms. Any nominal write-off, for instance, produces a loss that affects performance indicators and diminishes equity. However, following the methodology that assumptions should not be judged primarily by their realism but by their implications, the truly compelling argument for a monetary approach is that its conclusions concur with the evidence. As demonstrated in the preceding sections, nominal borrowing constraints entail stable prices, low unemployment, depressed interest and, crucially, the central bank's inability to generate inflation.

A further key implication has not been directly tested as yet. This implication, rewritten here as

$$(66) \qquad \frac{\partial F}{\partial K_t^d} - \delta > r_{t+1}^e,$$

was responsible for all the unconventional policy implications outlined here and deserves closer inspection. The inequality states that the marginal productivity of capital net of depreciation exceeds the expected real interest rate in a constrained equilibrium. Its right-hand side is observable as the yield of inflation-indexed treasuries. Measuring the left-hand side is more difficult. In a recent study, Knolle and Lehmann (2016) proposed weighted average cost of capital (WACC) as a proxy for the net marginal productivity of capital. The idea is that in reality, firms evaluate investment projects by calculating discounted cash flows. In doing so they employ WACC as a discount factor, an average of equity and debt cost; see Brealey et al. (2014: 479 ff.). Projects with a positive present value are pursued and other projects are rejected. Therefore, WACC represents the return of the marginal investment project. Correcting for taxes and inflation, the WACC measure is a valid proxy of the marginal capital productivity.

Importantly, objections against WACC and the underlying capital asset pricing model do not impair the usefulness of this empirical approach because its validity does not depend on whether or not producers select the "right" discount factor. And as long as one looks only at the trend of the WACC measure, it is immaterial whether single data points are biased. In practice, WACC are imposed by the CEO as an internal threshold. If credit becomes tighter, perhaps due to high indebtedness, the CEO will raise the WACC in order to distribute the available means efficiently; projects not reaching the required threshold are then refuted.

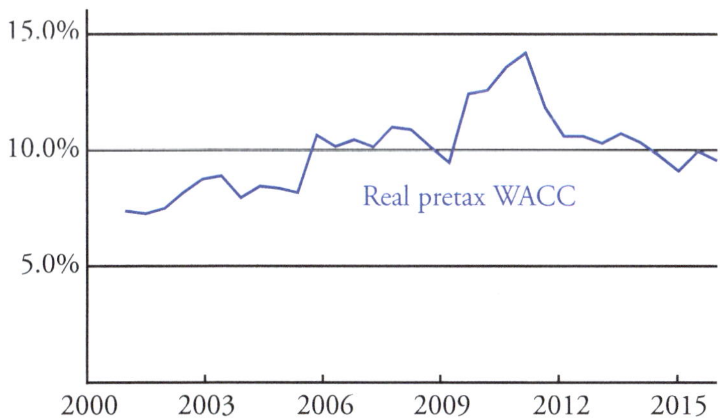

Figure 4.6: Marginal productivity of capital. *Notes*: Semiannual data, 30 June and 31 December. Real pretax WACC was compiled from a sample of over 3,700 firms from all OECD member states except Italy, cf. Knolle and Lehmann (2016: 7).

The sample considered by Knolle and Lehmann includes over 3,700 firms from all OECD countries except Italy. Figure 4.6 documents the results. For real pretax WACC, it suggests 10 percent as a typical value. Assuming a corporate tax rate of 30 percent, this finding is in accordance with long-run real stock returns of roughly 7 percent that are often reported in the literature; see Siegel (2014: 6). Furthermore, Figure 4.6 shows that capital productivity *increased* during the Great Recession and had no declining trend over the entire horizon. Given the global decrease in real interest rates, this pattern is difficult to reconcile with equality of the net marginal productivity of capital and the expected real interest rate. Moreover, real pretax returns of 10 percent contradict the very notion of secular stagnation according to which mature economies have simply run out of profitable investment opportunities and should engage in essentially costless government deficit spending.

Combined with decent corporate earnings and good stock market performances in the years after the Great Recession, the results suggest that declines in real interest rates do not point to economic decay but to a pronounced increase in profitability; the gap between producers' rates of return and the riskless interest rate has become wider. As mentioned previously, the size of the equity premium cannot be explained in terms of risk aversion; a fortiori, its increase is unlikely to be attributable to increased risk aversion. Tighter borrowing constraints provide a more compelling account: The gap between the net marginal productivity and the interest rate is not a risk premium but the shadow price of the constraint as defined in section 4.2. Moreover, constrained credit implies monetary policy ineffectiveness while risk aversion leaves the accustomed transmission channels unimpaired and provides no rationale for why central banks should be unable to boost nominal interest rates via higher inflation.

Regarding profits, it should be added that these are positive in a constrained equilibrium. Under competitive conditions, profits normally vanish because factor payments exhaust revenue. Introducing a borrowing constraint leaves output and factor demands unaffected, has no impact on real wages, and diminishes interest. Therefore, positive profits emerge. Because the model lacks a market for shares, all optimality and equilibrium conditions remain intact. The functional distribution is also unchanged. However, profit income rises at the expense of interest income, which may partly explain protests against an alleged exploitation of the ordinary saver.

A final remark concerns the interpretation of borrowing constraints in macroeconomic models. As is typical in macroeconomic reasoning, a uniform constraint represents a highly stylized representation of reality. At the micro level, there are always some individuals who cannot obtain credit, while credit is sufficiently available for others. Therefore, macroeconomic outcomes depend on the distribution of the credit limit and are governed by the position of the *marginal* borrowers. If the latter are unconstrained, credit supply and demand determine equilibrium interest in the accustomed fashion, and the marginal productivity of capital equals the expected real interest rate. But if borrowing limits are binding for the marginal borrowers, the net marginal productivity of capital will exceed the expected real interest rate, and the latter becomes irrelevant for investment demand.

4.5 Conclusion

Augmenting the standard framework with a borrowing constraint, this chapter discussed a coherent account of benign liquidity traps. The resulting equilibrium shows that unusually low interest rates need not indicate a secular stagnation but are fully consistent with stable prices and high employment. Regarding monetary theory, the most important finding was a qualification of the statement that "inflation is always and everywhere a monetary phenomenon". In the absence of a binding borrowing constraint, this proposition is almost a truism, since money creation and credit creation go hand in hand: As demonstrated in Chapter 3, any central bank open market purchase increases the money stock and the credit stock concurrently.

However, matters are different in the presence of a binding borrowing constraint. This financial friction blocks the normal transmission of monetary policy because increases in money leave total credit unaffected. Central bank open market purchases induce consumers to diminish their credit supply in such a way that total credit still coincides with the limit. During the adjustment process, consumers replace bond holdings by money balances, which necessitates a decrease in the equilibrium nominal interest rate.

Under a binding constraint, two key implications emerge that help reconcile theory and evidence. First, expansionary monetary policies actually diminish nominal and real interest rates. Second, inflation becomes independent of the money stock and responds only to changes in the borrowing limit. To put the entire chapter in a nutshell, inflation is not a monetary but a credit phenomenon.

Chapter 5

Net Worth

Chapter 2 introduced a functional distinction between consumers and producers. Producers were envisioned as abstract units that employ workers and acquire capital goods in order to produce output. They did not use own capital but borrowed all the required means by issuing bonds. Producers' net worth, the difference of assets and liabilities, was always zero. In reality, it is generally not feasible for producers to rely exclusively on debt financing. Owing to asymmetric information in financial markets, bond holders are unwilling to provide unlimited credit. Since the 1970s, the finance literature has developed many models of principle-agent problems in capital markets that rationalize the need for positive net worth under asymmetric information.

The purpose of the present chapter is not to repeat this strand but to feed the main result into the present framework and study its macroeconomic implications. Positive net worth also brings the model a step closer to reality because the use of own capital is quantitatively important. This refinement of the baseline framework is conducted in two steps. First, section 5.1 introduces net worth by considering entrepreneurs, such as single proprietorships or unlimited liability partnerships, who finance investment only partly with debt. Second, section 5.2 considers corporations with positive net worth whose shareholders have no obligation to make additional capital contributions in the case of losses. Section 5.3 employs the latter premise to analyze the general equilibrium consequences of stock manias. Section 5.4 combines the assumptions of the previous and the present chapter and considers endogenous borrowing constraints. The chapter is concluded with an informal discussion of Fisher's debt-deflations in section 5.5.

5.1 Entrepreneurs

The balance sheet $P_t K_t^d = B_t^s$, introduced in section 2.4, states that entrepreneurs finance investment exclusively by external debt. This assumption is now relaxed by allowing nonzero net worth and internal financing. *Net worth* (or own equity, E) is the difference of assets and liabilities and calculated as a residuum:

$$E_t = P_t K_t^d - B_t^s. \tag{67}$$

In any period t, a single entrepreneur can sell the capital goods, repay the debt, and pocket the remaining amount, E_t. In this sense, net worth represents a fundamental value. Positive net worth does not affect the definition of economic profit but changes the profit level: Under pure debt financing, expected profit vanishes in a competitive equilibrium; this is a direct consequence of the familiar adding-up theorem. Positive net worth implies a lower debt level at the profit maximizing capital stock. Interest payments are reduced by $i_t E_t$ and expected profits equal $\Pi^e_{t+1} = i_t E_t$ rather than zero.

If the entrepreneurs disburse an amount Z_t in period t, the evolution of net worth is given by the following equation of motion:

$$E_t = E_{t-1} + \Pi_t - Z_t . \tag{68}$$

Thus, net worth is increased by economic profit and diminished by disbursements. Only if $E_0 = 0$ and $\Pi_t = Z_t$ for all t holds, net worth vanishes identically, and the baseline scenario results as a special case. The more general model used here satisfies the *clean surplus* principle of accounting, according to which changes in net worth equal profit in the absence of disbursements. To the extent that entrepreneurs abstain from disbursements, *retained profits* emerge that can be used to finance an expansion or to reduce debt. This is referred to as self-financing.

Turning to consumers, who are the beneficial owners of the production entities, it may be helpful to stress in advance that the distribution of wealth among consumers is immaterial in this setting. Owing to identical homothetic utility functions (except in subsection 3.1.5), individual demands are linear functions of individual wealth, and consumers' aggregate behavior depends solely on aggregate wealth. At the micro level, some consumers may be acting as entrepreneurs while others are workers, some may be rich while others are poor, and some may hold bonds while others hold shares. On this basis, the only required change in modeling consumer behavior consists in replacing profit income by disbursements in the aggregate budget constraint, (12):

$$P_t C_t + B^d_t + M^d_t = (1 + i_{t-1}) B^d_{t-1} + M^d_{t-1} + \sigma_{t-1} + W_t N_t + Z_t . \tag{69}$$

The reformulated budget constraint takes account of the fact that it is not total profits but only disbursements that are available for individual expenditure. Without further changes, however, the model's behavior would change drastically, and in an implausible manner. To see this, consider a period with positive profits and zero disbursements. Compared with the original model, consumers' budget constraints become tighter, which diminishes demands. This is implausible because the entrepreneurs could obtain additional means by increasing disbursements. Setting $E_t = 0$ in (68) shows that entrepreneurs can realize disbursements of the amount $Z_t = E_{t-1} + \Pi_t$ if they liquidate or sell their businesses. This maximal disbursement exceeds profit income by the value of the initial net worth.

In what follows, individuals are assumed to make their intertemporal choices in accordance with the maximum disbursement. Put differently, they *perceive* net worth as part of their personal wealth. Using this assumption, appendix H derives the following consumption function for logarithmic utility:

(70) $$C_t = \frac{A_t + X_t + \sigma_t^r + E_{t-1} / P_t}{1 + \beta + \mu}.$$

Compared with the consumption function of the baseline model, equation (22), initial net worth enters the right-hand side, while profit is still included in the variable X_t. This makes sense because consumers' initial financial assets, A_t, which encompass producers' bond issues, are lower in a model with equity financing. Reminiscent of the Modigliani-Miller theorem, consumption and the equilibrium value of $A_t + E_{t-1}/P_t$ are in fact independent of the financing structure, and the latter's composition does not affect the allocation. Regarding monetary policy, a higher money growth rate that turned out to be superneutral in the basic framework is also superneutral here. In the long run, such a policy change increases the nominal interest rate but has no further effects on real variables other than real balances. The higher seigniorage is remitted to the consumers and enables them to stick to their original consumption plans. Moreover, debt and net worth move in proportion to the money stock.

Summarizing, this introductory section has shown that adding net worth as such does not change the model's properties, provided that consumers regard it as a part of their personal wealth. Net worth becomes only significant if additional assumptions are introduced. Such assumptions are considered step by step in the following sections.

5.2 Corporations

Many producers are organized as corporations. These are legal entities that must keep net worth positive or file for insolvency. A distinguishing feature of corporations is that their disbursements, referred to as *dividends*, are non-negative because shareholders cannot be forced to make additional contributions:

(71) $$Z_t \geq 0.$$

Of course, shareholders could conclude a capital increase and let the corporation issue new shares. Under asymmetric information, this is a rare occurrence especially in difficult times; and it comes with a notable tax disadvantage. While some authors consider external equity financing, this text focuses on the two predominant instruments of corporate finance: retained profit and external debt.

In practice, corporations will often target a specific *loan-to-value ratio*, $ltv = B_t^s / (E_t + B_t^s)$, whose value results from complex optimizations involving agency costs and tax considerations. Thus, corporations pay dividends if the current loan-to-value ratio falls short of the target. Otherwise, no dividends are paid. Under these assumptions, monetary policy affects the capital structure even in the absence of other frictions.

Figure 5.1 portrays a restrictive monetary policy that reduces the money stock by 2 percent per period. In the initial stationary state, the corporation maintains a target loan-to-value ratio of 75 percent. The deflation diminishes the value of the capital stock and induces losses. With net worth reduced, corporations miss the target loan-to-value ratio and cease to pay dividends. After a while, net worth recovers, and real dividends are restored at their original level. This pattern is due to the course of the nominal interest rate, which declines gradually while deflation expectations approach their new equilibrium level of –2 percent. The debt reduction is driven by zero dividends combined with lower interest on debt.

Notably, although monetary policy affects dividend streams and debt, it is still superneutral. This follows from the Modigliani-Miller theorem: Under the present assumptions, capital structures do not affect the allocation, nor do they influence prices. Specifically, the paths of nominal and expected real interest rates are identical to those in the basic framework.

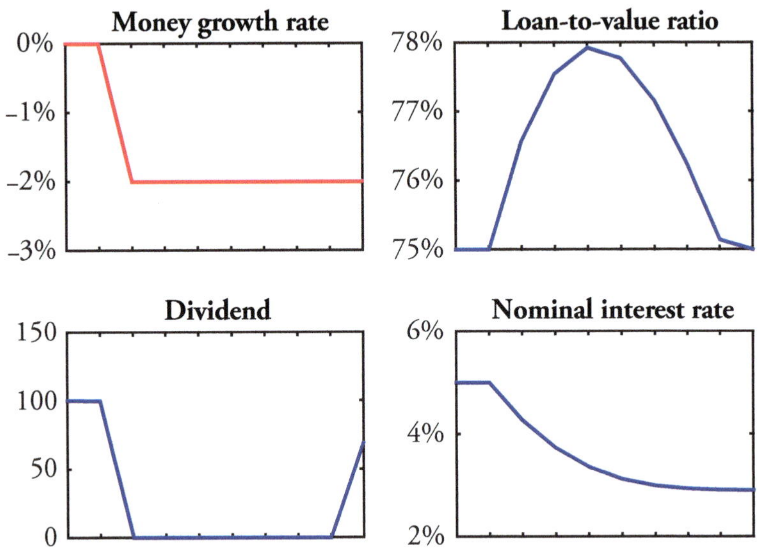

Figure 5.1: Dividend path during deflation. *Notes*: Horizontal axes represent time. The initial value of the dividend is normalized at 100. Other variables are measured in percent.

5.3 Stock Manias

In the broadest sense, manias can take two forms. The first form was studied in subsection 3.1.3, which showed that sudden increases in expected inflation are buffered by corresponding changes in the nominal interest rate. Anticipations of higher prices make investment more profitable and increase credit demand. In the case of a constant credit supply, which presumes a passive monetary policy, nominal interest rates are bound to rise. This restores equilibrium in the credit market and leaves the allocation unaffected. One can easily check that the foregoing reasoning carries over to a setting with corporations. Hence, there is no need for a detailed repetition.

The second form of manias concerns stock market behavior. Since Shiller's (1981) original contribution, research in finance has consistently found that stocks are characterized by excess volatility. Actual stock price behavior contradicts the RE premise because stocks rise too steeply during a boom and drop too sharply during a recession; see Gomme et al. (2011). According to a common explanation of this pattern, increases in stock prices foster investor confidence and induce additional stock purchases. The latter, in turn, stimulate investors to update their subjective beliefs about future stock prices, and this sets into motion a self-reinforcing process of "irrational exuberance"; see Adam et al. (2016).

In the preceding section, stock manias were not an issue because shareholders valued corporations at their fundamental value, E_t. Stock manias are now modeled as exogenous shocks $u_t > 0$ such that investors value corporations erroneously at $(1+u_t)E_t$, which may be due to an inability to anticipate corporate profits correctly. Such a premise points to a subtle problem of many general equilibrium models. In Arrow-Debreu economies, for instance, consumers make optimal choices subject to budget constraints that comprise quantities, prices, and profits. While it appears perfectly reasonable to assume that consumers know the quantities they choose and are able to observe the prevailing prices, the implicit assumption that they also make perfect profit forecasts is less innocuous because profits are the result of the equilibration process. Therefore, it is interesting to investigate the macroeconomic consequences of erroneous valuations.

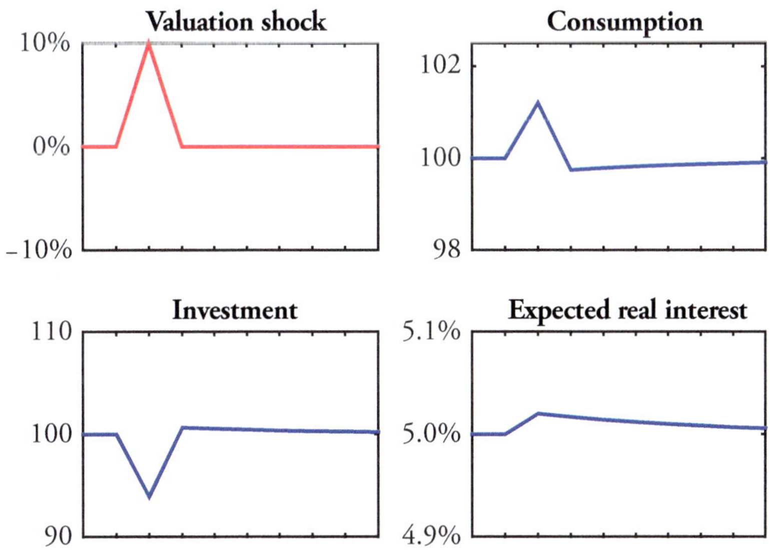

Figure 5.2: Stock mania. *Notes*: Horizontal axes represent time. The valuation shock and expected real interest are measured in percent. The initial values of the other variables are normalized at 100.

Although a positive valuation shock makes shareholders feel richer and changes their behavior, it is important to keep in mind that increases in perceived net worth have no influence on the consumers' aggregate budget constraint, (69). Corporate net worth, perceived or actual, does *not* show up on the right-hand side of the budget constraint because it is not available for spending. Possible sales of shares are not a valid counter-argument, since they constitute a receipt for the seller and an equal expense for the buyer. The resulting cash flows cancel each other out and do not influence consumers' aggregate means.

Figure 5.2 illustrates the consequences of a transient valuation shock that raises perceived net worth by 10 percent. As expected, consumers increase consumption demand. The other effects are strongly at variance with popular narratives. In particular, investment plummets sharply. This reaction is not due to changes in investment and credit demand but results from a reduction in credit supply: If consumers increase commodity purchases, they must reduce bond purchases. Thus, consumption crowds out investment via a temporary increase in the expected real interest rate, as depicted in the bottom right panel. Initially, output stays constant because it only depends on employment and the previous capital stock. The drop in investment matches the surge in consumption, whereas the relative change in investment is stronger because consumption makes up a larger fraction of output. In the following periods, output falls slightly as a result of diminished investment.

These are the pure effects of stock manias in a flexible price model. Interestingly, the results are not nullified but are reinforced if one assumes sticky prices instead. The reason is that rises in perceived wealth increase money demand. Remembering that increases in money demand have the same effects as decreases in the money stock, deflation sets in. Hence, if prices and wages are sticky, the resulting contraction diminishes output and employment.

The key finding of this section concerns the common refrain of *wealth effects* as drivers of economic activity. Increases in perceived wealth alone cannot cause a boom. If anything, they induce a real contraction, resulting from disinvestment, price rigidities, and the need to shift resources between consumption and investment sectors. The argument that higher expected profits and higher perceived wealth stimulate the economy is delusive and unconvincing in a general equilibrium framework. With constant income and a constant money stock, higher consumption necessitates lower bond purchases, hence lower credit for producers. This result—which underscores the importance of budget constraints for consistent macroeconomic reasoning—will be reiterated and qualified later.

5.4 Limited Leverage

Chapter 4 presented settings with constrained credit. Its main contribution was to show that strong money growth and stable prices can co-exist for an extended time if borrowers are restricted. In these models, investment was exclusively financed by debt. The present section merges the concepts of net worth and constrained credit, which yields three important insights. First, while credit and prices move in strict proportion under pure debt financing, the effect of credit on prices is less pronounced in a model with net worth. Second, the accumulation of net worth represents a natural escape route from a liquidity trap. Third, positive net worth allows the construction of endogenous credit limits. The following paragraphs provide the details.

Credit and Prices

Augmenting the net worth model with an exogenous borrowing limit is easy because it does not require any change in equilibrium conditions. From the point of view of the individual producer, bond issues are restricted in the following manner:

(72) $$B_t^s \leq \overline{B}_t .$$

This borrowing constraint repeats the inequality (59) and expresses that bond buyers do not accept unlimited leverage. Since producers have net worth of the amount E_{t-1} at the start of the period, they can finance any investment satisfying the following inequality, discussed in appendix H:

(73) $$P_t K_t^d \leq E_{t-1} + \overline{B}_t .$$

Assuming that producers keep net worth constant, changes in the borrowing limit produce effects that closely resemble those discussed in section 4.2. Like in Figure 4.1, a credit crunch diminishes the price level and the nominal interest rate but leaves the real variables unchanged under flexible prices. The quantitative impact of credit on prices is less pronounced, however, and can be characterized by a crisp formula:

(74) $$\frac{\Delta P_t}{P_t} = ltv \times \frac{\Delta \overline{B}_t}{\overline{B}_t}.$$

Here, *ltv* represents the loan-to-value ratio defined in section 5.2, a number between zero and one. With a loan-to-value ratio of 50 percent, for instance, prices decline by just one half of the decline in the credit limit. This is easy to prove. Because net worth and real capital are constant, equation (73) entails $\Delta P_t K_t^d = \Delta \overline{B}_t$. Dividing this by (73) and using $ltv = B/(E+B)$ yields (74). Naturally, a loan-to-value ratio of one, which corresponds to full debt financing, reproduces the result from section 4.2 that relative changes in credit and prices coincide.

Escaping from a Liquidity Trap

The previous finding can be summarized in the following way: With a given amount of net worth, indefinite liquidity traps are still possible in general equilibrium but the effect of credit on prices is weaker. While the conclusion of this proposition is convincing, its premise appears questionable. Intuitively, the very existence of a binding borrowing constraint means that producers cannot attain their preferred positions—the constraint prevents them from executing all profitable investment opportunities. Therefore, producers have an incentive to get rid of the credit restriction, and an obvious way to do this is self-financing: Retention of profit increases net worth and facilitates more investment. The following formula, derived in appendix H, sustains this intuition and characterizes profitable self-financing:

$$\text{(75)} \qquad \frac{\Pi_{t+1}^{e}}{E_t} = i_t + \xi_t \left(1 + \frac{B_t}{E_t}\right).$$

The left-hand side of this equation represents the expected *return on equity*. The variable ξ_t is the shadow price of the borrowing constraint, defined in (196), which indicates the increase in profit following a marginal relaxation of the constraint. Depending on whether or not the constraint binds, the formula describes two distinct situations that are well known from the literature but seldom related to each other:

- If $\xi_t = 0$, the borrowing limit does not bind. The second summand vanishes, and the return on equity equals the nominal interest rate. Moreover, the return on equity is independent of the finance structure, so that the Modigliani-Miller theorem applies.
- If $\xi_t > 0$, the borrowing limit binds, the second summand is strictly positive, and the return on equity exceeds the interest rate. The Modigliani-Miller theorem fails, and profit becomes an increasing function of debt (*leverage effect*).

While the first case renders the level of disbursements irrelevant, there is a compelling case for profit retention in the second case: Full disbursements leave the borrowing constraint unchanged and enable the owners to invest the proceeds at the going interest rate, i_t. Profit retention, by contrast, strengthens net worth and yields the higher return $\Pi_{t+1}^{e} / E_t > i_t$, as indicated in the above formula. Therefore, paying no dividends at all would theoretically be optimal. However, as Lintner (1956) noted in a thoughtful early study, shareholders often prefer stable over fluctuating dividends, and corporations must also include tax considerations into their decisions. Hennessy and Whited (2005) provide a comprehensive partial equilibrium treatment of optimal dividend and debt choices.

The following simulation focuses on the general equilibrium effects of constrained credit. It assumes that producers disburse total profit in the absence of a binding credit limit, but retain a constant fraction if borrowing is restricted. The value of this fraction governs the adjustment speed. Figure 5.3 considers a borrowing limit that just binds at the outset and then drops by 1 percent. This reduces actual bond issues and elevates the shadow price into positive territory. According to formula (75), the return on equity exceeds the nominal interest rate, which makes retention profitable and causes producers to increase net worth, as shown in the middle left panel. During the deleveraging, producers build up net worth and reduce debt. This process lasts until the desired bond issues fall below the borrowing limit, whereupon producers keep net worth constant. As opposed to a setting with pure debt financing, the economy has a built-in mechanism to recover from a liquidity trap that is caused by an exogenous borrowing limit. The price level and the nominal interest rate become temporarily depressed, as familiar from Chapter 4. These variables also overshoot in both directions since inflation expectations adjust only gradually. The fall in the price level induces a pursuant decrease in nominal bond issues. While the credit level becomes permanently depressed after adjustment is complete, the price level returns to its original position. This is due to the Modigliani-Miller theorem that holds at the outset and after completion of deleveraging. The capital stock does not change at all in this flexible price model.

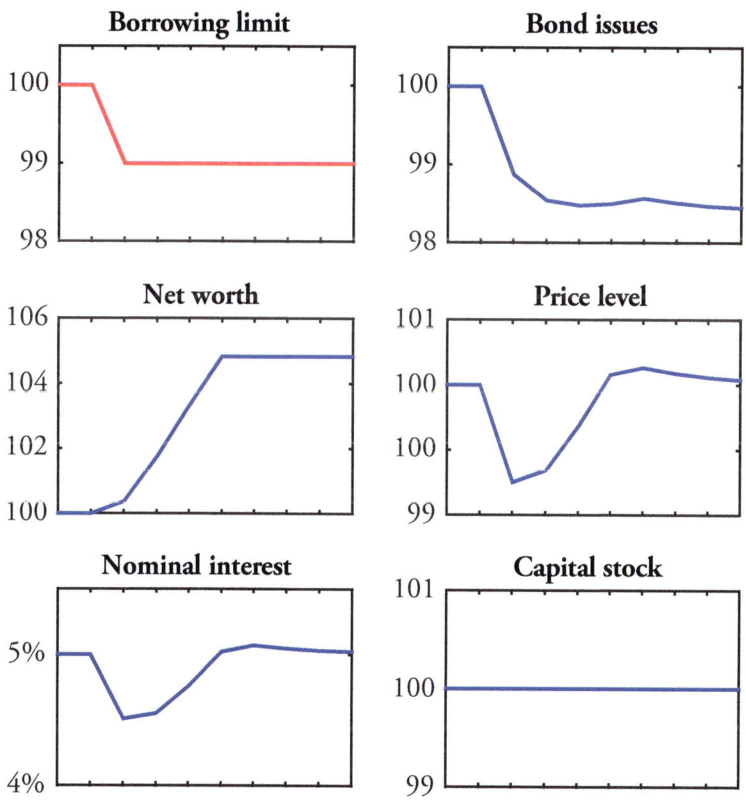

Figure 5.3: Deleveraging in a liquidity trap. *Notes*: Horizontal axes represent time. Nominal interest is measured in percent. The initial values of the other variables are normalized at 100.

Deleveraging is sometimes seen as a painful disease that depresses aggregate demand. According to this argument, debt repayments force individuals to spend less. Judged from the perspective of a consistent general equilibrium model where everyone's expenditure is another one's receipt, such a view appears misleading. To illustrate this key point, assume that prices are not fully flexible but sticky. Compared with the preceding simulation, credit tightening would have a smaller impact on prices but would also diminish output, initiating a recession. During deleveraging, output and prices recover simultaneously. This implies that the pain is exclusively due to the credit contraction, whereas deleveraging represents the relieving cure.

Recognizing the recessionary effects of credit tightening in a sticky price model raises the question of whether monetary policy could alleviate the adjustment. The answer has already been given in Chapter 4 but deserves to be noted again. Recessions resulting from a fall in the borrowing limit make monetary policy ineffective as long as the limit binds. If the central bank responded to a decrease in the borrowing limit through timely open market purchases, this would have no effect on output and prices before deleveraging is complete. Output and prices would rise only after the recession is over, that is, when a monetary stimulus is no longer needed.

Endogenous Borrowing Limits

While the foregoing text kept borrowing limits exogenous and made no attempt to deduce them from deeper principles, a large strand of macro models, including those proposed by Kiyotaki and Moore (1997), Aiyagari and Gertler (1999), Kocherlakota (2000), and Mendoza (2010), derives endogenous borrowing limits from collateral requirements.

The basic idea of this approach is that in modern societies—which have abandoned debtors' prisons and other cruel forms of punishment—promises to repay debt are unreliable. In the resulting incomplete contract setting, creditors ask for collateral, which can take various forms: Mortgage loans involve an explicit pledge of real property. Commercial loan contracts provide security assignments of inventory, reservations of property rights, or repos. Small consumer loans such as overdrafts are implicitly collateralized by the part of disposable income that is not exempt from execution. As a result, borrowers' capacity to obtain credit is limited by the value of collateral. The latter is determined in general equilibrium, and any plunge in collateral values tightens the borrowing constraint.

Net worth opens up the possibility to endogenize borrowing limits naturally. In the RE models cited, creditors compute future values of collateral and use these to set borrowing limits. In reality, creditors impose certain loan-to-value ratios. Of course, one could also assume they imposed minimum equity ratios or maximum debt-to-equity ratios; these representations are all equivalent. The following approach defines the borrowing limit as a given multiple of initial net worth:

$$\text{(76)} \qquad \frac{\overline{B}_t}{E_{t-1}+\overline{B}_t} = ltv \quad \Leftrightarrow \quad \overline{B}_t = \frac{ltv}{1-ltv}E_{t-1}\,.$$

Producers enter period t with initial net worth E_{t-1}, the difference of assets and liabilities. Bond holders, or creditors, can observe this magnitude and are ready to tolerate loan-to-value ratios up to ltv in order to keep a safety margin. Subject to initial net worth and feasible bond issues, producers can finance any capital stock satisfying $P_t K_t^d \leq E_{t-1} + \overline{B}_t = E_t / (1 - ltv)$. This borrowing constraint binds if optimal investment exceeds the available means; otherwise, producers select the profit maximizing capital stock. With capital demand determined in such a way, the equilibrium is computed subsequently. Terminal net worth, E_t, results from this process. Because this variable is not known for bond holders at the beginning of the period, when they make their credit commitment, creditors request the upfront payment E_{t-1} and restrict credit.

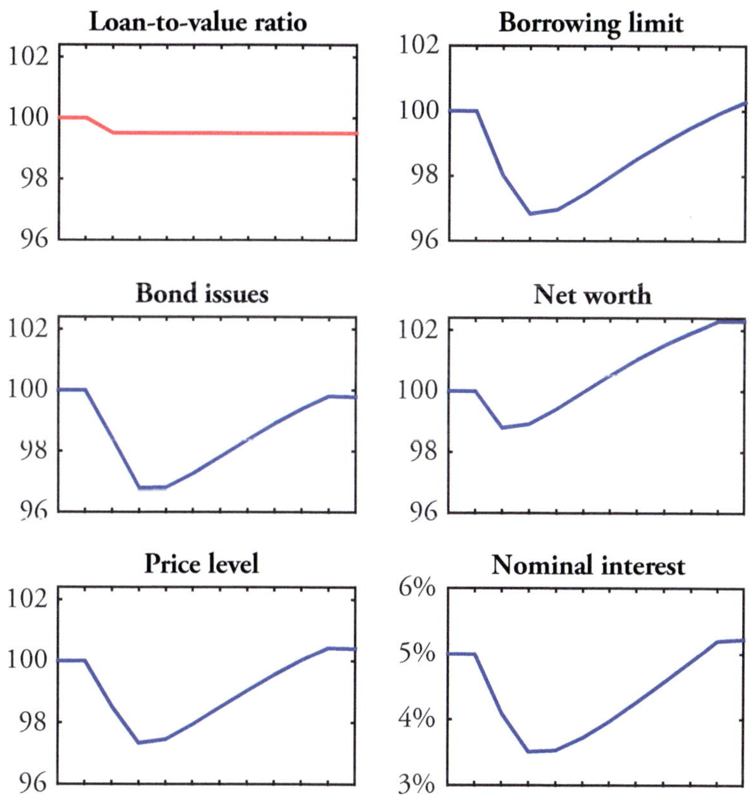

Figure 5.4: Credit tightening. *Notes*: Horizontal axes represent time. Nominal interest is measured in percent. The initial values of the other variables are normalized at 100.

Figure 5.4 presupposes again that producers distribute profits in the absence of a binding borrowing constraint. When the constraint binds, however, they retain profits partly because the return on equity exceeds the nominal interest rate. The simulation also assumes non-negative dividends, as motivated in section 5.2. The impulse is not a decrease in the absolute borrowing limit but a fall in the loan-to-value ratio, which has complex consequences.

While the qualitative reaction of the variables should be clear from the preceding paragraphs, an eye-catching feature of Figure 5.4 is the sharp decline in credit. Following a minimal decrease in the loan-to-value ratio of just 0.5 percent, borrowing falls by 3.2 percent. The reason is that prices drop so sharply that producers incur a loss. This loss, in turn, diminishes net worth and triggers a second round of credit tightening. Borrowing falls by 1.6 percent in the first round and by another 1.6 percent in the second round, as indicated in the middle left panel.

Thus, endogenous borrowing limits *amplify* and *propagate* an initial shock. Conversely, the accumulation of net worth promotes investment possibilities twice. As in the preceding section, more equity means more funds available for investment. But more equity also improves borrowing possibilities, such that every additional dollar of net worth increases feasible investment. Assuming a loan-to-value ratio of 75 percent, for instance, every $1 of net worth allows financing an amount of $4.

Figure 5.4 also helps to understand *asymmetry* as a key business cycle feature that has not yet been mentioned. Asymmetry means that cycles are often characterized by sharp downturns followed by slow recoveries. This characteristic pattern shows up if net worth is abruptly reduced by credit tightening and gradually rebuilt during the following periods through retained profit.

The general takeaway from this simulation is that sporadic inflations and deflations can result from revised credit conditions, while money demand and the money stock stay perfectly constant. The two features of the underlying process—amplification, propagation, and asymmetry—result from the interaction of two premises: endogenous borrowing constraints and non-negative disbursements. Importantly, the former assumption alone does not suffice to produce the results, since net worth could be preserved by negative disbursements.

5.5 Fisherian Debt-deflations

How do the previous results relate to Irving Fisher's (1933) celebrated debt-deflation theory of depressions? Fisher's approach is often summarized by the statement that deflation increases real debt and induces borrowers to spend less. This is a simplistic account that holds only with respect to unexpected deflations and assumes implicitly that the spending propensities of lenders and borrowers differ.

In fact, Fisher's theory was more sophisticated. He saw new investment opportunities as the ultimate starter of a debt-deflation. Such opportunities seduce corporations and lenders into increasing leverage. With conservative debt at the outset, higher loan-to-value ratios make corporations more vulnerable. Then, an adverse shock—for example, a sudden fall in the money stock—will produce a recession. This is clear from Figure 5.4 if one adds some price and wage rigidities to obtain declines in real output after reductions in debt or the money stock. With additional frictions outside the above model's scope, like specific capital goods (that are of no use to others) or damages of going concern (such as customer relationships), insolvencies would diminish aggregate net worth even more sharply. Therefore, Fisher advocated price level stabilization as a remedy, a policy goal not generally accepted in his time.

To generalize, non-negativity constraints on net worth and disbursements introduce crucial non-linearities: Even with identical constant returns to scale production functions, producers' aggregate behavior is not only affected by aggregate variables but also by their *distribution*. For instance, if all corporations were equally indebted, only an implausibly strong deflation that wiped out total net worth would entail insolvencies. By contrast, if loan-to-value ratios were uniformly distributed between zero and one, then even the mildest unexpected deflation would cause some corporations to go bust.

Chapter 6

Real Estate

For a long time, real estate—property consisting of land and buildings—largely disappeared from the macroeconomic script. Up to the middle of the nineteenth century, no economic writer failed to highlight the triad of land, labor, and capital. These inputs were presented not in alphabetical but in hierarchical order: Land is productive even in the absence of human action, labor *is* human action, and capital results from human action. While Ricardo saw landlords as the principal profiteers of economic development, Marx was the first who dropped land from the model and focused on class struggles between labor and capital. After World War II, land was considered an annoying impediment to constructing growth models—an input in fixed supply contradicted prevailing growth optimism. As a result, most contemporary books and research papers mention land only in passing or ignore it altogether.

The purpose of this chapter is to reintroduce land into the standard macro framework. Land is considered as a core feature whose neglect cannot be justified as an approximation. This is because its presence changes the model's long-run and short-run conduct qualitatively. As shown in the theoretical sections below, a fixed input tends to stabilize the economy in the long run but is apt to destabilize it in the short run. The chapter starts with an empirical overview that accentuates the quantitative significance of real estate and shows the way in which it is integrated and measured in the national accounts.

6.1 Empirical Overview

The system of national accounts, SNA (2008), embodies a distinction between financial and nonfinancial wealth. In a closed economy, or in the world as a whole, net financial wealth is zero since financial assets and liabilities are valued correspondingly. Therefore, the entire 'wealth of nations' consists of nonfinancial assets, which are subdivided into produced and nonproduced assets. *Produced* assets are mainly composed of tangible fixed assets, summarized by the symbol K. *Nonproduced* assets consist mainly of land that is measured in square meters and whose quantity is represented by the symbol $\bar{L}$. The bar indicates that land is non-augmentable and non-depletable. Q denotes the money price per square meter, and $q = Q/P$ is the real land price, measured in commodity units per square meter. With this notation, an economy's nonfinancial wealth in period t equals

$$K_t + q_t \bar{L}. \tag{77}$$

According to the SNA standard, land consists solely of the ground. Its value excludes any buildings or other structures situated on it; all land improvements and structures are fixed assets. Developed land is mainly used for agriculture, traffic, and residential or nonresidential construction. In each case, the owner combines a plot of raw land with produced assets such as seed, asphalt, concrete, or bricks to obtain a useful composite known as *real estate*. Similarly, a home buyer acquires a bundle consisting of a produced building and a nonproduced plot of land. Land prices are empirically inferred from the actual sales of vacant plots. If such sales are rare, as in densely populated regions, implicit land values can be obtained by subtracting the construction costs of comparable buildings, corrected for depreciation, from the observed total price of the property; see Davis and Heathcote (2007). Alternatively, if an old building is to be demolished after sale, the implicit land value equals the selling price of the property plus the cost of demolition.

To facilitate international comparisons, the components of nonfinancial wealth are usually represented as multiples of GDP. Specifically, K/Y is the capital–output ratio, qL/Y denotes the *land–output ratio*, and $(qL+K)/Y$ represents the *wealth–output ratio*. The following outline starts with countries that provide balance sheets of nonfinancial assets in accordance with SNA. Unfortunately, countries such as Germany, the United Kingdom, and the United States do not publish such figures.

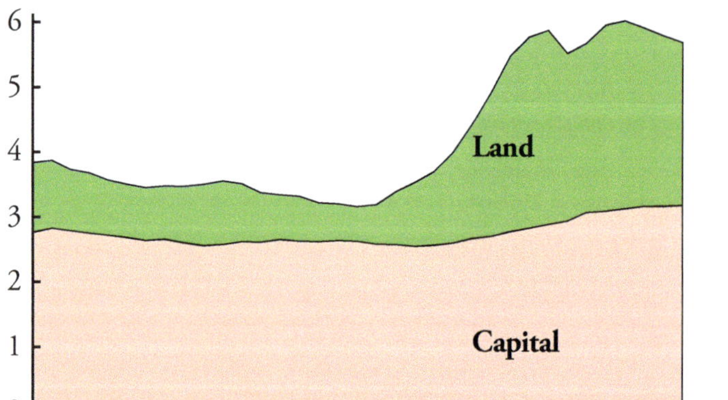

Figure 6.1: French nonfinancial wealth components as multiples of GDP. *Notes*: Annual data, retrieved April 2016 from <http//:stats.oecd.org>, Table 9B (balance sheets for nonfinancial assets), series N111 (tangible fixed assets), N211 (land) and B1_GE (gross domestic product).

Figure 6.1 relates to France, the country with the longest tradition of producing national balance sheets of nonfinancial assets. Since 1980, its capital–output ratio has remained close to 3, with little short-term volatility. The latter feature is typical of many countries: While investment fluctuates, its integral, the capital stock, moves steadily. Capital stock reductions are bounded below by the rate of depreciation, and increases are bounded above by capacity restrictions.

It is very informative to decompose France's nonfinancial wealth into its main components. The total amount of 12.2 trillion euros in 2014 included the following items: Land 44 percent; dwellings 34 percent; buildings other than dwellings 17 percent; machinery, equipment, weapon systems, and cultivated biological resources 5 percent. Thus, real estate made up 95 percent of nonfinancial wealth, while machines and equipment alone came to about 3 percent. This does not mean that capital in the conventional sense is unimportant in modern times. No technology firm and no service provider can do without some capital inputs. However, from a macroeconomic perspective, the bulk of nonfinancial wealth consists of real estate.

While Figure 6.1 documents a steady capital–output ratio, the land–output ratio fell from 1 in 1980 to 0.5 in 1997 and then surged to 3 in 2011, with a slight decrease thereafter. Compared with the capital–output ratio, the land–output ratio is much more volatile. This is possible because changes in qL/Y are driven by changes in the real land price, q, while the real price of capital goods essentially equals 1. Figure 6.1 also shows that, concurrently with the announcement and implementation of the euro, France's wealth–output ratio almost doubled from 3.2 in 1998 to a peak of 6.0 in 2011. This rally has led some to believe that "capital is back"; see Piketty and Zucman (2014). Figure 6.1 suggests the different view that "land is back", at least for a while. The last reservation should be kept in mind because what appears to be a permanently high plateau may well turn into a subsequent bust.

Japan illustrates this well. Between 1970 and 1991, its land–output ratio surged from 2 to almost 6; see Noguchi (1991: 15) and Stone and Ziemba (1993: 149). At the peak, Japan's total land value exceeded 20 percent of the entire world's wealth, and the land under the Emperor's Palace in Tokyo was estimated to be as valuable as all land in California or Canada. Following the 1991 crash, the land–output ratio fell for decades; by 2013, it had almost returned to its 1970 level. The plunge of the land–output ratio from 6 to 2 means that nonfinancial wealth of the amount of four annual outputs vaporized. It is true that some booms, including the Dutch tulip mania of 1637, were followed by even more pronounced busts in relative terms. Regarding the absolute decrease in nonfinancial wealth, however, Japan's land price cycle has no parallel.

Figure 6.2 shows capital–output ratios and land–output ratios for a group of countries that provide SNA data. Capital values regularly exceed land values, but Korea represents a counterexample. The United States has not been included because it does not provide comparable data. However, various measures of land values are available for the United States. Larson (2015) estimates a total land value of \$23 trillion in 2009. Relating this to the corresponding GDP of \$14.4 trillion yields a land–output ratio of 1.6. The same source shows that the land–output ratio came close to 2 in 2006, just before the house price crash. United States time series data are discussed in section 6.5 below. All of the preceding figures suggest that capital and land values are of the same order of magnitude. As a very rough estimate, models without land miss about one half of an economy's nonfinancial wealth.

Because dwellings and land make up the bulk of nonfinancial wealth, it is not surprising that housing markets have stimulated a lot of active research in recent years. Davis and Heathcote (2007) investigate United States house prices and estimate that land accounts for 36 percent of the existing housing stock. Of course, this share will normally be lower at the time of acquisition of a new house. However, it will gradually rise to 100 percent when the building deteriorates over time while the land remains intact. In a broad international study, Knoll et al. (2014: 50) find somewhat higher shares of land in home values, with 50 percent as a benchmark and considerable variation between countries. They also note a hockey-stick pattern of house price developments: In real terms, house prices remained roughly constant between 1870 and 1950, and then surged by 80 percent during the following decades.

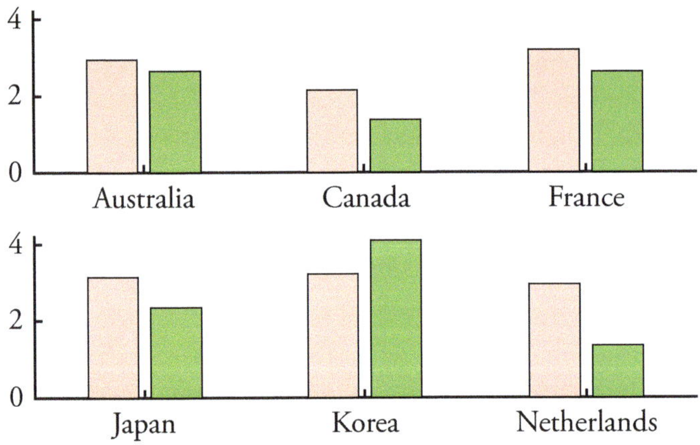

Figure 6.2: Capital (left bars) and land (right bars) as multiples of GDP, 2013. *Notes*: Annual data, retrieved April 2016 from <http//:stats.oecd.org>, Table 9B (balance sheets for nonfinancial assets), series N111 (tangible fixed assets), N211 (land), and B1_GE (gross domestic product).

Davis and Heathcote (2007), Jordà et al. (2014), and Knoll et al. (2014) also emphasize that the rise in real house prices is primarily due to real land price increases, while the real prices of buildings have no notable trend. This is consistent with the conduct of the broader measures considered above, which included not only residential but also agricultural and commercial land.

6.2 Modeling Real Estate

Land can be modeled as a consumption commodity, as in Richter (1993), or as a factor of production, as in Homburg (1991). The second method is preferred here because it parallels national accounting conventions and strengthens the model's empirical orientation. As indicated, national accounts treat real estate as a bundle of produced capital and nonproduced land. The construction of a new home, for instance, counts as a productive activity that yields a long-term output stream after completion. This holds irrespective of whether the construction is undertaken by a private household or a commercial firm. Hence, the functional distinction between consumers and producers used here is not identical with the more familiar sectoral distinction between households and firms. Construction of new homes always counts as investment, and a household that establishes a new home is treated as a producer in the theoretical model.

The service stream of real estate is remunerated either by explicit rents, as with tenants' flats, or by imputed rents, as with owner-occupied housing or nonresidential property used by the owner firm. In a one-sector model, rents are not treated separately but are a part of total output. However, since the model lacked land as an explicit factor of production, this will now be added:

$$Y^s_{t+1} = F(N^d_{t+1}, K^d_t, L^d_t). \tag{78}$$

The new production function is assumed to be linear homogeneous, smooth, strictly increasing, strictly quasi-concave, and Inada. Producers maximize expected profit, whose definition reads

$$\begin{aligned} \Pi^e_{t+1} = {} & P^e_{t+1}Y^s_{t+1} + (P^e_{t+1} - P_t)K^d_t - \delta P^e_{t+1}K^d_t + (Q^e_{t+1} - Q_t)L^d_t \\ & - W^e_{t+1}N^d_{t+1} - i_t B^s_t . \end{aligned} \tag{79}$$

As in the baseline model, profit includes revenue from sales plus revaluation of the capital stock minus current cost depreciation, wages, and interest. The only additional term, $(Q^e_{t+1} - Q_t)L^d_t$, represents revaluation of land: Producers acquire land in period t at price Q_t and sell it one period later at the expected price Q^e_{t+1}. Dividing the land prices, Q, by the respective price levels, P, the ratios q^e_{t+1} and q_t represent the real land prices, and

$$\hat{q}^e_{t+1} = \frac{q^e_{t+1} - q_t}{q_t} \tag{80}$$

is referred to as *expected appreciation*. Expected appreciation vanishes in a stationary state or, more generally, if producers believe that nominal land prices will experience the same relative change as commodity prices; otherwise, expected appreciation becomes positive or negative. With producers financing all investment by debt issues, their balance sheets read

$$P_t K^d_t + Q_t L^d_t = B^s_t . \tag{81}$$

Introducing real estate into the basic framework does not require any further modification. Specifically, central bank behavior is still as described in section 2.3, consumer behavior is still as described in section 2.5, producer behavior obeys the new equations (78) to (81), and the model is closed by the following equilibrium conditions:

$$\left.\begin{aligned} C_t + I_t &= Y_t^s \\ B_t^d + B_t^{cb} &= B_t^s \\ N_t^d &= \bar{N} \\ L_t^d &= \bar{L} \end{aligned}\right\} \Rightarrow (P_t, i_t, W_t, Q_t). \tag{82}$$

This system of equations determines the three accustomed endogenous variables and the equilibrium land price, Q_t. Solutions depend on expected appreciation, of course. This will be specified below. In a competitive equilibrium, the marginal productivity of labor equals the real wage rate. Moreover, the marginal productivity of capital equals the user cost:

$$\frac{\partial F}{\partial K_t^d} = r_{t+1}^e + \delta. \tag{83}$$

And as shown in appendix I, differentiating profit with respect to land yields the following new first-order condition:

$$\frac{\partial F}{\partial L_t^d} = q_t (r_{t+1}^e - \hat{q}_{t+1}^e). \tag{84}$$

This states that the marginal productivity of land equals the *user cost of land*, the term on the right-hand side. The two preceding formulas, (83) and (84), include expected real interest because acquisitions of capital and land are financed by interest-bearing bonds. They differ in three respects. First, the rate of depreciation, δ, appears only in the user cost of capital as capital deteriorates over time while land is non-depletable. Second, expected appreciation, $\hat{q}_{t+1}^e$, is subtracted from real interest in the second formula; expected increases in real land prices make land acquisitions more attractive. Third, the real land price enters the user cost of land since it influences the amount necessary to acquire a certain plot of land. The same holds true for capital, of course, but capital's real price equals one in this framework.

The simulations employ a conventional Cobb-Douglas production function,

$$F(N_{t+1}, K_t, L_t) = \theta_{t+1} N_{t+1}^{1-\alpha-\rho} K_t^{\alpha} L_t^{\rho}, \tag{85}$$

with parameters $\alpha = 2/9$ and $\rho = 1/9$. These choices leave the labor income share at 2/3 and split the residual between capital and land in such a way that the equilibrium values of the corresponding stocks are of equal size at an expected real interest rate of 5 percent. To produce this rate, the time preference parameter, β, is lifted to 5. The rest of the specification outlined in section 2.7 remains unchanged. As a side remark, there are two obstacles to directly measuring the *land income share* $\partial F/\partial L \times L/Y$, which equals ρ under a Cobb-Douglas production function. First, landlords lease composites of land

and buildings. Second, land rents must be imputed for owner-occupiers and are hidden in profit for commercial owners. Appendix I shows that optimal land and capital stocks are characterized by the following equation:

$$\frac{q_t L_t^d}{K_t^d} = \frac{\rho}{\alpha} \frac{r_{t+1}^e + \delta}{r_{t+1}^e - \hat{q}_{t+1}^e}. \tag{86}$$

The left-hand side displays the equilibrium ratio of the values of the two stocks of nonfinancial assets, land and capital. This ratio is obviously proportional to the two income shares, ρ and α. Dividing by the relative land price shows that the physical ratio L/K is also inversely proportional to the respective user cost given by (84) and (83). Relative to capital demand, land demand increases in land productivity, ρ, and decreases in its user cost.

6.3 Dynamic Inefficiency

Infinite horizon economies are vulnerable to a specific inefficiency problem whenever individuals plan over finite horizons. Diamond (1965) was the first to demonstrate this so-called dynamic inefficiency in a model with real capital but without land. In the context of an overlapping generations model, he showed that governments, by use of debt, can achieve a Pareto improvement if the growth rate exceeds the real interest rate in the steady state.

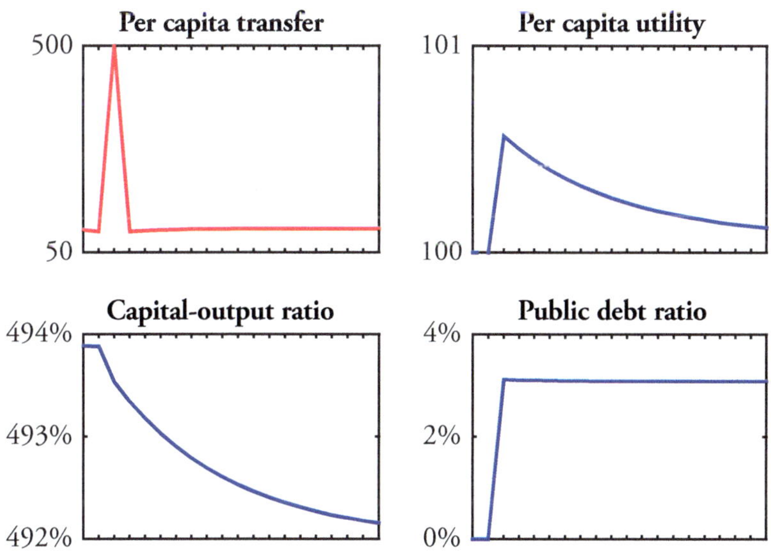

Figure 6.3: Dynamic inefficiency. *Notes*: Horizontal axes represent time. The two ratios are measured in percent. The initial values of the per capita variables are normalized at 100.

This has a simple intuition: Debt financed transfers increase individual consumption and diminish the capital stock. Marginal capital stock reductions entail an income loss of r since the real interest rate measures the net marginal productivity of capital. With n denoting the growth rate, a constant capital–output ratio requires net investment of the amount nK; capital and output must grow at the same rate. Hence, reducing the capital stock allows diminishing investment by n at the margin. Under the condition $r<n$, the output loss obviously falls short of the spared investment so that consumption can be increased forever, making all generations better off.

The economies studied so far are also susceptible to dynamic inefficiency since they evolve from the present to eternity. As an illustration, Figure 6.3 employs the fiscal model from section 3.3, modified twice: Population grows at a constant rate of $n=3$ percent, and the time preference parameter, β, is fixed at 8. The ensuing steady state involves an equilibrium real interest rate of $r=1.95$ percent. This path is inefficient since $r<n$. In the second period, therefore, the government disburses a transfer to consumers, financed by debt, but keeps the public debt ratio constant beforehand and thereafter. Public debt crowds out real capital in the usual manner. As indicated in Figure 6.3, this increases utility and leads to a new steady state with a lower capital–output ratio. Imagining a generational structure at the micro level, the policy measure represents a Pareto improvement.

Following this brief summary, it will now be shown that land precludes dynamic inefficiency. The basic idea goes back to Jacques Turgot (1766) and his ingenious insight that land keeps real interest strictly positive in a stationary state. In a stationary state, (86) assumes the following simple form:

(87) $$\frac{q\bar{L}}{K}=\frac{\rho}{\alpha}\times\frac{r+\delta}{r}.$$

With given parameters ρ, α, and δ, the real interest rate must be strictly positive in a stationary state, since otherwise, the left-hand ratio would become infinite. This outcome is of fundamental importance because it holds irrespective of consumers' preferences and denies the possibility of a "savings glut" that induces overaccumulation of real capital. Increasing the consumers' time preference parameter, β, will not drive the marginal productivity of capital net of depreciation into negative territory but results in ever increasing aggregate land values.

There are two alternative ways to understand this intuitively. First, investors calculate land values using the formula of a perpetual annuity, with the expected real interest rate in the denominator. If this rate vanished, land would become infinitely valuable, which cannot constitute an equilibrium as land buyers have finite means. The second explanation is an arbitrage argument. In a stationary state with real estate, investors can choose between depletable capital and non-depletable land. Selecting capital yields $\partial F/\partial K-\delta$ as the net return, and selecting land yields $1/q\times\partial F/\partial L$. Arbitrage requires

(88) $$\frac{\partial F}{\partial K}-\delta=\frac{1}{q}\frac{\partial F}{\partial L}.$$

In the presence of a non-depletable store of value, no investor needs to accept a negative net return on capital. Thus, land crowds out inefficient capital and renders overaccumulation impossible.

Extending the previous observations to a growing economy, it is clear that land becomes increasingly scarce. Recalling that the Cobb-Douglas production function implies a fixed land income share, the rent income and the relative land price, q, must grow at the common rate n in a steady state. With investors aware of this long-term trend, expected appreciation equals the growth rate. Substituting $\hat{q}^e = n$ into formula (86) yields

$$\frac{q\overline{L}}{K} = \frac{\rho}{\alpha} \times \frac{r+\delta}{r-n}. \tag{89}$$

This expression implies that the real interest rate exceeds the growth rate in a steady state, $r > n$; otherwise, land values would diverge. Land ensures dynamic efficiency and precludes scenarios such as those outlined above. In fact, the landless economy depicted in Figure 6.3 had a growth rate of 3 percent and a real interest rate of only 1.95, resulting from the choice of a high time preference parameter, β. In the presence of real estate, the same parameter gives rise to an equilibrium real interest rate of 5.1 percent in the steady state, well above the growth rate. The key message, however, is not that dynamic efficiency obtains for this special parameter but that it obtains for *any* parameter one may choose.

The point that non-depletable assets rule out overaccumulation is not valid only for stationary or steady states but can be considerably generalized. In a nutshell, if n_t denotes the growth rate and r_t the corresponding interest rate, a sufficient condition for dynamic efficiency reads

$$\frac{(1+n_1)(1+n_2)\dots(1+n_\infty)}{(1+r_1)(1+r_2)\dots(1+r_\infty)} = 0. \tag{90}$$

With constant interest and growth rates, this is equivalent to $r > n$, the efficiency condition for steady states. Along more general paths, (90) is fulfilled if interest exceeds growth on average. Notably, dynamic efficiency does not require that interest exceed growth in each period. As the formula indicates, it is actually immaterial what happens over any finite horizon; only the economy's limit behavior counts. If real interest rates fall short of growth rates for a while, this does not per se indicate dynamic inefficiency. The bottom line is that the general efficiency condition (90) holds in a model with land if the land's income share is bounded away from zero; see Homburg (2014).

To summarize, real estate changes the model's long-run properties in an attractive fashion. It precludes overaccumulation and easily absorbs any potential "savings glut". As documented, land values can soak up several annual incomes within a few years, by simple increases in land prices. Because land–output ratios were larger in the nineteenth century than they are today, there is still much scope for this adjustment mechanism. At the same time, Japan's example warns that rising land prices do not necessarily reflect lasting preferences for future consumption but can stem from speculation, credit easing, or international capital movements. Some of these treacherous incidents will be considered in section 6.5.

6.4 Quasi-Ricardian Equivalence

Section 3.3.2 reviewed fiscal policies in Ricardian and non-Ricardian economies. It demonstrated that tax reductions left the allocation unchanged if consumers perceived public debt as a future tax liability. This neutrality proposition was referred to as Ricardian equivalence. Myopic consumers regard public debt as net wealth. Under this premise, which underlies the present text and the national accounts, debt financed tax reductions induce consumers to spend more and enable the presently living to shift tax burdens into the future, where they hurt subsequent generations. The aim of this section, which merges the fiscal model of section 3.3 with the land model, is to demonstrate that an asset like land partly recovers Ricardian equivalence even if consumers make short-sighted plans and have no clue about future tax liabilities.

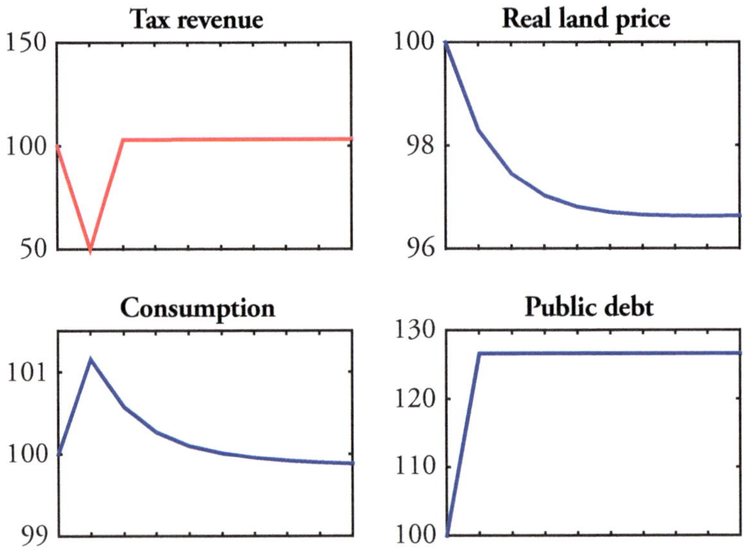

Figure 6.4: Quasi-Ricardian equivalence. *Notes*: Horizontal axes represent time. The initial values of all variables are normalized at 100.

Figure 6.4 illustrates a fiscal policy that preserves budget balance at the outset. In period 2, taxes are temporarily halved, but budget balance is re-established thereafter. The one-shot increase in public debt depresses real land prices and wipes out 3 percent of the value of real estate. The reason is that the private sector can invest in real capital, land, and public debt. If the government supplies more debt and consumers do not adjust consumption correspondingly, the economy's overall resource constraint necessitates a decrease in capital and land investments. While reductions in capital are only noticed later, through declines in output, reductions in land values diminish consumers' total wealth instantaneously. In the simulation, the fall in land values absorbs almost one half of the increase in public debt.

It has long been known that taxes are capitalized into land values even in the absence of immortal individuals; see Oates (1969). The same holds for public debt, which affects land in a similar fashion as taxes, although through a different channel: Rather than diminishing disposable income, public debt competes with investment and mortgage financing. From an empirical investigation of Swiss municipal debt, Stadelmann and Eichenberger (2009: 18) infer that local debt reduces local property values by a factor of about one half.

Two notable conclusions emerge. First, quasi-Ricardian equivalence questions the common view that present generations can easily exploit their successors by shifting tax burdens into the future. By attempting to do so, the presently living deprave their own property and reduce the money amount they can obtain from selling it when they are old. Second, the analysis casts doubt on the allegation that government bond issuance provides the private sector with safe assets, which is considered as a beneficial act in times of crisis. This argument overlooks the general equilibrium effects of public debt: To the extent that additional government bonds diminish land values, they contribute to making mortgage loans sour. New bonds effectively force the claimants of existing mortgages into a more junior position, which can have dire consequences for banks and buyers of mortgage-backed securities. In this respect, public debt exacerbates the problems it is assumed to resolve.

Before concluding this section, a further important relationship between land on the one hand and Ricardian equivalence on the other should be mentioned. Authors who use RE models with infinitely lived agents often dispute the view that housing and land prices affect consumer behavior. For instance, Sinai and Souleles (2005: 774) stress that "increases in house prices reflect a commensurate increase in the present value of expected future rents" so that "for homeowners with infinite horizons, this increase in implicit liabilities would exactly offset the increase in the house value, leaving their effective expected net worth unchanged." Put simply, expected increases in rents leave consumers' opportunity sets unchanged because the increase in wealth is fully exhausted by the present value of future rent payments.

This objection is formally correct. In denying that public debt and land are perceived as net wealth, Ricardian models contradict national accounting conventions that classify government bonds and land as private assets. These conventions, however, receive support from the observation that actual individuals have finite life spans. Rising land and housing prices make homeowners feel richer and induce them to spend more; it is immaterial for them whether or not their followers suffer from higher rents. Older homeowners are particularly happy to sell their property during a real estate boom since this makes more consumption affordable for them. Empirical studies have consistently found a significant positive correlation between house prices and consumption expenditure; see Case (2000), Case et al. (2013), Campbell and Cocco (2007), or Attanasio et al. (2011). The latter two studies also confirm that wealth effects are more pronounced for older households. As household debt generally decreases with age, these findings cast doubt on the view that house prices affect consumption exclusively through relaxations of liquidity constraints, as in Iacoviello (2005) and Liu et al. (2013). The evidence also constitutes a strong point against models with infinitely lived consumers.

6.5 Housing Manias

In a number of countries, the Great Recession of 2008–09 was foreshadowed by unprecedented increases in real estate prices. This is clearly true for the United States, Ireland, and Spain, but also for the United Kingdom and the Netherlands. The concurrence of rising land prices and prosperity, followed by land price busts and recessions, has led many researchers to investigate possible links.

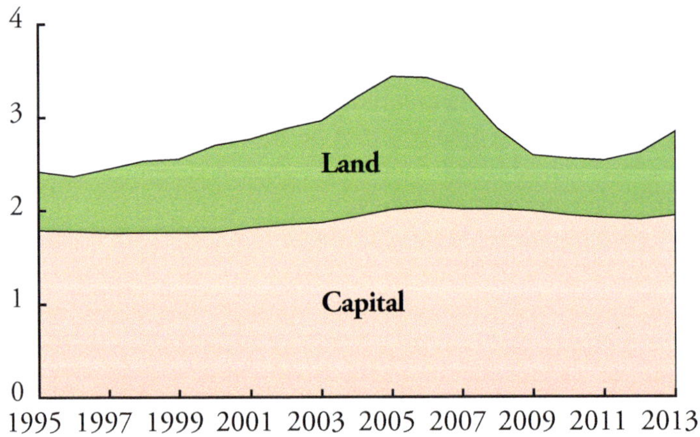

Figure 6.5: United States nonfinancial wealth components as multiples of GDP. *Source*: Homburg (2014).

Providing further empirical background, Figure 6.5 illustrates the United States' land price cycle. The numbers are not directly comparable with those of the countries referred to above because they do not comply with SNA conventions. This does not matter much, however, as long as one is interested in variations over time rather than in cross-country comparisons. Between 1995 and 2013, the capital–output ratio was roughly stable in the United States, paralleling the pattern known from other countries, whereas the land–output ratio surged from 0.6 in 1996 to 1.4 in 2006 and then fell back to 0.6 in 2009. In absolute terms, land values came to \$5 trillion in 1996, \$19 trillion in 2006, and \$9 trillion in 2009. These figures imply a plunge in nonfinancial wealth of $10 trillion within only three years. The data underlying Figure 6.5 are rather comprehensive. They include residential and nonresidential real estate owned by households and nonprofit organizations as well as by corporate and noncorporate nonfinancial businesses. At the same time, they exclude real estate owned by financial firms, which is small, and real estate owned by the government, which is more difficult to assess.

To relate the preceding figures to the vast housing literature, Figure 6.6 documents the house price index supplied by the Federal Housing Finance Agency. As already mentioned, the variation over time of house prices closely parallels that of real estate and land prices. Figure 6.6 also shows a pronounced positive correlation between real house prices and real investment. This raises the question of whether the present model allows reproducing such a pattern.

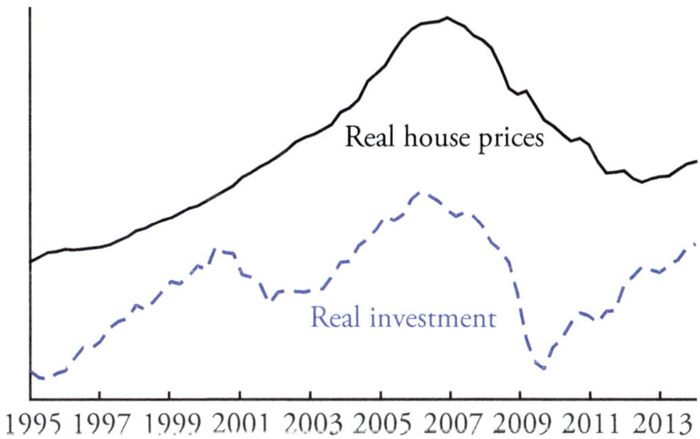

Figure 6.6: United States house prices and investment. *Notes*: Quarterly data, retrieved June 2016 from <https://fred.stlouisfed.org>, series GDPI (gross domestic private investment) and USSTHPI (Federal Housing Finance Agency house price index), both divided by the GDP deflator, GDPDEF.

To analyze the links between real estate and economic fluctuations, the land model introduced here must be closed with an expectation hypothesis. As with inflation, the present text assumes that individuals correct their prior of land price appreciation by what they observe:

$$\hat{q}^e_{t+1} = \hat{q}^e_t + \lambda_q(\hat{q}_t - \hat{q}^e_t) + u_t \,. \tag{91}$$

Expected appreciation on the left-hand side is determined by the prior $\hat{q}^e_t$, the deviation of actual appreciation from this prior, and an exogenous term, u_t, which represents an expectation shock. If one experiments with the model, it becomes clear that the inclusion of land has a highly destabilizing effect. Hence, a moderate value of 0.04 is selected for the learning parameter, λ_q.

Equipped with this framework, it is easy to analyze a *housing mania*, understood as an expectation shock $u_t > 0$ that is supposed to elevate house and land prices and to initiate a self-reinforcing process. Figure 6.7 proceeds from a stationary state and assumes that individuals, for whatever reason, come to expect real land prices to increase by 0.1 percent. This causes actual land prices to rise by 3 percent, which amplifies the impulse by a factor of thirty. Why is this effect so strong? First, since the actual land price feeds back into expected appreciation through (91), it has a minor effect on the user cost of land $q_t(r^e_{t+1} - \hat{q}^e_{t+1})$; a higher land price makes land less affordable but also more profitable. Second, the only further variable in the user cost formula is the expected real interest rate, which has multiple jobs to perform because it also affects the optimal capital stock and the bond market. As shown in the lower left panel, expected real interest rises but only by a small amount.

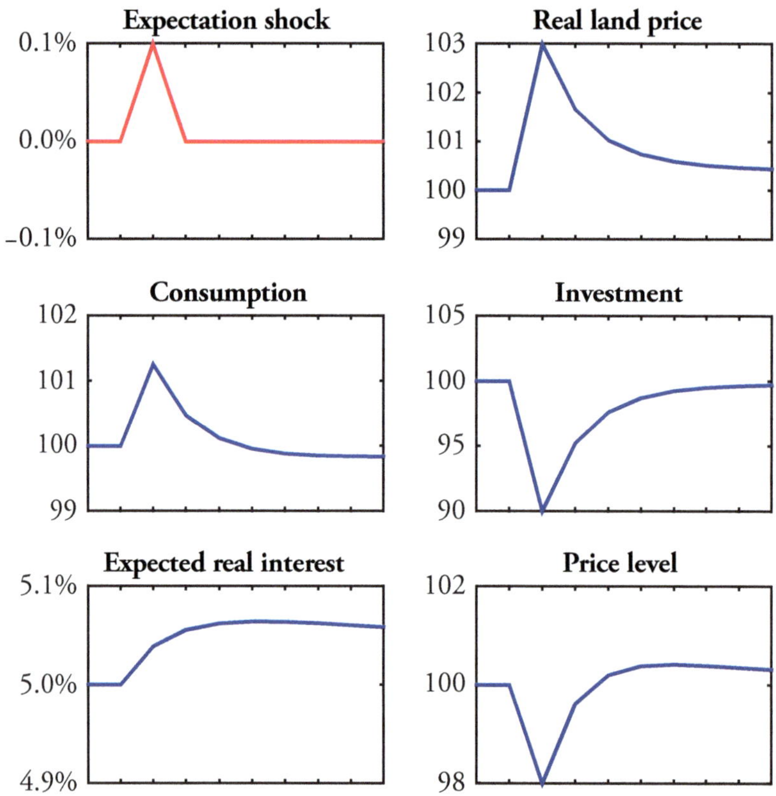

Figure 6.7: Housing mania. *Notes*: Horizontal axes represent time. The shock and expected real interest are measured in percent. The initial values of the other variables are normalized at 100.

The reaction of consumption to the expectation shock lends support to the housing mania narrative: Consumption immediately rises because consumers feel richer. For the same reason, money demand increases, depressing the equilibrium price level. As an intermediate result, shocks to land price expectations have real effects even in a model with perfectly flexible prices. This distinguishes them from erratic inflation expectations, as considered in subsection 3.1.3, that only entail commensurate changes in nominal interest rates and do not affect the allocation.

Regarding investment demand, the simulation brings to light a robust further result. As shown in the middle right panel, investment plunges sharply. With output given by the initial capital and land stocks as well as the natural level of employment, the increase in consumption necessitates a corresponding decrease in investment, as also noted by Deaton and Laroque (2001). In this respect, housing mania stories suffer from the same problem as the stock mania stories discussed in section 5.3. Irrespective of the assumed degree of price flexibility, both narratives suggest that optimistic expectations alone can trigger economic upturns but fail to account for the inevitable collapse in investment.

To avoid any misunderstanding, Figure 6.7 does not contradict empirical findings of a robust positive correlation between house prices and consumption. It only questions business cycle explanations that trace back changes in economic activity to expected appreciation alone or to housing demand shocks. The next section shows that something more is required to produce the desired result in a coherent fashion.

6.6 A Housing Cycle

According to a widely shared view, the United States Great Recession of 2008–09 was triggered by a housing bust that induced a subsequent financial crisis. The years preceding the recession witnessed concurrent increases in output, consumption, investment, employment, and real house prices. In 2004, the Securities and Exchange Commission (SEC) had weakened capital requirements for investment banks. Mortgage financing through emissions of asset-backed securities and collateralized debt obligations surged. Eventually, subprime mortgages became available for individuals that were previously denied credit access; see Brunnermeier (2009) and Hall (2011). When the bubble burst, credit standards became considerably tighter, and the five mentioned indicators—output, consumption, investment, employment, and real house prices—plunged.

While the preceding section showed that a simple model of housing manias, which relies on land price expectations alone, fails to imitate the data, this section employs a richer framework to reproduce the aforementioned stylized facts. It augments the real estate model with price and wage rigidities from section 3.5 and with net worth and endogenous borrowing constraints from section 5.4. Such a merger is straightforward since the various modules can be easily combined. However, the combination of land and constrained borrowing introduces a new feature. As demonstrated in appendix I, credit-constrained producers must distribute the available means on purchases of land and capital. Optimal decisions are characterized by the expression

$$\text{(92)} \qquad \frac{q_t L_t^d}{K_t^d} = \frac{\rho}{\alpha} \frac{r_{t+1}^e + \delta + \xi_t}{r_{t+1}^e - \hat{q}_{t+1}^e + \xi_t},$$

where ξ_t represents the shadow price of the borrowing constraint. If the constraint does not bind, the shadow price vanishes, and the formula becomes identical with condition (86). Tighter credit will generally diminish relative land demand. Conversely, any relaxation of the borrowing constraint stimulates relative land demand.

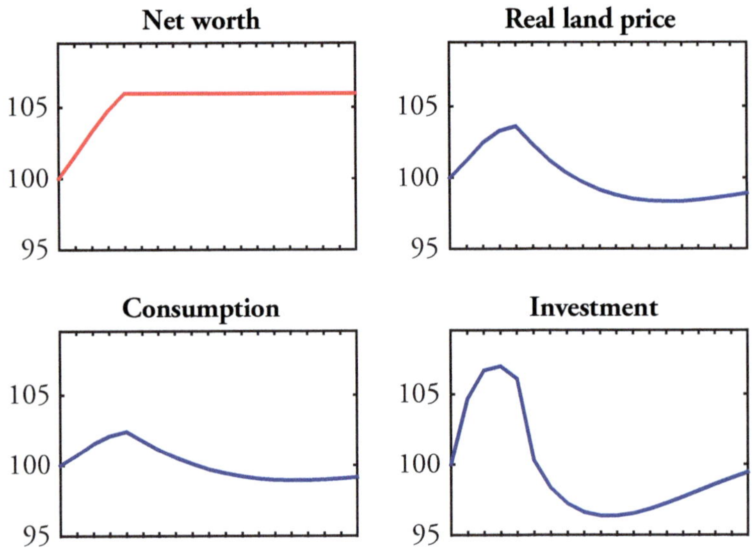

Figure 6.8: A leverage cycle. *Notes*: Horizontal axes represent time. The initial values of the variables are normalized at 100.

The simulation in Figure 6.8 is based on this extended model. Initially, producers are subject to a borrowing constraint and retain profits partly to get rid of the constraint (first panel). This relaxes the borrowing constraint and elevates real land prices (second panel). As a result, consumers as the beneficial owners feel richer and raise consumption (third panel). The crucial deviation from the model in the foregoing section regards investment (fourth panel), whose pronounced increase is made possible by the relaxed borrowing constraint: Rather than having to diminish investment in the presence of higher land prices, producers can finance *both* higher land acquisitions and higher capital purchases. This induces investment to move procyclically, with a volatility that exceeds the volatility of consumption and output. Owing to the assumed price and wage stickiness, the surge in consumption and investment demand raises output and employment.

Importantly, the model produces endogenous turning points. When the credit relaxation comes to a halt, the real land price will not remain at its higher level but will recede. This is the consequence of land appreciation expectations that become more cautious. A recession with strong declines particularly in investment follows. If lenders reacted to this unfavorable development by tightening credit, the recession would become even worse. Such an assumption appears reasonable but has not been incorporated because the simulation aims at highlighting an endogenous persistent cycle resulting from a single impulse. In fact, all variables recover in later periods and return slowly to their initial values.

Changes in the real land price are the driving force in this scenario. They result from the fixed land supply, which calls for strong price reactions, but also from the assumed rigidities in the price level and the nominal wage rate. With perfectly flexible prices and wages, credit relaxations would only entail commensurate changes in nominal variables. Moreover, expansionary monetary policies would still be superneutral under flexible prices and wage rates, as is clear from the conclusions of Chapter 3.

To summarize the main insight, the crucial element of a housing boom is *increased credit.* Erratic land price expectations alone—unaccompanied by soaring credit—would drive consumption and investment into opposite directions, contradicting the procyclical empirical pattern of these aggregates. Therefore, a sustained housing boom presupposes some form of monetary accommodation or a general relaxation of credit standards. In the case of the United States house price boom before 2007, the Fed and the SEC delivered both. Their choices were reinforced by creditors who made lending more favorable because they believed in permanent land price appreciations.

Chapter 7

Commercial Banks

The present chapter inserts commercial banks into the basic framework. This requires justification because macro models with banks are uncommon. The first reason for considering banks relates to the very process of money creation. Canonical models envisage fiat money as something that is exclusively supplied by a public agency, the central bank. In actual economies, however, the money stock is jointly produced by the central bank and many commercial banks. This public–private partnership has the important implication that the central bank cannot control the money stock directly but must incentivize banks to act in the intended manner. The second reason for taking account of commercial banks is also compelling. It leads back to Figure 2.1, which showed that short-term interest rates can diverge notably from long-term rates. The term structure of interest rates is of great importance for business cycle theory. While long-term interest rates normally exceed short-term rates, an *inverse term structure*—where short-term rates exceed long-term rates—is a good predictor of recessions.

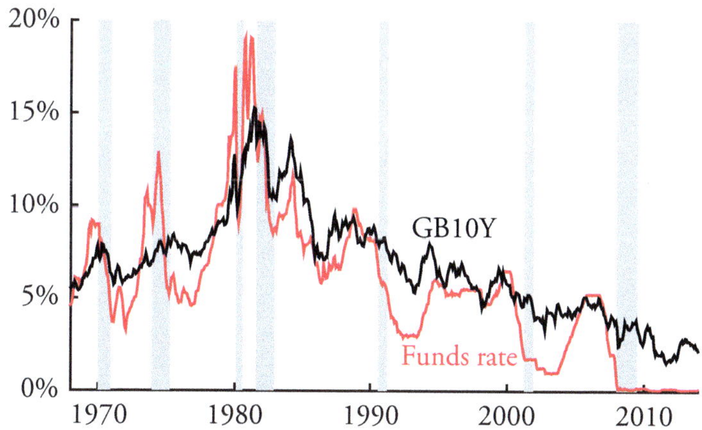

Figure 7.1: United States term structure of interest rates and recessions. *Notes*: The shaded areas indicate recessions. Monthly data, retrieved July 2016 from <https://fred.stlouisfed.org>, series DFF, WGS10YR, and USREC.

Figure 7.1 illustrates this intriguing fact. Taking the United States as an example, it shows the seven recessions that occurred between 1970 and 2015. Every recession succeeded, or coincided with, an inverse term structure of interest rates, that is, an excess of the funds rate over the 10-year government bond rate. Conversely, the figure does not document a single instance of a pronouncedly inverse term structure that was not followed by a recession. As the funds rate is determined in a competitive market for overnight interbank credit, one needs a model with banks to address this most interesting feature.

The chapter is organized as follows: Section 7.1 outlines the interactions between central banks and commercial banks in contemporary fiat money economies. Section 7.2 recalls the traditional banking model known from economic principles, but casts it in the form of an optimization problem. This lays the foundation for the core section 7.3, which introduces an explicit market for interbank credit and discusses the determination of the funds rate in such a setting. The material presented up to here would have sufficed until 2007. Since 2008, however, many central banks have been operating at the zero lower bound. An analysis of this extraordinary occurrence requires further tools that will be developed in section 7.4. Section 7.5 analyzes interest on reserves as a relatively new policy instrument. Section 7.6 introduces currency and the money base into the framework, and section 7.7 concludes.

7.1 Institutional Background

In the one-stage banking system presented in section 2.3, consumers maintained transfer and checking accounts with the central bank. They made payments by transferring money between these deposits (or by drawing cheques on the central bank). Real economies, by contrast, are characterized by two-stage banking where consumers have no direct access to the central bank. Idealizing somewhat, commercial banks are the central bank's only customers, while all nonbanks keep accounts with commercial banks. Abstracting from currency for the moment, the central bank creates *reserves*, $R_t \geq 0$, by acquiring bonds. If it does not pay interest on reserves, an assumption that will be relaxed in section 7.5, the central bank achieves a seigniorage that reflects its interest receipts. Equation (5) from section 2.3 is replaced by

$$B_t^{cb} = R_t \quad \text{and} \quad \sigma_t^{cb} = i_t B_t^{cb}. \tag{93}$$

Comparing (93) with (5) reveals two differences. First, money has been replaced by reserves. Just as the former symbol M_t represented consumers' money balances, R_t represents commercial banks' reserve balances with the central bank that are used for interbank settlements. Second, the seigniorage symbol comes with superscript "*cb*" to distinguish it from commercial bank seigniorage.

Assuming a unit continuum of identical commercial banks, all variables referring to this sector can be used interchangeably to represent individual or aggregate values, which simplifies the notation. In reality, banks perform many tasks. They arrange IPOs and M&As, manage savings accounts, and give advice to their customers. The "microeconomics of banking", cf. Freixas and Rochet (2008) or Degryse et al. (2009), analyzes the key role of banks in credit intermediation, screening, and monitoring. Macroeconomic models, by contrast, can compress all these services into the single output variable that also includes wheat, wine, and nursing care. However, banks are unique in that they provide deposit money, and this activity merits a distinct treatment. The following exposition does not aim at delivering a comprehensive bank theory but focuses on banks as *creators of money*. With this objective in mind, commercial banks are modeled as producers that buy bonds (or make loans) of amount B_t^b, keep reserves, and create deposits, $D_t \geq 0$. The assumption that they do not pay interest on deposits gives rise to the following balance sheet and earnings statement:

$$B_t^b + R_t = D_t \quad \text{and} \quad \sigma_t^b = i_t B_t^b . \tag{94}$$

The banks' seigniorage, σ_t^b, stems from the acquired bonds and the granted loans. Payments between consumers are arranged directly or indirectly in this setting. Specifically, if consumer *A* wishes to transfer money to consumer *B* and both keep accounts with the same bank, *A* simply orders the bank to debit *A*'s own account and to credit *B*'s account. If *A* and *B* maintain accounts with different banks *a* and *b*, then bank *a* debits *A*'s account, orders the central bank to transfer reserves from its account to *b*'s account and sends a notice to bank *b* to credit *B*'s account. For consumers, deposits assume the former role of money, and consumers are willing to keep positive deposit balances without interest because the convenience of deposits yields direct utility.

Occasionally, the determination of reserves is debated in a way that resembles philosophical discourses on Free Will—some authors treat reserves as an exogenous variable while others see them as endogenous. Beyond doubt, however, bank reserves are a policy variable. They constitute the liabilities side of the central bank asset sheet, and their total amount is determined by central bank decisions to buy or sell bonds. If the central bank decided to sell all its bonds, bank reserves would necessarily shrink to zero. More importantly, commercial banks cannot defend themselves against mounting reserves. Even if every single bank refused to sell bonds, the central bank could acquire the bonds from individuals. In this case, the central bank would credit the reserve account of the bank whose customer was the bond seller, while the bank would credit the customer's deposit account.

For banks, the total amount of reserve balances is exogenous. Banks cannot lend out reserves in the aggregate since each transfer of reserves from one bank to another leaves the sum total unaffected; the system is a closed loop. However, the plain fact that only central banks decide on the total amount of reserves does not dispute that they may feel compelled to do so. For instance, if a central bank pursues an interest rate target or is obedient to government pressure, it forfeits its capacity to set the level of reserves autonomously. Nonetheless, the central bank's *policy instrument* is still the volume of reserve balances it creates through open market operations or comparable credit instruments. Modern central banks do not fix short-term rates outright.

As a summary, Figure 7.2 represents the model's financial sector by means of the balance sheets of the central bank, the commercial banks, and the consolidated bank sector. The consolidated balance sheet indicates that deposits are virtually backed by bonds in hands of the central bank and the commercial banks. In reality, commercial banks also accept longer-term deposits that yield interest and cannot be used as means of payment. The resulting funds are utilized by banks to buy additional bonds (or make additional loans). In the present model, which comes with only a single bond interest rate, saving deposits and additional loans are disregarded because they represent pass-through items that vanish upon consolidation. Analyzing them properly would require an extended model with interest differentials and a greater variety of financial assets. The key feature of the bonds considered here is that banks acquire them by creating money out of thin air. Money created in this way is often referred to as *inside money* because D, as opposed to the former variable M, represents not a net financial asset of the private sector as a whole but a claim of consumers against private banks.

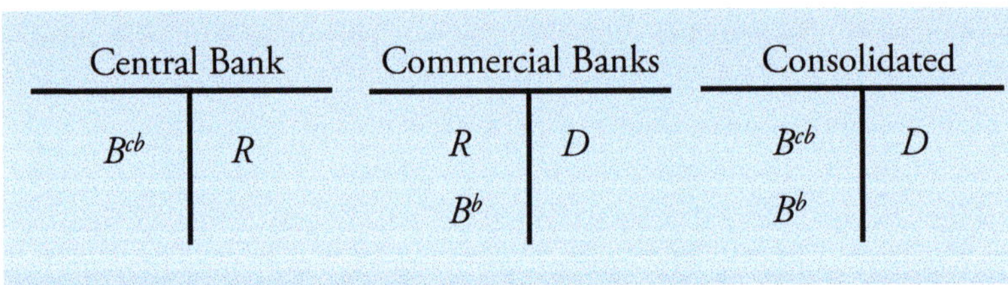

Figure 7.2: Balance sheet representation of the model's financial sector.

7.2 Traditional Banking Model

The traditional banking model, which can be traced back to Phillips (1920), is the best-known approach to determine the equilibrium quantity of deposits. In their role as financial firms, banks produce deposits subject to a cost function, $J(D_t)$, whose first and second derivatives are strictly positive. Bank profit, $i_t B_t^b - J(D_t)$, is the difference between bank seigniorage and nominal costs. Banks' choices are restricted by a reserve requirement according to which the amount of deposits must not exceed a given multiple of reserves, $rr \times D_t \leq R_t$. Here, $rr \in (0;1)$ denotes the *required reserve ratio* that is set by lawmakers or the central bank. According to the model's key assumption, reserves are given not only in the aggregate but also individually. Therefore, each single bank maximizes profit subject to the reserve requirement:

$$(95) \qquad \begin{aligned} \max_{B_t^b}! \quad & i_t B_t^b - J(D_t) \\ \text{s.t.} \quad & rr \times D_t \leq R_t \, . \end{aligned}$$

To solve this problem, one substitutes deposits from the balance sheet, (94), and forms a Lagrange function:

(96) $$\mathcal{L} = i_t B_t^b - J(R_t + B_t^b) - \xi_t^R \left(rr(R_t + B_t^b) - R_t \right).$$

With reserves exogenous for banks, the bonds are their only choice variable. Differentiating with respect to the bonds yields the first-order condition

(97) $$\xi_t^R = \frac{i_t - J'(D_t)}{rr}.$$

The numerator on the right-hand side represents the net return of an increase in credit and deposits. According to the traditional approach, this marginal net return is strictly positive, $i_t - J'(D_t) > 0$, an assumption that is maintained here. Intuitively, banks would like to increase credit and deposits indefinitely, but the reserve requirement prevents them from doing so. As a consequence, the Lagrange multiplier, ξ_t^R, must be strictly positive at an optimum, and the reserve requirement binds.

Three principal conclusions emerge. First, banks do not keep *excess reserves* in equilibrium. The constraint holds as an equality, $rr \times D_t = R_t$, because a hypothetical bank that has excess reserves available could increase its profit by expanding credit and deposits. Second, solving the preceding equality for deposits gives $D_t = R_t / rr$, the familiar money multiplier. With a required reserve ratio of one-third, for instance, equilibrium deposits would come to thrice the amount of reserves. Third, as noted by Gurley and Shaw (1960: 271), banks are situated in a characteristic disequilibrium. They would like to expand their business but cannot do so because of a legal restriction. The positive Lagrange multiplier, referred to as the *shadow price of reserves*, indicates the increase in bank profit that would result from a marginal relaxation of the reserve requirement.

Monetary policy is simple in such a setting. To induce banks to create a specific amount of deposits, the central bank must only adjust reserves through appropriate open market operations. Alternatively, it could change the required reserve ratio, but this variable is normally fixed for years or decades and not used as a policy instrument.

7.3 Funds Rate Determination

The traditional model outlined in section 7.2 shapes economic thinking through its eminent role in textbooks. However, the premise that each bank accepts its reserves as given is highly unsatisfactory. Commercial banks are profit-seeking firms that can be expected to look for additional reserves if they need some. In reality, reserves are traded in dense and highly competitive interbank markets. These markets differ from ordinary credit markets in that loans are regularly made for only one day. The typical transaction is an overnight repurchase agreement (or repo), where the borrower sells an asset to the lender with the promise to buy it back the next morning. Congruently, the lender conducts a reverse repurchase agreement. The interbank market is largely segmented from other credit markets because investors, or home buyers, have no access to it and, for that matter, do not find overnight credit useful. In the United States, the interbank market is referred to as the (federal) funds market, a term that is used generically here since similar markets exist in all advanced economies.

The following model, using Homburg (2016), introduces a separate market for reserves, with an interest rate i_t^F, the *effective funds rate*. The variable i_t, known hitherto as the nominal interest rate, is now referred to as the *bond interest rate* to avoid confusion. Thus, the effective funds rate is an interest rate for overnight interbank loans, while the bond interest rate is an interest rate for longer-term credit. The model builds on the *market segmentation hypothesis* that treats short-term and long-term credit markets as entirely separated. This assumption is opposed to the *expectations hypothesis*, which assumes perfect arbitrage opportunities and determines long-term rates as averages of expected short-term rates.

A bank that plans to increase its reserves can borrow an amount $F_t^d > 0$ from other banks; F_t^d denotes the demand for funds. Conversely, a bank with excess reserves can lend the amount $F_t^d < 0$. Typically, small banks that attract a lot of deposits are lenders in the funds market, while large banks with plenty of investment opportunities are borrowers. In the present model with identical banks, the effective funds rate is determined by the equilibrium condition $F_t^d = 0$. With an additional market now open, each bank determines its optimal choices of lending in the bonds market and borrowing in the funds market by solving

(98)
$$\max_{B_t^b, F_t^d}! \quad i_t B_t^b - i_t^F F_t^d - J(D_t)$$
$$\text{s.t.} \quad rr \times D_t \leq R_t + F_t^d .$$

Interbank borrowing diminishes profit by $i_t^F F_t^d$ and relaxes the constraint by the amount F_t^d. If a bank with reserves R_t borrows in the interbank market, it extends its balance sheet to $(R_t + F_t^d) + B_t^b = D_t + F_t^d$; borrowing increases both the bank's reserves and its liabilities. Lending, by contrast, constitutes an asset swap since the bank exchanges reserves for a claim against a fellow bank. Keeping in mind the negative sign of F_t^d for a lender, the balance sheet reads $(R_t + F_t^d) + B_t^b - F_t^d = D_t$. As neither borrowing nor lending affects the identity $R_t + B_t^b = D_t$, deposits can still be substituted by reserves and bonds in forming the Lagrange function

(99)
$$\mathcal{L} = i_t B_t^b - i_t^F F_t^d - J(R_t + B_t^b) - \xi_t^R \left(rr(R_t + B_t^b) - R_t - F_t^d \right).$$

Differentiating with respect to the bonds recovers (97). Differentiating with respect to the demand for funds yields the additional optimality condition

(100)
$$i_t^F = \xi_t^R .$$

In the preceding section, ξ_t^R represented the shadow price of reserves. Opening a market for funds converts the shadow price into an observable market price. The effective funds rate so characterized induces each bank to keep its reserves voluntarily; the disequilibrium highlighted by Gurley and Shaw disappears. Equating the optimality conditions (97) and (100) makes it possible to get rid of the shadow price and reveals an explicit *term structure of interest rates*:

$$i_t^F = \frac{i_t - J'(D_t)}{rr}. \tag{101}$$

Assuming a given bond interest rate for the moment, three important conclusions emerge. First, the effective funds rate is an increasing function of the bond interest rate, $\partial i_t^F / \partial i_t > 0$. The positive relationship between the two rates accords with Figure 7.1. Second, the effective funds rate is a decreasing function of reserves, $\partial i_t^F / \partial R_t = -J'' / rr^2 < 0$. When the central bank provides additional reserves, deposits rise because they are still determined by the multiplier formula, $D_t = R_t / rr$. As a result, marginal costs increase and the effective funds rate declines. Third, the formula admits an inverse term structure of interest rates because the denominator on the right-hand side is a number between zero and one. Such an inference seems highly counterintuitive as it implies that banks are willing to pay more for overnight loans than they receive for long-term credit commitments. However, consider a scenario with $rr = 1/3$ and $J'(D_t) = 2\%$, which implies $i_t^F = 3(i_t - 2\%)$. At a bond interest rate of 5 percent, banks would be offering up to 9 percent in the interbank market. Such a conduct is perfectly rational because each additional reserve unit, borrowed for 9 percent, allows expanding credit and deposits by three units earning a net return of 3×3 percent.

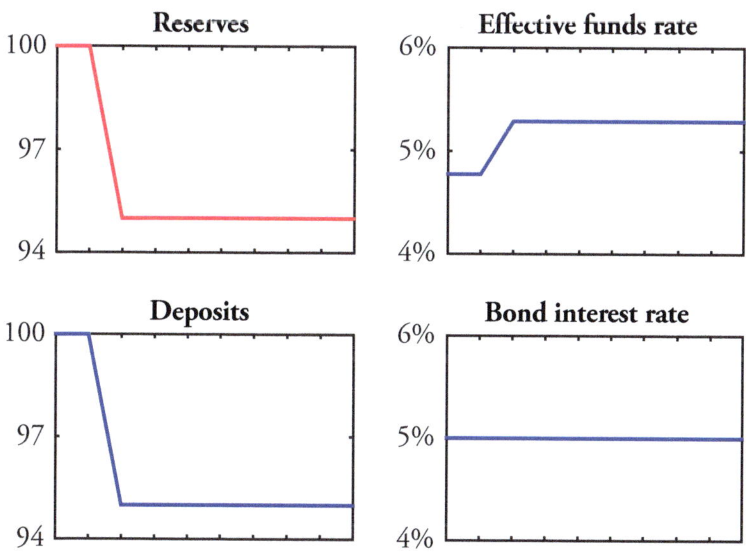

Figure 7.3: Restrictive monetary policy. *Notes*: Horizontal axes represent time. The interest rates are measured in percent. The initial values of the other variables are normalized at 100.

Figure 7.3 documents a partial equilibrium simulation with a given bond interest rate of 5 percent and an initial effective funds rate of 4.8 percent. This constitutes a normal term structure of interest rates. When the central bank diminishes reserves through open market sales, banks are legally required to reduce deposits. Reserves become scarce, which increases the effective funds rate to 5.3 percent, well above the bond interest rate. The resulting inverse term structure indicates a restrictive monetary policy. Recalling Figure 7.1 above, which shows that all United States recessions since 1970 were related to an inverse term structure of interest rates, the present finding suggests monetary restrictions as a possible cause for recessions.

Banking in General Equilibrium

The banking model considered so far can easily be integrated into any of the preceding general equilibrium models. Appendix J shows how this is done. For an analysis of monetary policy in the very short-run, the model with price and wage rigidities from section 3.5 appears particularly attractive. After including commercial banks, the system of equilibrium conditions takes the following form:

$$(102) \qquad \left.\begin{aligned} &\pi_t = \pi_t^e + \varphi^P \hat{Y}_t \\ &B_t^d + B_t^{cb} + B_t^b = B_t^s \\ &\pi_t^W = \pi_t^e + \varphi^W \hat{N}_t \\ &F_t^d = 0 \end{aligned}\right\} \Rightarrow (P_t, i_t, W_t, i_t^F).$$

The first and third equations are the familiar Phillips curves for the commodity and labor market, respectively. In the second equation, bank bonds appear as an additional source of credit. The fourth equation is new and represents equilibrium in the funds market. On the right-hand side, the effective funds rate shows up as an additional endogenous variable that is simultaneously determined with the price level, the bond interest rate, and the nominal wage rate. Based on these modifications, Figure 7.4 illustrates the impact of an expansionary monetary policy.

At the outset, the central bank conducts an open market purchase. The resulting increase in reserves makes them less valuable for banks and exerts downward pressure on the effective funds rate. This liquidity effect accords well with the intuition that an expansionary monetary policy lowers interest. With a reserve requirement that binds before and after the open market operation, banks expand credit and deposits. As discussed in section 3.5, such an expansion boosts output, prices, and expected inflation, which increases bond interest through the Fisher effect and the expected output effect. In this richer model, the two nominal interest rates move in opposite directions: The liquidity effect diminishes the short-term funds rate, while higher inflation and output expectations elevate the long-term bond interest rate. As the two rates can be considered as polar ends of the entire *yield curve*—a function that relates credit yields to credit durations—the monetary expansion steepens the yield curve. Conversely, monetary restrictions would flatten the yield curve and possibly invert its slope.

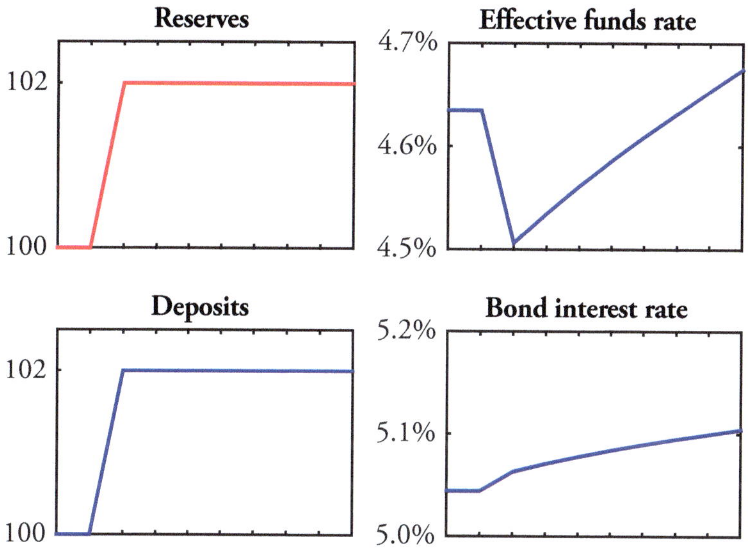

Figure 7.4: Expansionary monetary policy. *Notes*: Horizontal axes represent time. The interest rates are measured in percent. The initial values of the other variables are normalized at 100.

Figure 7.4 also illustrates that the initial impact becomes reverted soon. While changes in reserves have a lasting impact on the effective funds rate in partial equilibrium (see Figure 7.3), the present general equilibrium model grasps the repercussions of the bond interest rate on the effective funds rate: Higher bond yields make reserves more precious for banks and pull up the effective funds rate, as is clear from formula (101). To keep the effective funds rate down, the central bank would have to provide additional rounds of liquidity injections.

The Target Funds Rate

The foregoing model provides a reasonably realistic account of how monetary policy is actually conducted in the United States and many other economies. The objective of this subsection is to refine the argument and, in particular, to show that monetary policies are often misrepresented in macro models. In a sense, the literature lags behind advances in monetary policy that haven taken place over decades and can be characterized as a stronger market orientation. What does this mean?

Owing to its monopoly power, a central bank can influence interest rates in one of two ways. The first way involves fixing the overnight interbank rate outright at a level beneath the equilibrium rate and to ration access to central bank credit through bidding procedures. This method is cumbersome and may result in inefficient credit allocation or unwelcome distributional effects. Alternatively, the central bank can accept the interbank interest rate as determined by demand and supply and influence it through small-scale open market operations.

In the United States, the Fed uses the second strategy. At regular meetings, its Federal Open Market Committee (FOMC) decides on a *target funds rate*. Thereafter, the Open Market Desk (OMD) conducts bond sales and purchases to adjust bank reserves and keep the effective funds rate close to the target. In the 1970s, as former Fed Governor Henry Wallich (1984: 25) reported, the Fed set a range of between 0.5 and 1 percentage point around the target rate and sought to keep the effective funds rate within this range. After 1979, when the Fed started targeting reserves, the corridor was temporarily widened to 4 percentage points. Ennis and Keister (2008) and Ihrig et al. (2015) provide detailed contemporary descriptions of monetary policy implementation. Only occasionally does a second policy instrument become relevant: When an individual bank is unable to meet reserve requirements, it can borrow directly from the Fed at the so-called discount rate. As the discount rate is normally set 1 percentage point above the target rate, borrowing in the discount window penalizes banks and gives them an incentive to find reserves in the funds market.

The present model neglects *borrowed reserves* (obtained in the discount window) and concentrates on *non-borrowed reserves* (obtained in the funds market) that are much more important quantitatively. Non-borrowed reserves, R_t, always equal the value of bonds acquired by the central bank. Borrowed reserves could be introduced as an additional symbol, F_t, which designates the volume of credit the central bank grants to commercial banks. In this case, the last equilibrium condition in (102) would have to be replaced by $F_t^d = F_t$; in equilibrium, borrowed funds would not vanish but would coincide with central bank liquidity injections. Without an explicit discount rate that differs from the target funds rate, however, the instruments R_t and F_t are obviously equivalent. In models with only two interest rates, i_t^F and i_t, borrowed reserves constitute a redundant instrument and can safely be neglected.

For decades, the effective funds rate fluctuated smoothly around its target. This changed dramatically in fall 2008, when the effective funds rate collapsed to almost zero, where it has remained ever since. Figure 7.5 contrasts the weekly values of the effective funds rate and the target rate during this interesting period. Until September 2008, the effective funds rate followed the target funds rate closely, with only short-lived deviations. Evidently, the target was frequently changed. Without detailed knowledge of the underlying operations of the OMD and deliberations of the FOMC, one can never be sure whether the effective funds rate followed the target funds rate (proper targeting) or vice versa (dirty targeting). In any case, the effective funds rate deviated sharply from the target funds rate between September and 13 December 2008, when the Fed repealed the target funds rate and set a corridor of 0–0.25 percent that remained in place until December 2015. The decline in the effective funds rate to essentially zero contradicts received wisdom and requires an extended model, which is developed in section 7.4.

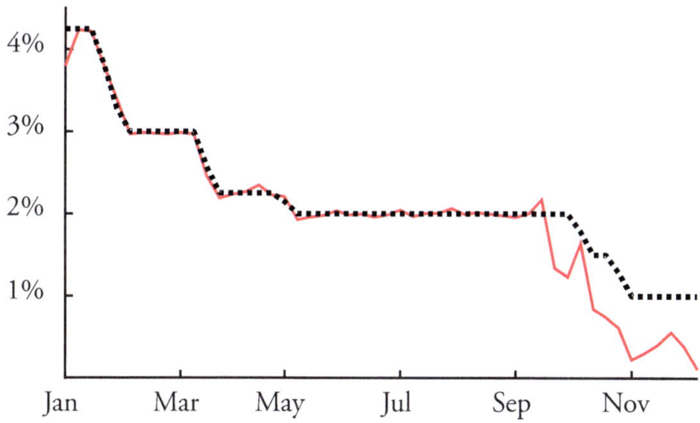

Figure 7.5: Effective funds rate (solid line) versus target funds rate (dotted line), United States, 2008. *Notes*: Weekly data, retrieved August 2016 from <https://fred.stlouisfed.org>, series DFF and DFEDTAR.

7.4 Excess Reserves

The preceding approach derived the effective funds rate from the reserve requirement $rr \times D_t \le R_t + F_t^d$. At equilibrium, the effective funds rate was strictly positive and the reserve requirement held with equality. These results were obtained in a model where reserves constituted the only restriction that prevented banks from expanding credit and deposits indefinitely. In the presence of *other* restrictions, the reserve requirement may well have slack at an individual bank's optimum. Such a possibility presents itself because equation (100) characterized the effective funds rate as a Lagrange multiplier. To see the connection, recall Kuhn-Tucker's complementary slackness condition, which reads $\xi_t^R \times (rr \times D_t - R_t - F_t^d) = 0$ in this context. If $\xi_t^R > 0$, the reserve requirement holds with equality. Conversely, the Lagrange multiplier vanishes if $rr \times D_t - R_t - F_t^d > 0$.

From this perspective, the emergence of excess reserves would make the observed decline in the effective funds rate consistent with the above model. Such an empirical implication is easily testable because the Fed publishes monthly averages of banks' excess reserves. These are depicted in Figure 7.6. Before fall 2008, banks kept essentially no excess reserves. To be entirely accurate, excess reserves ranged between \$1 and \$2 billion because intraday payments follow a stochastic process that prevents banks from satisfying the reserve requirement exactly. Following Poole (1968), an extensive body of literature has studied stochastic reserve management and intraday trading; see, for example, Afonso and Lagos (2015). These analyses concern small stochastic residuals that are important for financial economics. From a macroeconomic viewpoint, the record reserves created since 2008 are much more interesting.

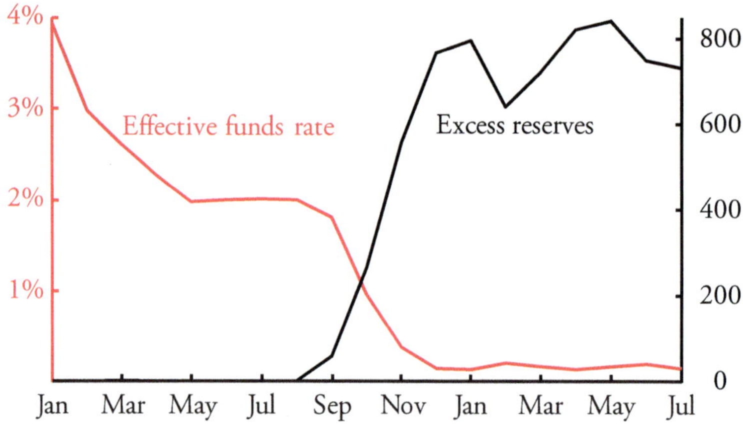

Figure 7.6: Effective funds rate in percent (left-hand scale) and excess reserves in billion dollars (right-hand scale), United States 2008–09. *Notes*: Monthly data, retrieved August 2016 from <https://fred.stlouisfed.org>, series DFF and EXCSRESNS.

In September 2008, the Fed began buying enormous amounts of assets of all sorts and increased its balance sheet abruptly. Banks became awash with reserves they did not need. As a consequence, the effective funds rate declined sharply. As is evident from Figure 7.6, the fall in the effective funds rate coincided with the emergence of excess reserves of an unprecedented scale. With excess reserves exceeding $800 billion, one may wonder whether banks could push the effective funds rate below zero. This was generally regarded as impossible because reserves can be held in the form of cash. If one neglects the costs of storing and insuring cash, the effective funds rate is subject to a *zero lower bound*,

$$i_t^F \geq 0. \tag{103}$$

As an intermediate result, the effective funds rate is a Lagrange multiplier that vanishes as soon as the reserve requirement slackens. Empirically, the emergence of large excess reserves aligned with the decline in the effective funds rate to zero. Bech and Monnet (2013) document analogous inverse relationships between excess reserves and overnight interbank rates for a broader country sample, including Canada, the eurozone, and the United Kingdom. In this respect, the evidence strongly supports the preceding theoretical reasoning.

Leverage Requirement
While the model studied so far accords with the inverse relationship between the funds rate and the level of reserves, it suggests that banks would see excess reserves as a good opportunity to increase deposits so as to earn higher seigniorage. As is well known, that did not happen. Hence, the model needs an extension in the form of another restriction that occasionally supersedes the reserve requirement and prevents banks from expanding deposits. An obvious candidate is a *leverage requirement* that limits bank borrowing. Both market forces and regulations hinder banks from becoming overleveraged. The Basel III framework, for instance, provides an explicit leverage requirement according to which a bank's net worth must exceed 3 percent of its balance sheet total (plus certain off-balance liabilities). In a simple model without explicit net worth, such a restriction translates into the postulate that liabilities are bounded from above by some exogenous number, *LR*.

A tricky part of the argument regards the determination of bank liabilities. For a bank planning to borrow in the funds market, liabilities equal $D_t + F_t^d$, the sum of deposits and borrowed funds. For a bank planning to lend in the funds market, liabilities coincide with deposits. As outlined in connection with the Lagrange function, (99), interbank lending does not diminish a bank's liabilities but constitutes an asset swap, an exchange of reserves for an interbank claim. Therefore, a leverage requirement imposed by counterparties or regulators takes the form

$$D_t + \max\{F_t^d; 0\} \leq LR. \tag{104}$$

In what follows, banks solve (98) subject to this additional constraint. Substituting deposits with reserves and bonds leads to the Lagrange function

$$\begin{aligned}\mathcal{L} = i_t B_t^b - i_t^F F_t^d - J(R_t + B_t^b) - \xi_t^R \left(rr(R_t + B_t^b) - R_t - F_t^d \right) \\ - \xi_t^L \left(R_t + B_t^b + \max\{F_t^d; 0\} - LR \right).\end{aligned} \tag{105}$$

To simplify semantics, the subsequent discussion neglects the non-generic case where both restrictions bind (which renders one of them redundant). Depending on which restriction binds, two regimes emerge:

- *Regime R*, $\xi_t^R > 0$ and $\xi_t^L = 0$: The reserve requirement binds while the leverage requirement has slack. As a result, the effective funds rate is strictly positive, and excess reserves vanish. In the United States, this regime prevailed during the entire postwar period before 2008. It underlies the preceding section and does not need further comments.
- *Regime L*, $\xi_t^R = 0$ and $\xi_t^L > 0$: The reserve requirement has slack while the leverage requirement binds. The effective funds rate becomes zero, and banks keep excess reserves.

In fall 2008, the United States economy moved from regime R to regime L, which constitutes unchartered territory and merits a detailed analysis. In a first step, the above Lagrange function is differentiated with respect to the bonds, yielding

(106) $$\xi_t^L = i_t - J'(D_t).$$

This condition resembles condition (97) that applies in regime R. After September 2008, the multiplier ξ_t^L became strictly positive because the Fed slackened the reserve requirement through its expansive open market operations. Commercial banks could not keep pace with increases in lending because the financial crisis and the emerging recession depressed their net worth and diminished the leverage tolerated by counterparties and regulators. Importantly, the bond interest rate fluctuated in 2008 and 2009, but did not nearly decline to zero (see Figure 2.1). This finding suggests that the decline in the effective funds rate cannot be attributed to decreases in the bond interest rate; rather, it was actually triggered by the rise in reserves.

Characterizing the effective funds rate encounters the problem that the maximum function in the second constraint is non-differentiable at the origin, which violates the assumptions of the Kuhn-Tucker theorem. However, a direct argument allows identifying the unique equilibrium. If $i_t^F > 0$, a funds demand $F_t^d = 0$ would be suboptimal because lending a small amount increases profit, leaves the first constraint unaffected ($\xi_t^R = 0$) and has no influence on the second constraint. If $i_t^F = 0$, however, $F_t^d = 0$ is weakly optimal for each bank: Interbank lending has no effect on profit and the constraints, whereas interbank borrowing leaves profit and the first constraint unaffected but tightens the second constraint. Hence, an effective funds rate at the zero lower bound is the unique equilibrium. In this equilibrium, the leverage constraint binds, $R_t + B_t^b = LR$, and central bank liquidity injections do not boost deposits but rather depress commercial bank credit, $B_t^b = D_t - R_t$.

Figure 7.7 illustrates the evolution of reserves, deposits, and the deposit counterpart, the difference between these two items. Between 2000 and summer 2008, bank credit and deposits developed in parallel. As indicated by the small spike, reserves rose only temporarily in September 2001 when the Fed feared a panic after the 9/11 terrorist attacks. From fall 2008 onward, reserves surged, deposits did not keep pace, and the deposit counterpart plunged. Starting October 2014, when QE was terminated, reserves fell somewhat, and the counterpart recovered, but deposits grew steadily at a slow pace.

To summarize, this section has revealed an asymmetry in central bank operations. Central banks can restrict deposit money as sharply as they wish. However, in accordance with the aphorism "you can't push on a string", expansionary policies may fail to produce commensurate increases in deposit money. If the policy overstretches the financial system's capacity, reserves and deposits become detached, and further accelerations neither affect the real economy, nor produce inflation. In such a case, referred to as regime L here, QE entails that central bank credit crowds out commercial bank credit and shifts seigniorage from commercial banks to the central bank.

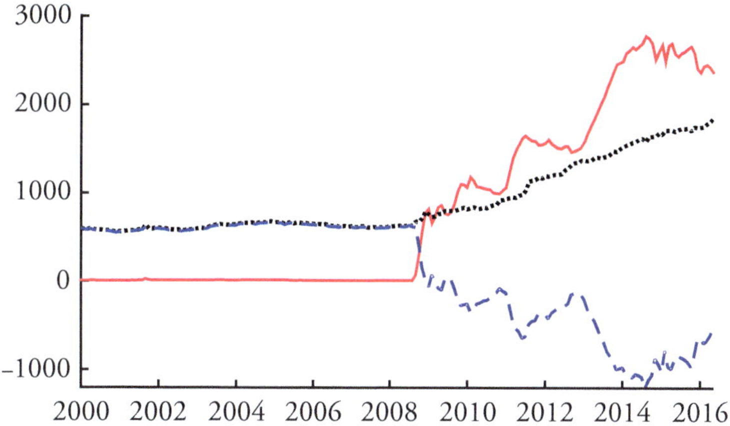

Figure 7.7: United States reserves (solid line), deposits (dotted line), and counterpart (dashed line), billion dollars. *Notes*: Monthly data, retrieved August 2016 from <https://fred.stlouisfed.org>. Reserves are RESBALNS, deposits are M1SL minus CURRSL, counterpart is deposits minus reserves.

7.5 Interest on Reserves

Traditionally, central banks do not pay interest on reserves. This is beginning to change. In the United States, for instance, the Fed introduced interest on reserves in 2008. After an experimental period with varying rules, the Fed fixed interest both on required and excess reserves at a uniform rate of 0.25 percent, effective starting January 2009. In December 2015, it raised the uniform rate to 0.50 percent. The objective of this section is to outline the influence of interest on reserves on the effective funds rate.

This requires two changes in the model. Denoting the *interest rate on reserves* as i_t^R , the payment $i_t^R R_t$ is subtracted from central bank seigniorage, (93), and added to bank seigniorage, (94). As a result, total seigniorage, which is remitted to consumers, remains unaffected, so the amendment has no influence on consumer behavior. The second change concerns bank profit, the objective in the foregoing optimization problems. Because a bank's planned reserves equal $R_t + F_t^d$, the new objective reads

(107) $$i_t B_t^b + i_t^R R_t + (i_t^R - i_t^F) F_t^d - J(D_t) .$$

Interest on reserves appears twice in this formula. While $i_t^R R_t$ represents a pure income effect, $i_t^R F_t^d$ changes bank incentives in that it alters the cost of interbank borrowing. Substituting the new profit function for the original in formula (98) yields the following characterization of the effective funds rate:

(108) $$i_t^F = \xi_t^R + i_t^R .$$

A comparison with the former characterization, $i_t^F = \xi_t^R$, shows that any increase in interest on reserves lifts the effective funds rate one-to-one. This has a simple intuition. From the banks' perspective, higher interest on reserves reduces the effective cost of borrowed funds. Hence, the effective funds rate must rise commensurately to maintain equilibrium in the funds market.

The preceding remarks apply to section 7.3, where banks were only restricted by the reserve requirement. In terms of section 7.4, this was referred to as regime R. Analyzing interest on reserves in regime L, where banks are restricted by the leverage requirement, is more complicated because of the mentioned non-differentiability problem. In regime L, the Lagrange multiplier, ξ_t^R, vanishes, and formula (108) suggests that the effective funds rate coincides with the interest rate on reserves, $i_t^F = i_t^R$. Although this observation is correct, it fails to take into account an intriguing indeterminacy. With an operative zero lower bound, the full set of effective funds rates compatible with market equilibrium is given by

(109) $$\left\{ i_t^F \geq 0 \,\middle|\, i_t^F \in [i_t^R - \xi_t^L ; i_t^R] \right\}.$$

Any effective funds rate exceeding the interest rate on reserves, the upper limit in the preceding formula, violates profit maximization because an individual bank could increase profit by lending a small amount, $F_t^d < 0$. Such a maneuver would leave the reserve requirement unaffected ($\xi_t^R = 0$) and would not influence the leverage requirement because lending does not change leverage.

Conversely, any effective funds rate falling short of the lower limit would also contradict profit maximization. Rewriting $i_t^F < i_t^R - \xi_t^L$ as $i_t^R - i_t^F > \xi_t^L$ shows that borrowing in the funds market would increase profit by an amount that exceeds the costs arising from the associated tightening of the leverage constraint.

For any effective funds rate between the lower and upper limit, however, $F_t^d = 0$ is individually optimal: Lending in the funds market diminishes profit strictly, whereas the advantage from borrowing falls short of the shadow price, ξ_t^L. The main implication of this theory is that in regime L, the effective funds rate varies between the zero lower bound and the interest rate on reserves. Figure 7.8 confirms this prediction. It shows that in December 2015, when the Fed raised the interest rate on reserves from 0.25 to 0.50 percent, the effective funds rate increased but remained below the interest rate on reserves.

What about negative interest rates on reserves? These are not an abstract possibility; they have already been implemented. The European Central Bank (ECB), for instance, the Danish National Bank, the Swiss National Bank, and the Swedish *Riksbank,* charge interest on banks' reserve balances. Theorists long overlooked such a possibility, presuming that negative interest rates on reserves were inconceivable. However, as storing and insuring cash is costly, central banks can actually charge negative interest at moderate rates.

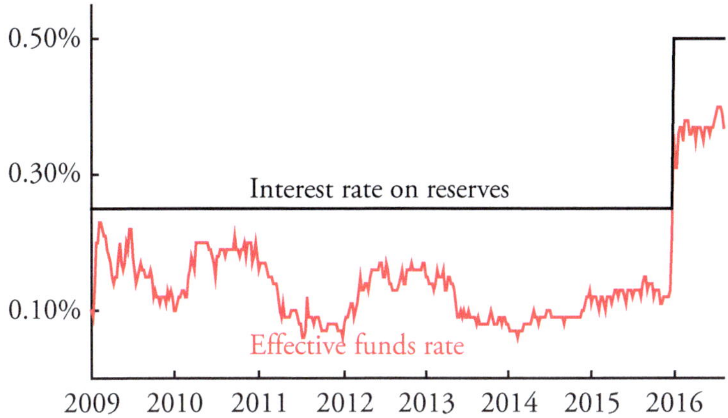

Figure 7.8: United States interest on reserves. *Notes*: Monthly data, effective funds rate retrieved August 2016 from <https://fred.stlouisfed.org> as series DFF; interest rate on reserves retrieved July 2016 from <https//:www.federalreserve.gov/monetarypolicy/reqresbalances.htm>.

With the effective funds rate determined by formula (108) in a regime where only the reserve requirement binds, negative interest on reserves depresses the effective funds rate beneath the shadow price of borrowed funds but not necessarily into negative territory. This is different under a binding leverage constraint. In formula (109), the entire interval would become located in the negative quadrant. If one relaxes the zero lower bound to take into account hoarding costs, the effective funds rate should become strictly negative. Evidence confirms this prediction in that the Eonia, the eurozone's equivalent to the effective funds rate, staggered around –0.30 percent in 2016. The analysis of the virtues and vices of negative interest rates on reserves is still in its infancy. With banks restricted by a leverage requirement rather than by scarce reserves, the effects of such a policy on bank behavior will probably be contained.

7.6 Currency and the Money Base

The models studied in the foregoing sections lack currency. The purpose of this section is to fill this gap. Introducing notes and coins makes it easier to relate the models to reality and shows that currency restricts bank lending even in the absence of a statutory reserve requirement. Such a demonstration is important because a number of countries—Canada, New Zealand, and the United Kingdom, for instance—do not explicitly require banks to hold minimum reserves.

In an economy with currency, money demand consists of demand for deposits and demand for currency. Representing the latter by the new symbol *CC*, this yields

(110) $$M_t^d = D_t + CC_t \,.$$

While money demand derives from the optimization problem outlined in Chapter 2, the following approach assumes that consumers keep currency and deposits in a fixed proportion, referred to as the *currency-to-deposit ratio*, $cr = CC_t / D_t$. Hence, for any money demand, the demands for currency and deposits follow as

(111) $$D_t = \frac{M_t^d}{1+cr} \quad \text{and} \quad CC_t = \frac{cr \times M_t^d}{1+cr} \,.$$

Currency is created in accordance with three rules to which economists are so accustomed that they are rarely pointed out. First, since Peel's bank act of 1844, central banks are the only producers of currency. Second, banks obtain currency in exchange for reserve deposits at a fixed rate of 1:1, in unlimited amounts, and with no strings attached. The *vault cash* so acquired, which is stored in banks' vaults and ATMs, counts as reserve. Therefore, reserves include both bank deposits with the central bank and vault cash. In the United States, many retail banks fulfill their reserve requirement with vault cash and lend out the excess in the funds market.

According to the third and final rule, nonbanks obtain currency from banks in exchange for deposit money, again at a fixed rate of 1:1 and in unlimited amounts. After having moved from the bank sector to the nonbank sector, notes and coins are referred to as *currency in circulation*, *CC*. As opposed to vault cash, currency in circulation is not a part of reserves. Together with reserves, currency in circulation constitutes the *money base*, designated by *H* for "high-powered money":

(112) $$H_t = R_t + CC_t \,.$$

The central bank creates base money by acquiring bonds. Its liabilities consist of reserves and currency in circulation. While the central bank controls the money base through its open market operations, it cannot influence its composition, as is clear from the rules stated above.

Recalling the assumption of identical banks, it is easy to outline the impact of currency demand on bank behavior. Each bank that contemplates creating deposits, D_t, knows that its customers will request currency in the amount $cr \times D_t$ to preserve a constant currency-to-deposit ratio. The bank can satisfy this currency drain with available reserves, including vault cash, or with additional reserves from the funds market. Thus, currency entails a separate demand for reserves in addition to statutory required reserves. The bank's optimization problem (98) becomes

(113) $$\begin{aligned} &\max_{B_t^b, F_t^d}! \quad i_t B_t^b - i_t^F F_t^d - J(D_t) \\ &\text{s.t.} \quad (rr + cr) \times D_t \le H_t + F_t^d \,. \end{aligned}$$

The differences between this problem and (98) regard the added currency drain, *cr*, and the replacement of reserves by the money base. In the special case $cr = 0$, the two optimization problems coincide as (112) implies $H_t = R_t$. In the special case $rr = 0$, the constraint reads $cr \times D_t = CC_t + F_t^d$ if it binds at the optimum; and banks will hold no reserves. In the general case with positive currency demand and an explicit reserve requirement, the demand for funds vanishes in equilibrium, and deposits amount to $D_t \leq H_t / (rr + cr)$. Substituting $M_t = D_t \times (1 + cr)$ yields

$$(114) \qquad M_t \leq \frac{1 + cr}{rr + cr} H_t .$$

The preceding formula resembles the textbook multiplier but is written more carefully as a weak inequality. As long as the reserve requirement binds, the money stock equals $(1+cr)/(rr+cr)$ times the money base; the currency drain restricts deposit creation even in the absence of a statutory reserve requirement. This enables the central bank to influence the money stock indirectly through its control over the liabilities side of its balance sheet. Succinctly, the money base *anchors* the monetary system in this case. However, if banks are not constrained by scarce reserves, the multiplier formula becomes meaningless, and the economy loses its nominal anchor.

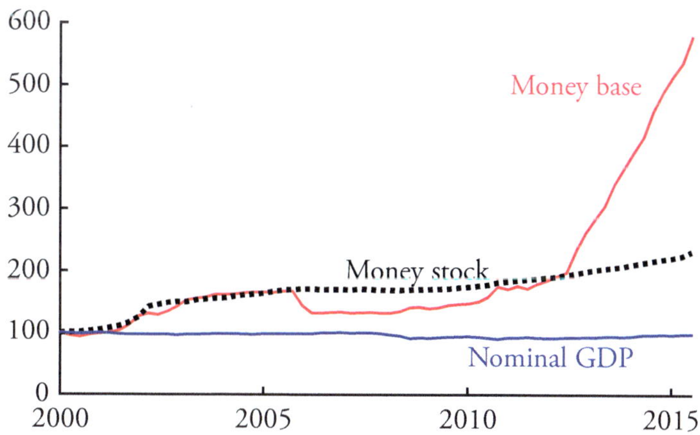

Figure 7.9: QE in Japan. *Notes*: Quarterly data retrieved August 2016 from <http//:stats.oecd.org> (money stock M1 and nominal GDP) and <http//:www.stat-search.boj.or.jp> (money base).

Figure 7.9 illustrates the latter instance for Japan, a country with a relatively long record of QE policies. The graphs show that the evolution of the money base, the money stock, and nominal GDP diverged starting at the turn of the century. In particular, nominal GDP remained almost unchanged. While a moderate dose of QE in 2003 succeeded in elevating the money stock somewhat, the subsequent stronger acceleration proved more or less ineffectual; commercial banks could not keep pace with commensurate increases in credit and deposit creation. The theories developed in this study question whether expansive monetary policies of this sort produce useful macroeconomic effects. While the preceding sections focused on the link between the money base and the money stock, the missing connection between the money stock and nominal GDP is better explained in terms of the models in Chapter 4. Hence, transmission of monetary policy in Japan faces two obstacles: Increases in the money base do not entail increases in the money stock of a comparable magnitude, and increases in the money stock leave nominal GDP unaffected.

Similar graphs could be produced for the eurozone, Switzerland, the United Kingdom, and many other countries, which all are characterized by enormous increases in the money base, modest increases in the money stock, and reticent nominal GDP growth. As documented by high inflation rates in Russia, Turkey, and several Latin American countries, however, this pattern is not a universal phenomenon.

To summarize, in models without currency, the ratio of the money stock (deposits) and the money base (reserves) is bounded above by $1/rr$. In the present model, the ratio of the money stock (deposits plus currency in circulation) and the money base (reserves plus currency in circulation) is bounded above by $(1+cr)/(rr+cr)$. The latter expression can be written in equivalent form as $1/rr^*$, where $rr^* = (rr+cr)/(1+cr)$ represents an *effective* required reserve ratio. Because currency affects the equilibrium only through its influence on bank behavior, the upshot is that an economy with currency can be represented by an economy lacking currency if one properly redefines the effective required reserve ratio. In 2016, for instance, the United States was characterized by a statutory required reserve ratio of roughly 10 percent and a cash-to-deposit ratio of 75 percent. Substituting into the preceding formula yields an effective required reserve ratio of approximately one half. Sudden changes in currency demand—which occurred at the turn of the millennium when people feared the "Y2K bug", or in September 2008 when Lehman Brothers failed—alter the effective ratio and possibly the money stock.

7.7 Conclusion

The main takeaway of this chapter may be the characterization of the effective funds rate as a Lagrange multiplier. A strictly positive funds rate indicates that reserves are scarce and that the money base anchors the monetary system. With a zero funds rate, the reserve requirement gets slack and nominal magnitudes become detached from the money base. This is an exceptional situation. In United States history, it has happened twice.

As shown in Figure 7.10, excess reserves as a percentage of nominal GDP were essentially zero in 1930, at the start of the Great Depression. This remained so until May 1932, when the Fed began to purchase large amounts of government securities. As a result, the reserve constraint slackened and the effective funds rate approached the zero lower bound. In fact, the measures initiated in 1932 can be considered as the Fed's first "quantitative easing" program, notwithstanding that the term was unknown in those days and that a good deal of the expansion of reserves reflected unsterilized gold inflows. Excess reserves remained elevated and the effective funds rate stayed close to zero until the end of World War II. Thereafter, the economy returned to the normal state of zero excess reserves and a positive effective funds rate until 2008. Interestingly, the vast amount of total reserves, which rose almost sevenfold between 1930 and 1940, was never reduced. The gradual disappearance of excess reserves was entirely due to increases in required reserves that stemmed mainly from surges in deposits, but also from temporary increases in the required reserve ratio.

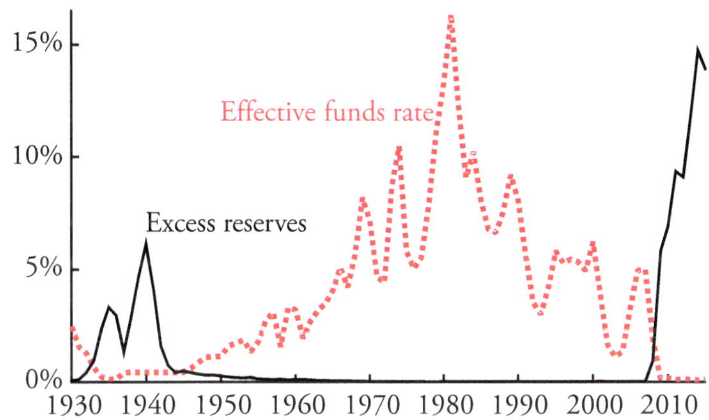

Figure 7.10: United States effective funds rate in percent, excess reserves as a percentage of GDP. *Notes*: Annual averages from Board of Governors of the Federal Reserve System (1943): Excess reserves (all member banks) p. 396. Prime bankers' acceptance p. 450. Board of Governors of the Federal Reserve System (1976): Excess reserves (all member banks), pp. 594–602. Prime bankers' acceptance p. 674. Excess reserves since 1959, effective funds rate since 1954, and GDP since 1930 retrieved August 2016 from <https://fred.stlouisfed.org> as EXCRESNS (EXCSRESNS), FEDFUNDS, and GDPA.

This largely forgotten episode suggests that the well-known criticism of Friedman and Schwartz, according to which the Fed contributed much to the severity and longevity of the Great Depression, should not be pushed too far; see Romer (1992). While Friedman and Schwartz (1963: 511) argue that between 1933 and 1941, "the Federal Reserve System made essentially no attempt to alter the quantity of high-powered money", Figure 7.10 indicates that an alternative course would have been ineffectual because commercial banks were already flooded with reserves. As an elementary principle of choice theory, widening slack in a non-binding constraint has no effect on behavior. Similar thoughts apply, of course, to the monetary measures taken after 2008, which overstretched the lending capacity of the banking sector.

A final remark pertains to Japan and the eurozone. Although these currency areas are also characterized by an overnight interbank rate, i_t^F, near the zero lower bound and by large excess reserves, they differ from the United States' experience in that the long-term bond interest rate, i_t, has also fallen to zero. Such an instance indicates credit abundance and leads back to Chapter 4, which analyzed scenarios where the obstacles to credit expansion are rooted in the nonfinancial sector. Bearing in mind Chapter 6, which showed that the bulk of investment and credit demand derives from real estate, Japan and the eurozone seem to be characterized by borrowing constraints and pessimistic land price expectations.

Chapter 8

Methods

Based on the framework outlined in Chapter 2, the preceding text presented a comprehensive macroeconomic theory. During the exposition, all required assumptions were explicitly spelled out. However, the text did not indicate why exactly these assumptions were made. The purpose of the present chapter is to fill this gap and to compare the chosen framework with alternatives. Such a meta-discussion may be particularly useful for model builders who are aware that small changes in assumptions made at an early stage have large consequences for the further development of a theory.

8.1 Expectations

Section 2.2 introduced adaptive expectations as forecasts that depend only on past and present experience. Specifically, it was assumed that individuals in period t expect the inflation rate $\pi^e_{t+1} = \pi^e_t + \lambda(\pi_t - \pi^e_t)$ to prevail in period $t+1$, where π^e_t denotes their inflation forecast for period t, π_t indicates actual inflation in period t, and λ represents a learning parameter. Output expectations were defined analogously in section 3.4. A large fraction of the current literature, by contrast, employs the RE hypothesis and specifies expected inflation as $\pi^e_{t+1} = E_t\{\pi_{t+1}\}$. The expression on the right-hand side is the mathematical expected value conditional on information available in period t. In a deterministic model, RE are equivalent to perfect foresight. In a stochastic setting, RE differ from the realizations by an error term with zero mean.

Comparing the two approaches, it should be stressed at the outset that the key difference is *not* whether individuals behave rationally in the economic sense. Rather, the key difference pertains to the specification of the information set. If individuals knew the true structural model, its parameters, and the nature of the stochastic processes (e.g., white noise, random walks, random walks with drift), and if all this information were available at zero cost, then one could safely assume that decisions were governed by RE. These informational requirements, however, are stringent to the extreme. Although it may be a painful insight, there is simply no consensus model used by all (or, at least, most) macroeconomists to make forecasts and to evaluate policy measures. On the contrary, how to model the overall economy is subject to debate.

As is well known, the premises of adaptive and rational expectations are not mutually exclusive. If inflation follows a random walk, adaptive inflation expectations are rational in the sense that they minimize the mean squared forecast error; see Muth (1960: 300), and Shepherd (2012) for a generalization. If the data-generating stochastic processes take different forms, adaptive expectations become suboptimal only if these processes are known to the decision-maker. Many researchers deem the assumption of known stochastic processes as overly strong and have argued that adaptive expectations are an acceptable forecast method if the said assumption is not met; see Evans and Ramey (2006: 250) and the literature cited therein. This is exactly the position taken here: In monetary macroeconomics, the true model is generally unknown. A decision-maker who forms adaptive expectations avoids persistent errors and does not place too much emphasis on random disturbances.

Evans and Honkapohja (2001) assume that individuals know the structural model and the stochastic processes but do not know the model parameters. In this case, often referred to as *adaptive learning*, expectations may converge toward RE in a stationary environment if they are continually revised. In a dynamic environment, however, the learning process is likely to be too slow to justify the RE assumption, as noted by Shiller (1978). The approach used here is still more agnostic. It sees macroeconomic models not as outright representations of reality but as tools that facilitate coherent thinking, highlight specific chains of causation, and prepare empirical testing.

As pointed out by Estrella and Fuhrer (2002) and Milani (2007), RE models not only are hard to justify with regard to their core assumption but also suffer from counterfactual implications. As a rule, disturbances in exogenous parameters or policy instruments cause *jumps* in endogenous variables that cannot be found in the data. At the same time, such disturbances fail to produce *persistent* variations. To reconcile theory and evidence, RE models need additional ingredients such as habit persistence, indexation, and investment or capital adjustment costs. Nevertheless, most of the persistence stems from the exogenous stochastic processes. Walsh (2010: 344), for instance, considers a policy where the central bank sets the bond market interest rate according to a Taylor rule, $i_t = \delta_\pi \pi_t + \delta_Y \hat{Y}_t + v_t$. The interest rate depends on the inflation rate, the output gap, and a monetary policy shock that is specified as an autoregressive process, $v_t = \rho_v v_{t-1} + \varepsilon_t$. As Walsh rightly observes, "all the persistence displayed by the responses arises from the serial correlation introduced into the process for the monetary shock v_t. If $\rho_v = 0$, all variables return to their steady-state values in the period after the shock".

A final important comment pertains to macroeconomic policy. To compute equilibrium paths in a RE model, individuals need to know the full sequences of future monetary and fiscal policies. These sequences are normally specified as announcements, a premise that is particularly hard to buy. Since the work of Kydland and Prescott (1977), it has been known that policy announcements are generally time inconsistent, or unreliable. No experienced policy observer could contest this view. Especially in democratic societies, even the smartest policy analysts often have no idea what their government will do after the next election. And while financial market participants may listen to central bank announcements, not necessarily believing them, price setters in actual markets for goods and services do not care about such proclamations but focus on current demand and cost conditions in their individual markets. Odyssean forward guidance policies in the sense of Campbell et al. (2012)—where governments and central banks commit to future actions just as Odysseus committed himself to resisting the sirens' call by having himself bound to the mast—are infeasible. It is difficult to see why ultra-rational individuals capable of computing equilibrium market outcomes over infinite horizons should take such a naive attitude in policy matters.

8.2 Intertemporal Choice

The basic framework contained two models of intertemporal choice, one for producers and the other for consumers. In section 2.4, producers' investment decisions were derived from the objective function

$$(115) \qquad \Pi^e_{t+1} = P^e_{t+1}Y^s_{t+1} + (P^e_{t+1} - P_t)K^d_t - \delta P^e_{t+1}K^d_t - W^e_{t+1}N^d_{t+1} - i_t B^s_t .$$

In period *t*, producers select real capital and external finance to maximize expected profit in period *t*+1. This is a dynamic optimization problem whose solutions depend on price expectations. Capital goods are produced in period *t* and used in period *t*+1, and their time index refers to the installation period. Parts of the literature follow a different notation and use as a time index the period where the capital goods become employed in production. Such a convention is innocuous as such, but can lead to misinterpreting the program as a static optimization problem. Ljungqvist and Sargent (2012: 467), for instance, conceive of (115) as a simultaneous choice of capital and labor demand.

To elaborate this point, one can represent the economy's overall resource constraint as $C_t + K_t \leq F(N_t, K_{t-1}) + (1-\delta)K_{t-1}$, where the time index of capital refers to the period when the capital goods are *produced*. This convention, employed here, warns that the capital stock used in period t is a predetermined variable. Alternatively, one may write the overall resource constraint as $C_t + K_{t+1} \leq F(N_t, K_t) + (1-\delta)K_t$ on the understanding that the time index of capital refers to the period when the capital goods are *used*. Such a notation is logically fine but apt to suggest that the controls N_t and K_t are chosen simultaneously. However, contrary to Ljungqvist and Sargent's treatment, K_t is predetermined and only the controls N_t and K_{t+1} can be adjusted in the current period.

Apart from this issue, it should be clear that (115), together with the static determination of labor demand, (6), is equivalent to maximizing net present value since there are no adjustment costs. Therefore, the present delineation of producer behavior deviates only slightly from the canonical setting in that it incorporates an explicit financing constraint, $P_t K^d_t = B^s_t$. Especially in Chapters 4 and 5, producers' need for external finance was shown to give rise to important coordination problems that become hidden if capital is absorbed into consumers' budget constraints.

Turning to consumers, money demand will be discussed in the next section, while this section considers intertemporal choice. Most of the current literature derives consumption decisions from an infinite horizon approach. In the canonical model, outlined in Ljungqvist and Sargent (2012: 4), consumers consider as given their initial financial assets, A_0, the (stochastic) streams of nonfinancial incomes, X_t, and real interest rates, r_t. With $\beta < 1$ as a time preference parameter (that obviously differs from the respective parameter introduced in section 2.7), consumers maximize (expected) utility

$$\sum_{t=0}^{\infty} \beta^t u(C_t), \tag{116}$$

subject to a sequence of periodic budget constraints,

$$A_{t+1} = (1 + r_{t+1})(A_t + X_t - C_t). \tag{117}$$

This infinite horizon program is more an advertisement because it generally yields no explicit solutions and requires the model to be placed in a steady state. However, solutions can be characterized by means of a value function, which gives the highest possible utility resulting from the initial level of assets and the constraints:

$$V(A_t) = \max_{C_s}! \quad \sum_{s=t}^{\infty} \beta^{s-t} u(C_s). \tag{118}$$

Writing the value function $V(A_{t+1})$ analogously and combining it with the previous expression entails Bellman's equation, according to which decisions after period t must constitute an optimal policy with regard to the state resulting from the initial choices:

$$\begin{aligned} &V(A_t) = \max_{C_t,\, A_{t+1}}! \quad u(C_t) + \beta V(A_{t+1}) \\ &\text{s. t.} \quad A_{t+1} = (1 + r_{t+1})(A_t + X_t - C_t). \end{aligned} \tag{119}$$

Bellman's equation represents the choice problem in recursive form and essentially transforms an infinite-dimensional problem into a two-dimensional one. The present text, by contrast, proceeds directly from two dimensions:

$$\begin{aligned} &\max_{C_t,\, A_{t+1}}! \quad U(C_t, A_{t+1}) \\ &\text{s. t.} \quad A_{t+1} = (1 + r_{t+1})(A_t + X_t - C_t). \end{aligned} \tag{120}$$

Comparing the two programs (119) and (120), it is obvious that they coincide if $U(C_t, A_{t+1}) = u(C_t) + \beta V(A_{t+1})$. Moreover, both approaches entail a Euler equation: At an optimum, the marginal rate of substitution between current and future consumption equals the reciprocal of the expected real interest factor. The representation of consumer choice proposed here simplifies the model enormously, allows dispensing with the steady state requirement, and avoids investing too much effort in a program that is arguable anyway. After all, behavioral economics suggests that individuals find it hard to make consistent intertemporal choices and prefer workable rules of thumb.

Combining the two-period program (120) with a logarithmic or CDC utility function yields a zero or low interest elasticity of savings that fits the empirics cited in section 2.7 and produces a model whose dynamics, as in reality, are mostly driven by investment rather than consumption demand. Put succinctly, the present modeling strategy reduces the complexity of consumers' intertemporal choice to get rid of the steady state straitjacket. Analytic solutions are then obtained using standard methods, without approximations of unknown quality.

A third way to model consumers' intertemporal choices is the well-known overlapping generations (OLG) model. Considering its simplest form with only two generations, older consumers passively spend their wealth *cum* interest, $C_t^2 = A_t$, while younger ones solve

$$\max_{C_t^1,\, A_{t+1}}! \quad u(C_t^1, C_{t+1}^2)$$

$$\text{(121)} \qquad \text{s.t.} \quad \text{i)} \quad A_{t+1} = (1 + r_{t+1})(X_t - C_t^1),$$

$$\text{ii)} \quad C_{t+1}^2 = A_{t+1}.$$

If the utility functions of the bounded horizon model and the OLG model coincide, that is, if $U(C_t, A_{t+1}) = u(C_t^1, C_{t+1}^2)$, the two models produce identical first-order conditions for a utility maximum. However, the numerical solutions differ due to an important difference in the specifications of the budget constraints: The two-period OLG model is bound to produce capital–output ratios below one, associated with very high real interest rates, because the capital stock falls short of wage income, and the latter falls short of output. Since output and wage income depend on the period length, reasonable values for the capital–output ratio and the real interest rate emerge if one assumes a period length of 30 years or so, as some researchers do. Such a period length, however, is unsuited for analyzing short-run fluctuations. To circumvent these difficulties one can assume models with dozens of generations rather than just two; see Ríos-Rull (1996) and Heer and Maussner (2009: 405). Such multi-generation models allow incorporating a demographic structure and appear most attractive for empirical applications.

8.3 Modeling Money

A common method to model money is to treat it as an argument of the utility function. This money-in-the-utility, or MIU, approach is followed here. Before comparing it with alternatives, it seems appropriate to consider a fundamental critique. According to Wallace (1980: 49), fiat money is *intrinsically useless*, that is, "never wanted for its own sake; it is not legitimate to take fiat money to be an argument of anyone's utility function". This view confounds the question of why consumers accept money flows as payments—which they do only because they believe others will also accept the money in exchange for goods—with the question of why consumers hold money stocks. The inclination to hold positive money balances in the presence of assets with higher returns can be rationalized by putting money into the utility function. This is in perfect accordance with subjective value theory, a cornerstone of economics since the second half of the nineteenth century. Subjective value theory holds that economists are not compelled to explain *why* individuals find certain commodities useful. Rather, economists infer usefulness from an observed willingness to pay.

When examining the market for electricity, for instance, an economist can safely put this commodity into the utility function to derive a demand curve. From a philosophical point of view, one may classify electricity as intrinsically useless since it is never wanted for its own sake; alas, it is even dangerous! Such an objection appears economically irrelevant, however, since consumers reveal a preference for electricity by their willingness to pay a certain amount per kilowatt-hour. No economist studying the respective market must specify the technical processes of converting electricity into ultimate services such as illumination or TV. No economist analyzing the demand for hot spices is required to scrutinize cooking recipes because hot spices are never wanted for their own sake. And in monetary economics, it is equally legitimate, though not necessarily optimal, to derive money demand from MIU. On this point, see also Feenstra (1986) and McCallum (1983).

The MIU framework together with the assumed utility functions was chosen to capture two stylized facts, namely, the negative interest elasticity of money demand and the absence of a long-run trend in the circular velocity. Notwithstanding numerous financial innovations in recent decades, the circular velocity of M1 money demand in the United States stood at 5.1 in 1970, rose to an all-time high of about 10.5 until the 2007 financial crisis, and receded to 5.5 in 2016. Correcting for sweep accounts—virtual retail deposits used to circumvent reserve requirements, see Board of Governors of the Federal Reserve System (1999: 59)—money demand has even somewhat risen over the last decades. Earlier hopes that the demand for money could be represented as a stable function of only a few variables have not been fulfilled, however, cf. Goldfeld (1976) and Laidler (1993). Much of the variance in money demand appears still enigmatic.

Instead of using MIU as a shorthand method, one can explicitly model frictions that induce consumers to hold positive money balances. A common way is Clower's (1967) cash-in-advance constraint (CIA), which assumes that consumers need sufficient money stocks to finance consumption expenditure. The above models can easily be converted into CIA models if one drops real balances from the utility function and adds the following inequality to the consumers' decision problem:

$$M_t \geq \mu P_t C_t . \tag{122}$$

Subject to an exogenous parameter, μ, whose value depends on the period length, consumers need a minimum of cash balances to finance current consumption. With a positive interest rate, (122) holds as an equality at an individual optimum. Money demand displays a unit elasticity with respect to consumption expenditure and a unit elasticity with respect to GDP if the consumption share of GDP remains constant. However, since the CIA determines money demand mechanically as an institutional necessity, consumers do not respond to rising nominal interest rates by economizing on money balances, which seems unnatural.

The transaction costs approach (TCA) developed by Baumol (1952) is superior in this respect. Baumol conceives of money demand as a problem of optimal lot size. Individuals can reduce average cash balances if they invest their income in interest-bearing bonds and sell a small fraction of the bonds each time they need cash. Every such transaction entails a fixed cost ("shoe leather effect") so that the decision problem boils down to weighing these costs against the opportunity costs of foregone interest. The result is a money demand function that decreases in the nominal interest rate but displays an income elasticity of only one half, contradicting the evidence of a near unit elasticity. More recently, Banerjee and Maskin (1996) as well as Lagos and Wright (2005) proposed full-fledged models that derive money demand from microeconomic structural relationships such as a double-coincidence of wants. While these approaches constitute interesting basic research, their complexity renders them less useful for discussing macroeconomic issues. Moreover, Camera and Chien (2013) argue that the Lagos and Wright approach, which requires a steady state assumption, yields the same theoretical and quantitative predictions as a simple CIA model if comparable assumptions are made.

All alternative approaches mentioned so far ascribe the demand for money to its role as a *means of payment*, and some economists think this is the only sensible way to rationalize positive balances. Another strand, however, treats money as a *store of value*. Mulligan and Sala-i-Martin (2000) note that the majority of United States households do not hold interest-bearing assets simply because their financial wealth is too low to warrant costly portfolio management. Brunnermeier and Sannikov (2016) consider individuals who select portfolios consisting of money and capital. Capital comes with a return that exceeds the return on money in expectation but is subject to idiosyncratic risk. If individuals maximize expected utility rather than expected yield, they will pick mixed portfolios even in the absence of any exchange frictions.

Figure 8.1 contains instructive evidence with regard to money as a store of value. It displays the demand for €50 and €500 notes, which together make up roughly two-thirds of the total currency in circulation. In the eurozone, €500 notes are not generally accepted as a means of payment. Jewelers and second-hand vehicle dealers aside, many shops explicitly state that they will not accept denominations larger than €100. Nevertheless, the demand for

€500 notes is obviously strong, and it spiked by about 10 percent in September 2008. The explanation for the discontinuity is obvious: After the collapse of Lehman Brothers, individuals recognized banknotes as a safe haven. On the other hand, the demand for €50 notes increases steadily and shows a strong seasonal pattern, with a peak in each December when more cash is required for Christmas shopping and presents. Such a pattern is also characteristic of all notes up to a denomination of €100, but not of notes of higher denominations. In sum, these findings suggest that money serves as an important store of value, notwithstanding that it cannot quantitatively compete with alternative stores such as real estate.

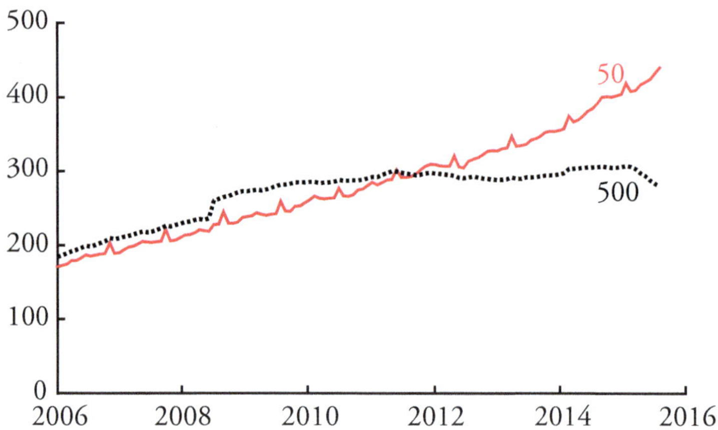

Figure 8.1: Eurozone net banknote circulation. *Notes*: Billion euros, monthly data, not seasonally adjusted, retrieved September 2016 from <http//:sdw.ecb.europa.eu>, series BKN.M.U2.NC10.B.10P1.01.S.E.

This leads to a final, and crucial, question: What makes money so interesting for macroeconomists? The answer proposed here holds that the significance of money is unrelated to its function as a means of payment and is independent of its suitability as a store of value. Rather, money is vital only if it serves as the *unit of account* in a sticky price setting. To develop the argument, consider a microeconomic general equilibrium model, condensed into a vector-valued excess demand function, $e(p)$, whose components, $e_j(p)$ represent the difference of demand and supply in the j-th market. Under a mild rationality assumption, the excess demands are null homogeneous in the price vector $p = (p_1, \ldots, p_n)$ representing the n market prices; a proportional increase in all prices does not affect individual choice. Taking commodity no. n as the unit of account, money, one obtains $p_n = 1$, and the other prices become money prices of the respective goods and services.

If an initial equilibrium, $e(p) = 0$, is disturbed in such a way that an excess demand in some market $j < n$ emerges, at least one money price must adjust to restore equilibrium. An excess demand for money, however, cannot be removed by adjusting p_n, which always equals one; rather, it requires changes in *all* other prices. Because prices in the real world are not set by an auctioneer but display different degrees of stickiness, as discussed in section 3.5, distortions are bound to emerge during the adjustment process. This is the proper reason why abrupt changes in money demand and the money stock are generally considered harmful. A policy that keeps excess money demand close to zero reduces the need for price adjustments in a multitude of markets. Of course, price level stability does not render such adjustments superfluous since economic dynamics require permanent changes in relative prices.

The above line of reasoning made no reference whatsoever to a double coincidence of wants or a related story. In fact, if individuals desired banknotes not to facilitate payments but because of their fragrance, this would not affect the argument as long as money served as the unit of account—changes in the preference for banknote sniffing would still affect the general price level. A related point is made by Fama (1980), who argues that if prices were expressed in gallons of oil, instead of in units of the means of payment, governments would be inclined to stabilize the oil price and would pay less attention to the price of coins and notes. Thrilling historical examples of the disastrous consequences of changes in the unit of account include the British *Great Recoinage* of 1694–1700, which entailed a strong deflation and riots; see Feavearyear (1931: 94), as well as France's redenomination in 1724, which was followed by an industrial sector contraction of 30 percent; see Velde (2009).

8.4 Labor Supply

As in growth theory, the present study assumed a constant labor supply. Many business cycle models, however, incorporate a labor supply decision. Canonically, consumers maximize

(123) $$\sum_{t=0}^{\infty} \beta^t u(C_t, 1 - N_t)$$

subject to a sequence of periodic budget constraints. Here, utility depends on consumption and leisure, which equals one minus working hours. Endogenous hours are a necessary ingredient not only of real business cycle model, or RBC, but also of sticky price DGE models that assume perfect wage flexibility, as many do. The reason is that with permanent labor market clearance, a constant labor supply contradicts one of the most robust business cycle features: the strong positive correlation between output and employment.

To highlight this point, Figure 8.2 depicts economic fluctuations in an RBC economy with a constant labor supply. The model coincides with the flexible price and wage framework developed in Chapter 2. Output changes are induced by random disturbances of the parameter θ from section 2.7, the so-called Solow residual. Fluctuations in this parameter induce similar fluctuations in output and the real wage rate, whereas employment stays constant by hypothesis. The three curves are not identical because the capital stocks adapt in the background.

Such a conduct is unsatisfactory because output and employment fluctuations are closely tied to one another. To fit the model to reality, a common procedure makes hours endogenous and assumes a large elasticity of labor supply with respect to the real wage rate. As a result, employment not only varies procyclically, as intended, but also dampens strong procyclical variations in the real wage rate that cannot be detected in the data. Owing to the underlying premise that consumers always operate on their labor supply curves, unemployment is voluntary in these models.

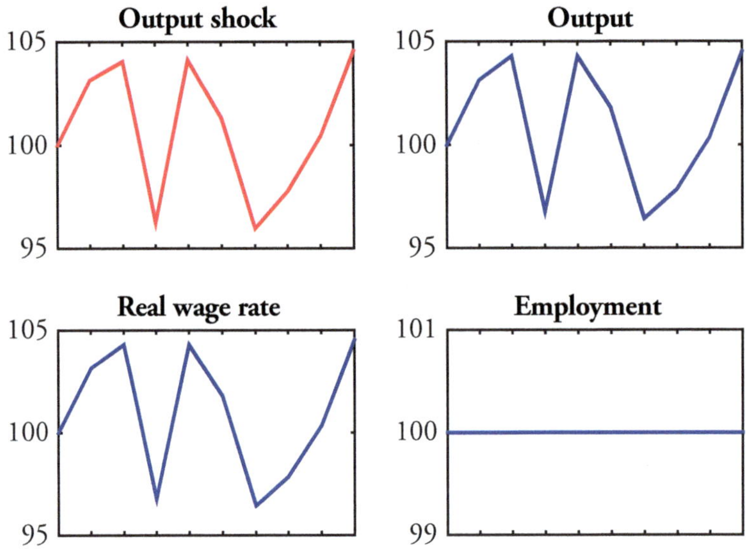

Figure 8.2: Real business cycle. *Notes*: Horizontal axes represent time. The initial values of the variables are normalized at 100.

In an empirical survey, Chetty et al. (2013: 6) note that the huge labor supply elasticities needed to make flexible wage macromodels meaningful are inconsistent with quasi-experimental microeconometric studies that typically obtain labor supply elasticities close to zero. Boppart and Krusell (2016: 2) document *negative* long-run elasticities of average hours worked with respect to the real wage rate. They show that between 1870 and 1998, average hours almost halved in a broad selection of industrialized countries.

The determination of labor supply elasticities is challenging because labor supply decisions have several dimensions. The first dimension relates to the margin of response: extensive choices (job quitting) versus intensive choices (varying hours conditional on employment). The second dimension concerns the timing of response: intertemporal substitution of leisure versus steady state leisure demand. And third, it is crucial whether changes in net wage rates result from changes in gross wage rates or tax amendments. Gross wage rates reflect the general productivity level and their changes entail the familiar substitution and income effects. Variations in tax rates, by contrast, alter the tradeoff between market production and household production. Because this tradeoff involves an additional substitution possibility that reinforces the impact on official hours, estimates derived from tax rate differentials are likely to overstate workers' responses to changes in gross wage rates.

As an intermediate summary, mainstream macromodels often employ counterfactual labor supply elasticities, and many of them presume that consumers are continually *on* their labor supply curves. The latter premise is acceptable in the context of a long-run analysis that washes out all temporary frictions. For business cycle analyses, however, labor market clearance is an inappropriate assumption. Therefore, the modeling strategy of sections 3.4 and 3.5 neglects short-run changes in labor supply as a second-order factor and ascribes employment fluctuations to changes in labor demand. Due to price and wage rigidities, labor markets can fail to clear, which pushes consumers *off* their labor supply curves. According to the findings of Chetty et al. (2013: 26), models generating unemployment this way are consistent with the evidence. They also accord with the presumption that mass unemployment after recessions does not result from clever intertemporal optimization on the side of consumers that reduce hours or quit jobs until better times, but constitutes a social dilemma.

8.5 Price Determination

Any macroeconomic theory determines prices either as solutions to a system of *equilibrium* conditions or by specifying a *disequilibrium* process. In the first case, researchers have a further choice between competitive and monopolistic equilibrium as two common concepts. As the preceding text focused on competitive equilibrium, it seems useful to briefly consider monopolistic price setting. Following Dixit and Stiglitz (1977), the customary approach to modeling monopolies in the commodity market is to contemplate C as an aggregate of many different consumption goods, $C(j)$, where j represents an index. Assuming a continuum, aggregate consumption is specified in CES form as

$$C = \left[\int_0^1 C(j)^{(\varepsilon-1)/\varepsilon} dj \right]^{\varepsilon/(\varepsilon-1)}, \tag{124}$$

where $\varepsilon > 1$ represents the elasticity of substitution. With such a symmetric treatment of individual commodities, the associated price vector equals

$$P = \left[\int_0^1 P(j)^{1-\varepsilon} dj \right]^{1/(1-\varepsilon)}, \tag{125}$$

and consumption expenditure, PC, is the product of the two integrals. In an equilibrium with monopolistic competition, each producer j sets the price $P(j)$ at the profit maximizing level. As a result, the equilibrium price level is higher under monopolistic competition than under perfect competition, while output is lower. Such an inference is most interesting for antitrust and competition policy.

From the standpoint of monetary economics, the difference between the two equilibrium concepts appears less profound: Blanchard and Kiyotaki (1987: 654) stress that assuming monopolistic competition alone does not impair neutrality of money. Put succinctly, if the monopolistic price level exceeds the competitive price level by 10 percent, this will remain so after a monetary shock has hit; changes in money will not affect output or employment. For this reason, the present text—with its focus on monetary economics—preferred perfect competition as the simpler concept.

Simplicity also guided the way that disequilibrium processes were represented. The basic premise specified price adjustments as the outcome of a trial-and-error process satisfying

$$\pi_t = \pi_t^e + \varphi^P \hat{Y}_t, \qquad (126)$$

where $\varphi^P > 0$ represents an adjustment speed and $\hat{Y}_t$ is the output gap. Sticky prices of this kind impair short-run money neutrality. The underlying behavioral assumption carries forward Arrow and Hurwicz's (1958, 1959) approach to price setting in microeconomic general equilibrium models. Arrow and Hurwicz describe an economy by a vector-valued market excess demand function, *e(p)*, and stipulate adjustments of the form $dp_j/dt = f_j(e_j(p))$, where the left-hand side represents the derivative with respect to time and f_j is a sign-preserving function. Thus, individual commodity prices rise in response to excess demands and fall in response to excess supplies. The macroeconomic assumption made here is perfectly analogous.

Alternative approaches to price setting developed in recent decades infer prices (or wages) within choice-theoretic frameworks. Mankiw (1985) assumes that altering prices is costly and derives individually optimal price rigidities from these "menu costs". Another strand considers staggered pricing. Taylor (1979) imposes that contracts last for one year and can only be changed semiannually. In Calvo (1983), the dates on which individual producers may change their prices follow an exogenous stochastic process. Clearly, both types of staggered pricing give rise to monetary non-neutralities because prices cannot adjust instantaneously to changes in monetary conditions.

The models of Taylor and Calvo, which both rest on the RE hypothesis, yield a number of counterfactual predictions, including that credibly announced monetary contractions induce economic booms. Mankiw and Reis (2002) review these problems and attack them with a *sticky information* model that takes into account the costs of acquiring and processing information. The solution proposed by Mankiw and Reis comes close, not only in spirit but also in its analytical form, to equation (126), which represents price setting as a tentative endeavor under incomplete information. In a sense, the results of Mankiw and Reis corroborate the view that the distinction between RE and adaptive expectations depends on the specification of information sets.

Appendices

A Producer Behavior

Section 2.4 introduced a static and a dynamic optimization problem of producers. The first is easy to solve by substituting the production function (7) into the profit definition (6) and differentiating with respect to employment, which yields the first-order condition (8). Regarding the dynamic problem, producers maximize profits

$$(127) \qquad \Pi^e_{t+1} = P^e_{t+1}Y^s_{t+1} + (P^e_{t+1} - P_t)K^d_t - \delta\, P^e_{t+1}K^d_t - W^e_{t+1}N^d_{t+1} - i_t B^s_t\,,$$

subject to the production function

$$(128) \qquad Y_{t+1} = F(N_{t+1}, K_t)$$

and the balance sheet

$$(129) \qquad P_t K^d_t = B^s_t\,.$$

Substituting the latter equations into the profit definition and dividing by the expected price level P^e_{t+1}, using (2), yields the following unconstrained optimization problem, where $w = W/P$ represents the real wage rate and r^e_{t+1} is the expected real interest rate defined in equation (4):

$$(130) \qquad \max_{N^d_{t+1}, K^d_t}! \quad F(N^d_{t+1}, K^d_t) - \delta\, K^d_t - w^e_{t+1}N^d_{t+1} - r^e_{t+1}K^d_t\,.$$

Differentiating with respect to the capital stock yields (11), the dynamic optimality condition.

With a Cobb-Douglas production function,

$$(131) \qquad F(N_{t+1,} K_t) = \theta_{t+1} N^{1-\alpha}_{t+1} K^{\alpha}_t\,,$$

the derivatives with respect to the factor demands read

$$(132) \qquad \frac{\partial F}{\partial N^d_t} = \theta_t(1-\alpha)\left(\frac{N^d_t}{K^d_{t-1}}\right)^{-\alpha} \quad \text{and} \quad \frac{\partial F}{\partial K^d_t} = \theta_{t+1}\,\alpha\left(\frac{N^d_{t+1}}{K^d_t}\right)^{1-\alpha}.$$

Substituting into the first-order conditions gives the following factor demand functions and, after inserting optimal labor demand into the production function, the commodity supply function:

$$(133) \qquad N^d_t = \left(\frac{\theta_t(1-\alpha)}{w_t}\right)^{\frac{1}{\alpha}} K^d_{t-1}\,,$$

(134)
$$K_t^d = \left(\frac{\theta_{t+1}\alpha}{r_{t+1}^e + \delta} \right)^{\frac{1}{1-\alpha}} N_{t+1}^d ,$$

(135)
$$Y_t^s = \theta_t^{\frac{1}{\alpha}} \left(\frac{1-\alpha}{w_t} \right)^{\frac{1-\alpha}{\alpha}} K_{t-1}^d .$$

In the simulations, however, labor demand is not calculated from (133) but from an inversion of the production function:

(136)
$$N_t^d = \left(\frac{Y_t}{\theta_t K_{t-1}^{\alpha}} \right)^{\frac{1}{1-\alpha}} .$$

With flexible prices, the output variable on the right-hand side is specified as commodity supply and otherwise as commodity demand. Thus, one and the same labor demand function can be used in all model variants.

Equation (134) determines capital demand as a function of expected labor demand in the next period. Raising all terms to the power of $1-\alpha$ and substituting employment from (136) makes it possible to express capital demand more conveniently as a function of expected output:

(137)
$$K_t^d = \frac{\alpha Y_{t+1}^e}{r_{t+1}^e + \delta} .$$

In the flexible price models, labor demand matches the natural employment level, and capital demand is given by (134), where $N_{t+1}^d = \bar{N}$. With wage or price rigidities, capital demand is instead determined by (137). The inverse determination of factor demands at given output levels represents an application of Clower's (1965) *dual decision hypothesis*. This hypothesis is also implicitly invoked with respect to consumers because the latter take employment as given and revise their consumption and saving decisions accordingly.

To ensure interior solutions, the text uses the Inada (1963) conditions. These have the following meaning: For any capital stock $K > 0$, the premise $N \to 0$ implies $\partial F/\partial N \to \infty$, and $N \to \infty$ implies $\partial F/\partial N \to 0$. Moreover, for any employment level $N > 0$, two analogous implications hold with respect to the marginal productivity of capital. With a positive depreciation rate, however, the net marginal productivity of capital may become negative.

B Consumer Behavior

As outlined in the text, consumers maximize the utility function

(138)
$$U\left(C_t, A_{t+1}^e, \frac{M_t^d}{P_t} \right)$$

subject to the budget constraint

(139) $$P_t C_t + B_t^d + M_t^d = P_t(A_t + X_t).$$

This constraint follows from substituting definitions (13) of financial assets and nonfinancial income into the original budget constraint, (12). An efficient way to obtain the first-order conditions is to transform the constrained optimization problem into an unconstrained problem. To do so, definition (13) of financial assets is shifted one period into the future

(140) $$A_{t+1}^e = \frac{(1+i_t)B_t^d + M_t^d + \sigma_t}{P_{t+1}^e}.$$

Solving for the bond demand

(141) $$B_t^d = \frac{P_{t+1}^e A_{t+1}^e - M_t^d - \sigma_t}{1+i_t},$$

inserting the result into (139) and rearranging terms yields

(142) $$P_t C_t + \frac{P_{t+1}^e A_{t+1}^e}{1+i_t} + \frac{i_t}{1+i_t} M_t^d = P_t(A_t + X_t) + \frac{\sigma_t}{1+i_t}.$$

This can be written in real terms if one divides both sides by the price level and uses definitions (4) and (21) of expected real interest and real seigniorage, respectively:

(143) $$C_t + \frac{A_{t+1}^e}{1+r_{t+1}^e} + \frac{i_t}{1+i_t}\frac{M_t^d}{P_t} = A_t + X_t + \sigma_t^r.$$

The requested unconstrained optimization problem is now obtained by substituting consumption from (143) into the utility function:

(144) $$\max_{A_{t+1}^e, M_t^d/P_t}! \quad U\left(A_t + X_t + \sigma_t^r - \frac{A_{t+1}^e}{1+r_{t+1}^e} - \frac{i_t}{1+i_t}\frac{M_t^d}{P_t}, A_{t+1}^e, \frac{M_t^d}{P_t}\right).$$

Differentiating with respect to financial assets and money balances as the two remaining control variables yields

(145) $$-\frac{\partial U}{\partial C_t}\frac{1}{1+r_{t+1}^e} + \frac{\partial U}{\partial A_{t+1}^e} = 0,$$

(146) $$-\frac{\partial U}{\partial C_t}\frac{i}{1+i_t} + \frac{\partial U}{\partial (M_t^d/P_t)} = 0,$$

from which the first-order conditions (15) and (16) follow, reproduced here for convenience:

(147) $$\frac{\partial U / \partial A_{t+1}^e}{\partial U / \partial C_t} = \frac{1}{1+r_{t+1}^e} \quad \text{and} \quad \frac{\partial U / \partial (M_t^d/P_t)}{\partial U / \partial C_t} = \frac{i_t}{1+i_t}.$$

Logarithmic utility: With a logarithmic utility function of the form

(148) $$U = \ln C_t + \beta \ln A^e_{t+1} + \mu \ln \frac{M^d_t}{P_t},$$

the first-order conditions (147) read

(149) $$A^e_{t+1} = \beta(1+r^e_{t+1})C_t \quad \text{and} \quad \frac{M^d_t}{P_t} = \mu \frac{1+i_t}{i_t} C_t.$$

Putting these values into (143) yields

(150) $$C_t + \beta C_t + \mu C_t = A_t + X_t + \sigma^r_t.$$

This equation can be solved for consumption, yielding (22). Money demand is obtained from (149), and bond demand follows from the budget constraint, (139), as

(151) $$B^d_t = P_t(A_t + X_t - C_t) - M^d_t \cdot$$

CDC utility: To simplify calculations, the outer exponent in (23) is dropped and the function itself is multiplied by $\eta/(1+\eta)$. This increasing transformation (consisting of two decreasing transformations) represents the same preferences as the original utility function:

(152) $$U = \frac{\eta(1+\beta)}{1+\eta}\left(C_t(A^e_{t+1})^\beta\right)^{\frac{1+\eta}{\eta(1+\beta)}} + \frac{\eta\mu^{-1/\eta}}{1+\eta}\left(M^d_t / P_t\right)^{\frac{1+\eta}{\eta}}.$$

Differentiating with respect to the three arguments gives

(153) $$\frac{\partial U}{\partial C_t} = \left(C_t(A^e_{t+1})^\beta\right)^{\frac{1-\eta\beta}{\eta(1+\beta)}}(A^e_{t+1})^\beta = C_t^{\frac{1-\eta\beta}{\eta(1+\beta)}}(A^e_{t+1})^{\frac{\beta(1+\eta)}{\eta(1+\beta)}},$$

(154) $$\frac{\partial U}{\partial A^e_{t+1}} = \left(C_t(A^e_{t+1})^\beta\right)^{\frac{1-\eta\beta}{\eta(1+\beta)}} C_t\beta(A^e_{t+1})^{\beta-1},$$

(155) $$\frac{\partial U}{\partial(M_t / P_t)} = \left(\frac{M^d_t / P_t}{\mu}\right)^{1/\eta}.$$

Inserting the former two derivatives into (147) yields

(156) $$A^e_{t+1} = \beta(1+r^e_{t+1})C_t,$$

just as in the logarithmic case. The derivative with respect to consumption can now be simplified by substituting A^e_{t+1} into (153):

(157) $$\frac{\partial U}{\partial C_t} = C_t^{1/\eta}\left(\beta(1+r^e_{t+1})\right)^{\frac{\beta(1+\eta)}{\eta(1+\beta)}} = \left(\Theta_t C_t\right)^{1/\eta},$$

where the new symbol is defined as

$$(158) \qquad \Theta_t = \left(\beta(1+r^e_{t+1})\right)^{\frac{\beta(1+\eta)}{1+\beta}}.$$

Optimal money demand follows upon substitution of this result together with (155) into the right-hand equation in (147):

$$(159) \qquad \frac{\partial U / \partial (M^d_t / P_t)}{\partial U / \partial C_t} = \left(\frac{M^d_t / P_t}{\mu \Theta_t C_t}\right)^{1/\eta} = \frac{i_t}{1+i_t}.$$

Solving for real balances,

$$(160) \qquad \frac{M^d_t}{P_t} = \mu \Theta_t \left(\frac{i_t}{1+i_t}\right)^{\eta} C_t.$$

This equation shows that η represents the elasticity of money demand with respect to the user cost of money at constant consumption (and a constant expected real interest rate). With the abbreviation

$$(161) \qquad \mu_t = \mu\, \Theta_t \left(\frac{i_t}{1+i_t}\right)^{1+\eta},$$

the demand for real balances becomes

$$(162) \qquad \frac{M^d_t}{P_t} = \mu_t \frac{1+i_t}{i_t} C_t.$$

Explicit solutions follow from putting terminal financial assets, (156), and money demand, (162), into the budget constraint, (143):

$$(163) \qquad C_t + \beta C_t + \mu_t C_t = A_t + X_t + \sigma^r_t.$$

Solving for consumption and money balances yields the final results

$$(164) \qquad C_t = \frac{A_t + X_t + \sigma^r_t}{1+\beta+\mu_t},$$

$$(165) \qquad M^d_t = \mu_t \frac{P_t(A_t + X_t + \sigma^r_t)}{1+\beta+\mu_t} \left(\frac{1+i_t}{i_t}\right).$$

In the two utility specifications, μ and μ_t are small relative to $1+\beta$. Therefore, consumption demand is essentially the same for logarithmic and CDC utility. Money demand, however, comes with an interest elasticity that can be freely selected. Bond demand as the third choice variable still follows from (151).

C Walras' Law

In the preceding period, consumers held the money stock, $M^d_{t-1} \equiv M_{t-1}$. Adding the central bank's balance sheet and earning statement, (5), with the time index shifted back, and substituting this identity yields the further identity

$M^d_{t-1} + \sigma_{t-1} \equiv (1+i_{t-1})B^{cb}_{t-1}$. Moreover, all bonds issued in the preceding periods were held by consumers and the central bank, giving rise to the identity $B^d_{t-1} + B^{cb}_{t-1} = B^s_{t-1}$. As a result, the consumers' budget constraint, (12), can be rewritten as

(166) $$P_t C_t + B^d_t + M^d_t = (1+i_{t-1})B^s_{t-1} + W_t N_t + \Pi_t.$$

The balance sheet (10) implies $P_{t-1}K^d_{t-1} = B^s_{t-1}$. Substituting this into the profit definition yields

(167) $$\Pi_t = P_t Y^s_t + (1-\delta)P_t K^d_{t-1} - W_t N^d_t - (1+i_{t-1})B^s_{t-1}.$$

In the next step, profit and the natural employment level are substituted into the budget constraint to yield

(168) $$P_t C_t + B^d_t + M^d_t = W_t \bar{N} + P_t Y^s_t + (1-\delta)P_t K^d_{t-1} - W_t N^d_t .$$

The equation of motion, (1), and the balance sheet can be combined and written as $(1-\delta)P_t K^d_{t-1} = P_t K^d_t - P_t I_t = B^s_t - P_t I_t$. Substituting this expression into (168), adding $B^{cb}_t = M_t$ from (5) and rearranging terms yields the final result:

(169) $$P_t(C_t + I_t - Y^s_t) + W_t(N^d_t - \bar{N}) + (B^d_t + B^{cb}_t - B^s_t) + (M^d_t - M_t) = 0.$$

D Existence

It is sometimes argued that monetary models with perfectly flexible wages and prices behave like RBC models, cf. Benassy (1995: 312). If true, such a view implied that monetary models would only become interesting if one added price or wage rigidities. The following considerations, however, suggest that the mere presence of money raises specific existence problems that do not show up in RBC models. This issue is often ignored in the literature.

Preparing this and a later proof, a useful identity is derived first. As the left-hand sides of equations (139) and (168) are identical, it follows that

(170) $$A_t + X_t = Y^s_t + (1-\delta)K^d_{t-1} + w_t(\bar{N} - N^d_t).$$

To simplify the exposition, the following proposition makes overly strong assumptions and reveals two distinct possible causes of nonexistence of equilibrium. After the proof, the assumptions are relaxed. Note that the proposition is not restricted to steady states but pertains to arbitrary temporary equilibria.

Existence of equilibrium: For all $\alpha, \beta, \theta, K^d_t > 0$ and $\eta \leq 0$, a unique temporary equilibrium exists if $\pi^e_t \geq 0$, $\delta = 0$ and $\lambda = 0$.

Proof: The proof proceeds in four steps and shows existence of a triple (P^*_t, i^*_t, W^*_t) such that all markets clear.

Step 1: The condition $N^d_t = \bar{N}$ is met for a unique real wage rate. This follows from $K^d_{t-1} > 0$ and the Inada properties of the production function. Hence, labor market equilibrium defines a function $W_t(P_t) = \partial F(\bar{N}, K_{t-1}^d) / \partial N_t^d \times P_t$. Equation (170) implies that $A_t + X_t$ is constant for $W_t = W_t(P_t)$ because its first summand depends only on the equilibrium real wage rate, the second is predetermined, and the third vanishes.

Step 2: Similarly, the equilibrium condition $M_t^d = M_t$ defines an implicit function $P_t(i_t)$. To see this, substitute $\sigma_t = i_t M_t$ into money demand, (165),

$$(171)\; M_t^d = \mu_t \frac{P_t(A_t + X_t) + \frac{\sigma_t}{1+i_t}}{1+\beta+\mu_t}\frac{1+i_t}{i_t} = \frac{\mu_t\left(P_t(A_t + X_t)\frac{1+i_t}{i_t} + M_t\right)}{1+\beta+\mu_t},$$

set money demand equal to the money stock,

$$(172)\qquad \frac{M_t}{P_t} = \mu_t \frac{A_t + X_t}{1+\beta}\frac{1+i_t}{i_t},$$

and solve for the price level:

$$(173)\qquad P_t(i_t) = \frac{M_t(1+\beta)}{\mu_t(A_t + X_t)}\left(\frac{i_t}{1+i_t}\right).$$

Since μ_t is independent of the price level for $\lambda = 0$ and $A_t + X_t$ is constant for $W_t = W_t(P_t)$, as shown in the first step, this represents an explicit solution for the price level as a function of the nominal interest rate.

Step 3: The commodity market is considered next. For any nominal interest rate, $i_t > 0$, consumption demand assumes a particularly simple form if the price level and the nominal wage rate are given by $P_t(i_t)$ and $W_t(P_t(i_t))$. This becomes evident from equating (162) and (172) and making use of the identity $A_t + X_t = K_{t-1}^d + Y_t^s$, which follows from (170) for $\delta = 0$ at labor market equilibrium:

$$(174)\qquad C_t = \frac{A_t + X_t}{1+\beta} = \frac{Y_t^s + K_{t-1}^d}{1+\beta}.$$

Excess commodity demand is defined as $EY_t = C_t + I_t - Y_t^s$. Substituting consumption and investment demand, which reads $I_t = K_t^d - K_{t-1}^d$ under zero depreciation, excess commodity demand satisfies

$$(175)\qquad EY_t = \frac{Y_t^s + K_{t-1}^d}{1+\beta} + K_t^d - K_{t-1}^d - Y_t^s.$$

With prices and wages set in accordance with $P_t(i_t)$ and $W_t(P_t(i_t))$, changes in the nominal interest rate only affect K_t^d. The following conclusions make use of the Inada properties of the production function: For $i_t \to 0$, the capital stock grows without bound owing to the above assumptions, such that the denominator in (134) vanishes. Consequently, EY_t becomes positive. For $i_t \to \infty$, the desired capital stock converges to zero, and the excess demand

$EY_t = K_t^d - \beta/(1+\beta) \times (Y_t^s + K_{t-1}^d)$ becomes negative. Continuity and strict monotonicity of the marginal productivity of capital ensure that there exists a unique $i_t^* > 0$ in between such that EY_t vanishes.

Step 4: Setting $P_t^* = P_t(i_t^*)$ and $W_t^* = W_t(P_t(i_t^*))$, the three equilibrium conditions $N_t^d = \bar{N}$, $M_t^d = M_t$ and $C_t + I_t = Y_t^s$ are fulfilled by construction. Walras' law implies a bond market equilibrium, $B_t^s = B_t^d + B_t^{cb}$, which completes the proof.

While the premise $\pi_t^e \geq 0$ is often fulfilled, the other two assumptions are really restrictive. Their function is to rule out two distinct existence problems:

First, if $\delta > 0$, the third step in the proof need not go through. This step makes use of the fact that capital demand diverges if the interest rate approaches zero. With a positive rate of depreciation, however, $i_t \to 0$ need not imply that the user cost of capital vanishes. If investment demand only becomes sufficiently large at a *negative* nominal interest rate, an equilibrium does not exist; the assumed utility function precludes such rates. This possibility is referred to as a malign liquidity trap. RBC models are not exposed to such a risk: In the absence of a nominal interest rate, the real rate can become negative by all means, which suffices to establish existence of equilibrium.

Second, if $\lambda > 0$, an altogether different problem emerges. Technically, the third step in the proof remains valid if

$$\lim_{i_t \to 0} r_{t+1}^e = 0 \quad \text{and} \quad \lim_{i_t \to \infty} r_{t+1}^e = \infty. \tag{176}$$

These conditions are obviously met under exogenous inflation expectations, $\lambda = 0$. With endogenous expectations, changes in nominal interest rates affect inflation expectations through $P_t(i_t)$ and can have adverse effects on the real rates. In such cases, price spirals emerge that rule out existence of equilibrium.

To conclude, the above proposition clarifies that competitive equilibria need not exist under all circumstances. They do exist if the parameters λ and δ are small enough; otherwise, price spirals and malign liquidity traps are conceivable in theory. As argued in subsection 3.1.3 and section 4.1, however, these instances of non-existence of equilibrium have implausible empirical implications.

E Superneutrality

Money is superneutral in the sense that changes in its growth rate have no impact on real variables other than real balances. This proposition can be shown to hold for temporary equilibria generally, not only for steady states. The proposition is now stated in formal terms and proven.

Superneutrality: Consider two unique temporary equilibria that are associated with two distinct money growth rates. Then, the two equilibria feature identical levels of output, consumption, investment, and employment.

Proof: The two corresponding equilibrium price levels are denoted as P_t^* and P_t^{**}, respectively. If nominal wage rates satisfy

$$\frac{W_t^{**}}{W_t^*} = \frac{P_t^{**}}{P_t^*}, \tag{177}$$

equilibrium real wages are the same. There is no change in labor demand and commodity supply, see (133) and (135), because these depend only on the real wage rate and the initial capital stock. Similarly, if nominal interest rates satisfy

$$\frac{1+i_t^{**}}{1+i_t^*} = \frac{1+\pi_t^{e**}}{1+\pi_t^{e*}}, \tag{178}$$

expected real interest rates are the same. There is no change in investment demand, see (134) and (1), because investment demand depends only on the expected real interest rate, the initial capital stock, and the exogenous future employment, $N_{t+1}^d = \bar{N}$.

To establish superneutrality, it remains to be shown that there is no change in equilibrium consumption. Labor market equilibrium and the constancy of the real wage rate imply, through (170), that the sum $A_t + X_t$ is identical in both equilibria. Equation (174), then, entails that consumption demand also remains unchanged.

While the proof made use of the baseline model, it can easily be generalized in two directions. First, superneutrality holds for any production function with constant returns to scale and strictly diminishing marginal productivities. This becomes obvious if one checks the above steps, which do not exploit the specific properties of Cobb-Douglas production functions. Second, the CDC utility function can be replaced by any utility function that is strictly monotonic, strictly quasi-concave, and separable in real balances, with indifference surfaces bounded away from the axes. Under these assumptions, the optimization program outlined in appendix B entails that consumers stick to their original intertemporal choices if the central bank accelerates money growth.

The superneutrality proposition holds for all real variables except real money balances. A simple corollary regarding the latter can be inferred from equation (172), which is rewritten here in the following form:

$$\frac{M_t}{P_t} = \mu\,\Theta_t \frac{A_t + X_t}{1+\beta}\left(\frac{i_t}{1+i_t}\right)^{\eta}. \tag{179}$$

Owing to superneutrality, all variables except real balances and the nominal interest rate are independent of the money growth rate. Since $\eta < 0$, it is obvious that an increase in money growth, which spurs inflation and the nominal interest rate, reduces equilibrium real balances.

F Fiscal Model

The fiscal model outlined in section 3.3 does not require any changes in producers' optimal response functions. As indicated in the text, consumers maximize

$$(180) \qquad U\left(C_t, \mathring{A}^e_{t+1}, \frac{M^d_t}{P_t}\right),$$

where $\mathring{A}^e_{t+1} = [(1+i_t)B^d_t + M^d_t]/P^e_{t+1}$, subject to the budget constraint

$$(181) \qquad P_t C_t + B^d_t + M^d_t = P_t(\mathring{A}_t + X_t) - P_t T_t .$$

Moving through the steps in appendix B shows that the budget constraint in real terms, (143), becomes

$$(182) \qquad C_t + \frac{\mathring{A}^e_{t+1}}{1+r^e_{t+1}} + \frac{i_t}{1+i_t}\frac{M^d_t}{P_t} = \mathring{A}_t + X_t - T_t .$$

With this modification, it is easy to show that consumers' optimal responses satisfy

$$(183) \qquad C_t = \frac{\mathring{A}_t + X_t - T_t}{1+\beta+\mu} \quad \text{and} \quad M^d_t = \mu \frac{P_t(\mathring{A}_t + X_t - T_t)}{1+\beta+\mu}\frac{1+i_t}{i_t}$$

for the logarithmic utility function. Solutions for the CCD utility functions are analogous; one only needs to substitute μ_t for μ in the preceding equations. In any case, bond demand can be inferred from the budget constraint:

$$(184) \qquad B^d_t = P_t(\mathring{A}_t + X_t - C_t - T_t) - M^d_t .$$

In the Ricardian version of the fiscal model, consumers maximize

$$(185) \qquad U(C_t, \mathring{A}^e_{t+1} - D^g_{t+1}, \frac{M^d_t}{P_t})$$

subject to the same budget constraint, (181). From the definitions of financial assets and public debt, (35) and (40), it follows that perceived financial assets, the second argument in the utility function, equal

$$(186) \qquad \mathring{A}^e_{t+1} - D^g_{t+1} = \frac{(1+i_t)(B^d_t - B^g_t) + M^d_t + \sigma_t}{P^e_{t+1}} .$$

Solving for the bond demand yields

$$(187) \qquad B^d_t = \frac{P^e_{t+1}(\mathring{A}^e_{t+1} - D^g_{t+1}) - M^d_t - \sigma_t}{1+i_t} + B^g_t .$$

Substituting into (181) and dividing by the price level yields an intermediate budget constraint in real terms:

$$(188)\qquad C_t + \frac{\mathring{A}^e_{t+1} - D^g_{t+1}}{1 + r^e_{t+1}} + \frac{i_t}{1+i_t}\frac{M^d_t}{P_t} = \mathring{A}_t + X_t + \sigma^r_t - T_t - \frac{B^g_t}{P_t}.$$

In the final step, B^g_t is replaced using (34) and (40):

$$(189)\qquad C_t + \frac{\mathring{A}^e_{t+1} - D^g_{t+1}}{1 + r^e_{t+1}} + \frac{i_t}{1+i_t}\frac{M^d_t}{P_t} = \mathring{A}_t + X_t + \sigma^r_t - G_t - D^g_t.$$

With a logarithmic utility function, the solutions follow from using (149), where $\mathring{A}^e_{t+1} - D^g_{t+1}$ replaces A^e_{t+1}, and this budget constraint:

$$(190)\qquad \begin{aligned} C_t &= \frac{\mathring{A}_t + X_t + \sigma^r_t - G_t - D^g_t}{1+\beta+\mu}, \\ M^d_t &= \mu\frac{P_t(\mathring{A}_t + X_t + \sigma^r_t - G_t - D^g_t)}{1+\beta+\mu}\frac{1+i_t}{i_t}. \end{aligned}$$

The treatment of the CCD function is perfectly analogous; one needs to substitute (156) and (162) into the budget constraint. The result parallels (183), with μ_t replacing μ. Bond demand follows from (184) in both cases.

Ricardian equivalence is a straightforward consequence: As taxes do not affect consumption and money demand and have no influence on producers' decisions, the only consequence of a change in taxes is a corresponding change in bond demand. By Walras' law, these two changes must coincide.

G Borrowing Constraints

The presence of an exogenous borrowing limit does not affect the static optimization problem that yields output and labor demand. To derive capital demand, one considers the intertemporal optimization problem where producers maximize

$$(191)\qquad \Pi^e_{t+1} = P^e_{t+1}Y^s_{t+1} + (P^e_{t+1} - P_t)K^d_t - \delta P^e_{t+1}K^d_t - W^e_{t+1}N^d_{t+1} - i_t B^s_t,$$

subject to the production function

$$(192)\qquad Y_{t+1} = F(N_{t+1}, K_t),$$

the balance sheet

$$(193)\qquad P_t K^d_t = B^s_t,$$

and the borrowing constraint

$$(194)\qquad B^s_t \le \overline{B}_t.$$

Combined, the balance sheet and the borrowing constraint constitute the financing constraint, $P_t K^d_t \le \overline{B}_t$. Substituting the production function and the borrowing constraint into the profit function and adding a multiplier times the financing constraint gives the Lagrangean

(195)
$$\mathcal{L} = P^e_{t+1}[F(N^d_{t+1}, K^d_t) + (1-\delta)K^d_t] - W^e_{t+1}N^d_{t+1} \\ -(1+i_t)P_t K^d_t - \xi_t(P_t K^d_t - \bar{B}_t).$$

Dividing by expected prices and differentiating yields the first-order condition

(196)
$$\frac{\partial F}{\partial K^d_t} = r^e_{t+1} + \delta + \frac{\xi_t}{1+\pi^e_{t+1}}$$

and the complementary slackness condition, $\xi_t(P_t K^d_t - \bar{B}_t) = 0$. The borrowing constraint's shadow price, ξ_t, vanishes if the constraint is not binding; in this case, the first-order condition reduces to (11). If the borrowing constraint binds, the shadow price becomes generically strictly positive, and the marginal productivity of capital exceeds the user cost. In either case, producers' effective capital demand can be calculated as

(197)
$$\min\left\{K^d_t, \bar{B}_t / P_t\right\},$$

where K^d_t equals conventional capital demand as determined by (134) in the baseline model and by (137) in models with price or wage rigidities.

Section 4.2 presented the following proposition that has not yet been proven. The proof below presumes logarithmic utility, which entails a very specific result.

Credit crunch: Assume a stationary state with unconstrained credit of the amount B^*. Introducing a borrowing limit $\bar{B} \in (0; B^*)$ leaves output, employment, capital and consumption unaffected, diminishes prices and wages by $\bar{B} / B^*$, and decreases interest. Moreover, the marginal productivity exceeds the user cost of capital.

Proof: The proposition assumes the existence of a triple (P^*, i^*, W^*) supporting the original unconstrained equilibrium and asserts the existence of a triple $(\bar{P}, \bar{i}, \bar{W})$ supporting the same equilibrium in the presence of a borrowing constraint. Moreover, it asserts

(198)
$$\bar{P} = \frac{\bar{B}}{B^*}P^*, \quad \bar{W} = \frac{\bar{B}}{B^*}W^*, \quad \bar{i} < i^*.$$

Step 1: Real wages are obviously the same, $\bar{w} = w^*$. Therefore, (133) and (135) imply that producers leave labor demand and commodity supply unchanged.

Step 2: Through (174), constancy of commodity supply and labor demand entails that consumers stick to their original consumption plan in equilibrium. As the money stock is constant and the price level becomes diminished by hypothesis, the demand for real balances, given by the right-hand equation in (149), increases, implying that the equilibrium user cost of money must fall. Because money demand is unit elastic in the case of a logarithmic utility function, $\bar{i}/(1+\bar{i}) = \bar{B}/B^* \times i^*/(1+i^*)$.

Step 3: Financing satisfies $P^*K = B^*$ in the unconstrained and $\bar{P}K = \bar{B}$ in the constrained case. With prices falling in proportion to credit, it is *feasible* for producers to stick to the original capital demand. Zero expected inflation implies that nominal and expected real interest rates coincide: The fall in nominal interest induces a corresponding reduction in expected real interest. As a result, it is also *optimal* for producers to stick to the original investment demand.

Step 4: Summarizing the preceding steps, optimal private choices remain unchanged, preserving equilibrium in the commodity and labor market. The reduction in nominal interest ensures that money demand equals the given money stock. From Walras' law, (169), bond demand and bond supply must coincide. Hence, all equilibrium conditions in (58) remain satisfied, which completes the proof.

The assumption of logarithmic utility was used in the second step where it implied that the borrowing limit reduces the user cost of money commensurately. With a more general CDC utility function, one only derives an unspecific reduction in the user cost of money. In this case, one must assume $i < 13.9$ percent under the standard parameterization. Beyond this threshold, money demand would increase in nominal and real interest, as can be inferred from (160). The qualification of a nominal interest rate below 13.9 percent seems innocuous in the neighborhood of the ZLB.

H Net Worth

As indicated in the text, consumers optimize in accordance with the following budget constraint, where actual disbursements replace profit income:

$$(199) \qquad P_t C_t + B_t^d + M_t^d = (1+i_{t-1})B_{t-1}^d + M_{t-1}^d + \sigma_{t-1} + W_t N_t + Z_t .$$

This reformulation of the original budget constraint, (12), respects that only disbursements constitute a cash inflow. Rational consumers, however, perceive initial net worth plus profit as part of their personal wealth, because the sum $E_{t-1} + \Pi_t$ makes up the maximal disbursement (or the revenue from selling the business) available for current and future consumption. Therefore, a consumer's perceived budget constraint in real terms parallels equation (143), with initial equity as an additional term:

$$(200) \qquad C_t + \frac{A_{t+1}^e}{1+r_{t+1}^e} + \frac{i_t}{1+i_t}\frac{M_t^d}{P_t} = A_t + X_t + \sigma_t^r + \frac{E_{t-1}}{P_t},$$

Applying the steps in appendix B analogously yields the following demand functions for logarithmic utility

$$(201) \qquad C_t = \frac{A_t + X_t + \sigma_t^r + E_{t-1}/P_t}{1+\beta+\mu},$$

(202) $$M_t^d = \mu \frac{P_t(A_t + X_t + \sigma_t^r) + E_{t-1}}{1+\beta+\mu}\left(\frac{1+i_t}{i_t}\right).$$

For CDC utility, one simply replaces μ by μ_t. Crucially, the bond demand is not calculated from the perceived but from the actual budget constraint to keep the model consistent and to preserve Walras' law.

Regarding producers, net worth does not change the profit definition, (9). Using the balance sheet, $P_t K_t^d = B_t^s + E_t$, this definition reads

(203) $$\Pi_{t+1}^e = P_{t+1}^e Y_{t+1}^s + (P_{t+1}^e - P_t)K_t^d - \delta P_{t+1}^e K_t^d - W_{t+1}^e N_{t+1}^d - i_t(P_t K_t^d - E_t).$$

The adding-up theorem for linear homogeneous functions allows output to be written in terms of marginal productivities:

(204) $$Y_{t+1}^s = \frac{\partial F}{\partial N_{t+1}^d} N_{t+1}^d + \frac{\partial F}{\partial K_t^d} K_t^d.$$

Substituting the latter equation into the former, labor drops out because of the first-order condition, $P_{t+1}^e \partial F / \partial N_{t+1}^d = W_{t+1}^e$. This yields

(205) $$\begin{aligned} \Pi_{t+1}^e &= P_{t+1}^e\left(\frac{\partial F}{\partial K_t^d} + 1 - \delta\right)K_t^d - (1+i_t)P_t K_t^d + i_t E_t \\ &= (1+\pi_{t+1}^e)\left(\frac{\partial F}{\partial K_t^d} + 1 - \delta\right)P_t K_t^d - (1+\pi_{t+1}^e)(1+r_{t+1}^e)P_t K_t^d + i_t E_t \\ &= (1+\pi_{t+1}^e)\left(\frac{\partial F}{\partial K_t^d} - \delta - r_{t+1}^e\right)P_t K_t^d + i_t E_t \end{aligned}$$

as an alternative representation of profit. Using the shadow price of the credit constraint defined in (196) and the balance sheet simplifies the expression:

(206) $$\Pi_{t+1}^e = i_t E_t + \xi_t P_t K_t^d.$$

This formula shows the two factors that render competitive profits positive in an equilibrium with fulfilled expectations: Net worth reduces interest payments, and a possible credit limit pushes the net marginal productivity of capital above the expected real interest rate. The formula can be used to derive the WACC in terms of constrained borrowing. The first summand equals $i_t(E_t + B_t) - i_t B_t$, the second equals $\xi_t(E_t + B_t)$. Substituting and rearranging gives

(207) $$i_t + \xi_t = \frac{\Pi_{t+1}^e}{E_t}\frac{E_t}{E_t + B_t} + i_t \frac{B_t}{E_t + B_t}.$$

The WACC on the left-hand side are defined as *interest plus shadow price*. They equal the weighted arithmetic average of the return on equity and the nominal interest rate, with the equity ratio and the loan-to-value ratio as weights.

Borrowing constraints of the form $P_t K_t^d \le E_{t-1} + \overline{B}_t$ do not raise difficulties in the net worth model and can be handled as described in the previous appendix. In particular, the emerging first-order conditions are the same. However, combining constrained credit with non-negative disbursements produces a tricky problem. In a consistent model, feasible investment satisfies the balance sheet, $P_t K_t^d = E_t + B_t^s$, introduced as equation (67) in the text. If the borrowing constraint and the non-negativity constraint both bind and if producer incur a loss, the equation of motion for net worth implies $E_t < E_{t-1}$, which means that the equity available at the end of the period does not suffice to finance the capital purchases made at the beginning. In this exceptional case, the model assumes that creditors grant emergency loans to avoid illiquidity of otherwise solvent producers. In practice, such concerns seem to be built into the loan-to-value ratio accepted by creditors. The lower this ratio, the more emergency credit can be granted without serious hazard.

I Real Estate

Following the assumptions made in the text, producers maximize profits

$$\begin{aligned} \Pi_{t+1}^e &= P_{t+1}^e Y_{t+1}^s + (P_{t+1}^e - P_t) K_t^d - \delta P_{t+1}^e K_t^d + (Q_{t+1}^e - Q_t) L_t^d \\ &\quad - W_{t+1}^e N_{t+1}^d - i_t B_t^s \end{aligned} \tag{208}$$

subject to the production function

$$Y_{t+1} = F(N_{t+1}, K_t, L_t) \tag{209}$$

and the balance sheet

$$P_t K_t^d + Q_t L_t^d = B_t^s . \tag{210}$$

Substituting the production function and the balance sheet into the profit function and dividing by the expected price level entails the following unconstrained optimization problem:

$$\begin{aligned} \max_{N_{t+1}^d, K_t^d, L_t^d}! \; & F(N_{t+1}^d, K_t^d, L_t^d) + (1-\delta) K_t^d + q_{t+1}^e L_t^d \\ & - w_{t+1}^e N_{t+1}^d - (1 + r_{t+1}^e)(K_t^d + q_t L_t^d). \end{aligned} \tag{211}$$

Differentiating yields the standard first-order conditions for optimal labor and capital demand as well as a new condition for optimal land demand:

$$\frac{\partial F}{\partial L_t^d} = q_t (r_{t+1}^e - \hat{q}_{t+1}^e) . \tag{212}$$

Employing the Cobb-Douglas production function assumed in Chapter 6, $F(N_{t+1}, K_t, L_t) = \theta_{t+1} N_{t+1}^{1-\alpha-\rho} K_t^{\alpha} L_t^{\rho}$, the first-order conditions read:

$$\frac{\partial F}{\partial N_t^d} = \theta_t (1-\alpha-\rho)\left(N_t^d\right)^{-(\alpha+\rho)} K_{t-1}^{\alpha} L_{t-1}^{\rho} = w_t,$$

(213) $$\frac{\partial F}{\partial K_t^d} = \theta_{t+1}\, \alpha \left(N_{t+1}^d\right)^{1-\alpha-\rho} \left(K_t^d\right)^{\alpha-1} \left(L_t^d\right)^{\rho} = r_{t+1}^e + \delta,$$

$$\frac{\partial F}{\partial L_t^d} = \theta_{t+1}\, \rho \left(N_{t+1}^d\right)^{1-\alpha-\rho} \left(K_t^d\right)^{\alpha} \left(L_t^d\right)^{\rho-1} = q_t (r_{t+1}^e - \hat{q}_{t+1}^e).$$

The first condition gives labor demand:

(214) $$N_t^d = \left(\frac{\theta_t (1-\alpha-\rho)}{w_t} K_{t-1}^{\alpha} L_{t-1}^{\rho}\right)^{\frac{1}{\alpha+\rho}}.$$

Dividing the second and third condition yields

(215) $$\frac{q_t L_t^d}{K_t^d} = \Phi_t, \quad \text{where} \quad \Phi_t = \frac{\rho}{\alpha} \frac{r_{t+1}^e + \delta}{r_{t+1}^e - \hat{q}_{t+1}^e}.$$

The last expressions make it possible to replace land demand in the second equation in (213) and to solve for capital demand. Analogously, it allows substituting capital demand in the third condition and to solve for land demand. This yields two explicit factor demand functions:

(216) $$K_t^d = \left(\frac{\theta_{t+1}\, \alpha (\Phi_t / q_t)^{\rho}}{r_{t+1} + \delta}\right)^{\frac{1}{1-\alpha-\rho}} N_{t+1}^d,$$

(217) $$L_t^d = \left(\frac{\theta_{t+1}\, \rho (\Phi_t / q_t)^{-\alpha}}{q_t (r_{t+1} - \hat{q}_{t+1}^e)}\right)^{\frac{1}{1-\alpha-\rho}} N_{t+1}^d.$$

Optimal commodity supply follows from substituting labor demand into the production function:

(218) $$Y_t = \theta_t^{\frac{1}{\alpha+\rho}} \left(\frac{1-\alpha-\rho}{w_t}\right)^{\frac{1-\alpha-\rho}{\alpha+\rho}} K_{t-1}^{\frac{\alpha}{\alpha+\rho}} L_{t-1}^{\frac{\rho}{\alpha+\rho}}.$$

As in the baseline model, labor demand is calculated from an inversion of the production function:

(219) $$N_t^d = \left(\frac{Y_t}{\theta_t K_{t-1}^{\alpha} L_{t-1}^{\rho}}\right)^{\frac{1}{1-\alpha-\rho}}.$$

With flexible prices, output equals the profit maximizing commodity supply, Y_t^s. Under price rigidities, output equals commodity demand. Analogously to the treatment in appendix A, the above capital and land demand functions assume that future labor demand coincides with the given labor supply, $\bar{N}$. Price and wage rigidities invalidate this assumption and require expressing the factor demands as functions of expected output, which is still determined by (49).

In this case, capital and land demand are obtained from inversions of the production function:

$$(220)\quad \begin{aligned} \frac{\partial F[F^{-1}(Y^e_{t+1},K^d_t,L^d_t),K^d_t,L^d_t]}{\partial K^d_t} &= r^e_{t+1}+\delta\,, \\ \frac{\partial F[F^{-1}(Y^e_{t+1},K^d_t,L^d_t),K^d_t,L^d_t]}{\partial L^d_t} &= q_t(r^e_{t+1}-\hat{q}^e_{t+1})\,. \end{aligned}$$

The assumed Cobb-Douglas production function yields the following explicit demand functions:

$$(221)\quad K^d_t = \frac{\alpha Y^e_{t+1}}{r^e_{t+1}+\delta}\,,$$

$$(222)\quad L^d_t = \frac{\rho Y^e_{t+1}}{q_t(r^e_{t+1}-\hat{q}^e_{t+1})}\,.$$

The model with land, net worth, and constrained borrowing combines the preceding approaches. Firms maximize profit

$$(223)\quad \begin{aligned} \Pi^e_{t+1} = {} & P^e_{t+1}Y^s_{t+1} + (P^e_{t+1}-P_t)K^d_t - \delta\, P^e_{t+1}K^d_t + (Q^e_{t+1}-Q_t)L^d_t \\ & - W^e_{t+1}N^d_{t+1} - i_t B^s_t \end{aligned}\,,$$

subject to the production function

$$(224)\quad Y_{t+1} = F(N_{t+1},K_t,L_t)\,,$$

the balance sheet

$$(225)\quad P_t K^d_t + Q_t L^d_t = E_t + B^s_t\,,$$

and the borrowing constraint

$$(226)\quad B^s_t \le \overline{B}_t = lr \times E_{t-1}\,.$$

A Lagrangean is formed by substituting the production function into profit and adding a multiplier times the combined financing constraint:

$$(227)\quad \begin{aligned} \mathcal{L} = {} & P^e_{t+1}[F(N^d_{t+1},K^d_t,L^d_t)+(1-\delta)K^d_t] + Q^e_{t+1}L^d_t - W^e_{t+1}N^d_{t+1} \\ & -(1+i_t)(P_t K^d_t + Q_t L^d_t) - \xi_t(P_t K^d_t + Q_t L^d_t - \overline{B}_t)\,. \end{aligned}$$

Dividing by the expected price level gives the first-order conditions for optimal capital and land demand:

$$(228)\quad \begin{aligned} \frac{\partial F}{\partial K^d_t} &= r^e_{t+1} + \delta + \frac{\xi_t}{1+\pi^e_{t+1}}\,, \\ \frac{\partial F}{\partial L^d_t} &= q_t\Big(r^e_{t+1} - \hat{q}^e_{t+1} + \frac{\xi_t}{1+\pi^e_{t+1}}\Big)\,. \end{aligned}$$

To get an explicit solution, one eliminates the Lagrangean multiplier:

(229)
$$\frac{\partial F}{\partial K_t^d} - \frac{1}{q_t}\frac{\partial F}{\partial L_t^d} = \delta + \hat{q}_{t+1}^e .$$

Using the derivatives for a Cobb-Douglas production function provided in (213) and substituting land demand $L_t^d = (\bar{B} - P_t K_t^d)/Q_t$ yields an equation whose left-hand side is strictly decreasing in capital demand. This can be solved numerically. The solution is relevant if the borrowing constraint binds; otherwise the explicit demand functions (216) and (217) apply. Optimal labor demand and commodity supply are still given by (213) and (218), respectively, since the borrowing constraint does not affect them. An intuitive characterization of the optimum that resembles (215) is obtained by dividing the first-order conditions to yield:

(230)
$$\frac{q_t L_t^d}{K_t^d} = \frac{\rho}{\alpha} \frac{r_{t+1}^e + \delta + \xi_t}{r_{t+1}^e - \hat{q}_{t+1}^e + \xi_t} .$$

In models with land and constrained credit, dynamic efficiency cannot be assessed by comparisons of interest and growth rates. Rather, one must compare the net marginal productivity of capital with the growth rate, bearing in mind that the former exceeds real interest in the presence of a binding borrowing constraint. The assertion that land ensures dynamic efficiency in a stationary state is true even if the real interest rate happened to be negative. In a stationary state, for instance, (229) can be rewritten as

(231)
$$\frac{\partial F}{\partial K^d} - \delta = \frac{1}{q}\frac{\partial F}{\partial L^d} > 0 .$$

Therefore, the net marginal productivity strictly exceeds the real growth rate, which is zero. However, (228) gives

(232)
$$r = \frac{\partial F}{\partial K^d} - \delta - \frac{\xi}{1+\pi} ,$$

an expression that turns negative for a large enough shadow price. Thus, a net marginal productivity of 2 percent is perfectly compatible with a real interest rate of –2 percent. Dynamic efficiency obtains notwithstanding that $r < n$.

J Commercial Banks

The banking sector introduced in Chapter 7 is easily integrated into any of the preceding general equilibrium models. To keep the necessary changes to a minimum, one defines total seigniorage as the sum of central and commercial bank seigniorage:

(233)
$$\sigma_t = \sigma_t^{cb} + \sigma_t^{b} .$$

On the understanding that total seigniorage is remitted to consumers, the latters' budget constraints, (142), remain unchanged in this respect. Bank profit is the difference between bank seigniorage and cost of deposits. If consumers are entitled to bank seigniorage distributions, they must also bear the cost. Hence, the definition of nonfinancial income from section 2.5 must be extended as follows:

$$X_t = \frac{W_t N_t + \Pi_t - J_t}{P_t}. \tag{234}$$

Finally, real cost J_t / P_t are added to consumption and investment as a part of aggregate demand. These changes keep the model consistent and ensure that equilibrium in the markets for commodities, bonds, labor, and federal funds implies coincidence of deposits and money demand, $D_t = M_t^d$. For the simulations, nominal costs were specified as $J = \gamma / P_t (D_t)^{2}$, where γ is a positive parameter.

K MATLAB Sample Codes

The sample program produces Figure 3.1. It should be easily readable by anyone with some MATLAB experience. Basically, the code declares constants, parameters, and variables first. In the following "output" section, each line refers to those parameters, variables, and functions that are to be included in the output data. By adding or deleting lines, the user can freely select and format the output data without affecting the rest of the program. Thereafter, the "action" function comprises all policy actions or exogenous shocks that influence the model's behavior.

The functions are then defined in a natural way just as in the text above. To prevent error propagation, the definition of initial financial wealth, A, uses the right-hand side of the identity $B_{t-1}^d + B_{t-1}^{cb} \equiv B_{t-1}^s$ because the algorithm finds only approximate solutions for the bond market equilibrium.

The main program loops over a finite set of periods, solves the system of market equilibrium conditions in each period, stores the results in an array, and shifts the state variables. It also calls the action function.

```
function Figure3_1
TMAX=10; NBAR=1; VAR=1;                                    % Constants

theta=1.0; alpha=1/3; delta=0.05; beta=4.0; mu=0.08;      % Parameters
eta=-0.1; lambda=0;

Bcb=3;                                                      % ExoVars
P=6.46862; i=0.05; W=7.87336;                              % EndoVars
P_1=P; i_1=i; K_1=6.085806; Bs_1=P_1*K_1; PiExp_1=0;       % StateVars

% Output to print and plot****************************************
Output = {'Bcb' 'Money stock' [100 103.5 1]          % Function, name,
          'P' 'Price level' [100 103.5 1]   % axes limits, increments
          'Ys' 'Output' [99 101 1]
          'i' 'Nominal interest' [4 6 1]};
```

```
% Periodical actions ***********************************************
function Action()                                   % Insert actions here:
   if t==2 Bcb=3.06; end;
end

% Demand and supply functions, auxiliaries *************************
function A=A()
  A = ((1+i_1)*Bs_1)/P; end
function X=X()
  X = (W*NBAR+PI)/P; end
function Mut=Mut()
  THETA = (beta*(1+rExp))^((beta*(1+eta))/(1+beta));
  Mut = mu*THETA*(i/(1+i))^(1+eta); end
function C=C()
  C = (A+X+i*Bcb/((1+i)*P))/(1+beta+Mut); end
function Md=Md()
  Md = (P*(A+X)+i*Bcb/(1+i))*Mut/(1+beta+Mut)*(1+i)/i; end
function Bd=Bd()
  Bd = P*(A+X-C)-Md; end
function Ys=Ys()
  Ys = theta^(1/alpha)*((1-alpha)/w)^((1-alpha)/alpha)*K_1; end
function Nd=Nd()
  Nd = (Ys/(theta*K_1^alpha))^(1/(1-alpha)); end
function Kd=Kd()
  Kd = (theta*alpha/(rExp+delta))^(1/(1-alpha))*NBAR; end
function I=I()
  I = Kd-(1-delta)*K_1; end
function Bs=Bs()
  Bs = P*Kd; end
function PI=PI()
  PI = P*Ys+(P-P_1)*K_1-delta*P*K_1-W*Nd-i_1*Bs_1; end
function Pi=Pi()
  Pi = P/P_1-1; end
function w=w()
  w = W/P; end
function PiExp=PiExp()
  PiExp = lambda*Pi+(1-lambda)*PiExp_1; end
function rExp=rExp()
  rExp = (1+i)/(1+PiExp)-1; end
function ExcDem=ExcDem(Root)
  Root=num2cell(Root); [P,i,W]=Root{:};           % Change EndoVars
  ExcDem=[C+I-Ys, Bd+Bcb-Bs, Nd-NBAR]; end

% Main program start ***********************************************
clc; clf;
for t=1:TMAX
  ComputeEquilibrium(t,@ExcDem,[P,i,W]);      % Try previous EndoVars
  for Var=1:numel(Output(:,VAR))
    Data(t,Var) = eval(Output{Var,VAR}); end          % Store results
  Bs_1=Bs; K_1=Kd; PiExp_1=PiExp; P_1=P; i_1=i;    % Shift state vars
  Action(); end                                      % Perform action
ShowResults(Output,Data,1,'');                       % Print and plot
end
```

The external function "ComputeEquilibrium" contains an error treatment and solves the system of equations through a call of the function "ExcDem", which returns the market excess demands. Using the fsolve command, the routine works like an auctioneer who adjusts prices in each period until a temporary equilibrium is established. In settings with sticky prices and wages, the auctioneer combines this price tâtonnement with a quantity tâtonnement.

```
function ComputeEquilibrium(t,ExcDem,Start)
  Options = optimoptions('fsolve','Display','none','TolX',1e-8,'Tol-
Fun',1e-7);
  [~,ED,Flag,Output] = fsolve(ExcDem,Start,Options);       Find root
  if Flag<1
    Output
    error('ERROR NO. %d in period %d. PROGRAM STOPPED.',Flag,t); end;
  if Flag>1
    fprintf('FSOLVE: WARNING NO. %d in period %3d. ExcDem = ,,Flag,t);
    fprintf('%+1.3f ',ED); fprintf('\n'); end;
end
```

The program terminates after calling the external function "ShowResults" that prints and plots the data. Each figure in the text is produced from a slight variation or extension of this model. The source codes of the "ShowResults" function and the other codes are available on request.

References

Abel, A. B. (1987) Optimal Monetary Growth. *Journal of Monetary Economics* 19: 437–450.

Adam, K., A. Marcet, and J. P. Nicolini (2016) Stock Market Volatility and Learning. *Journal of Finance* 71: 33–82.

Afonso, G. and R. Lagos (2015) Trade Dynamics in the Market for Federal Funds. *Econometrica* 83: 263–313.

Akerlof, G. A. and R. J. Shiller (2009) *Animal Spirits: How Human Psychology Drives the Economy, and Why It Matters for Global Capitalism.* Princeton: Princeton University Press.

Aiyagari, S. R. (1994) Uninsured Idiosyncratic Risk and Aggregate Saving. *Quarterly Journal of Economics* 109: 659–684.

Aiyagari, S. R. and M. Gertler (1999) "Overreaction" of Asset Prices in General Equilibrium. *Review of Economic Dynamics* 2: 3–35.

Arrow, K. J. and L. Hurwicz (1958) On the Stability of the Competitive Equilibrium, I. *Econometrica* 26: 522–552.

Arrow, K. J. and L. Hurwicz (1959) On the Stability of the Competitive Equilibrium, II. *Econometrica* 27: 82–109.

Attanasio, O., A. Leicester, and M. Wakefield (2011) Do House Prices Drive Consumption Growth? The Coincident Cycles of House Prices and Consumption in the UK. *Journal of the European Economic Association* 9: 399–435.

Azariadis, C. (1981) Self-Fulfilling Prophecies. *Journal of Economic Theory* 25: 380–396.

Bailey, M. J. (1956) The Welfare Cost of Inflationary Finance. *Journal of Political Economy* 64: 93–110.

Banerjee, A. V. and E. S. Maskin (1996) A Walrasian Theory of Money and Barter. *Quarterly Journal of Economics* 111: 955–1005.

Barro, R. J. (1974) Are Government Bonds Net Wealth? *Journal of Political Economy* 82: 1095–1117.

Barro, R. J. (1976) The Loan Market, Collateral, and Rates of Interest. *Journal of Money, Credit, and Banking* 8: 439–456.

Baumol, W. J. (1952) The Transactions Demand for Cash: An Inventory Theoretic Approach. *Quarterly Journal of Economics* 66: 545–556.

Bech, M. L. and C. Monnet (2013) The Impact of Unconventional Monetary Policy on the Overnight Interbank Market. *Reserve Bank of Australia Annual Conference Volume*: 147–177.

Benassy, J.-P. (1995) Money and Wage Contracts in an Optimizing Model of the Business Cylcle. *Journal of Monetary Economics* 35: 303–315.

Benhabib, J., S. Schmitt-Grohé, and M. Uribe (2001) The Perils of Taylor Rules. *Journal of Economic Theory* 96: 40–69.

Berentsen, A., S. Huber, and A. Marchesiani (2015) Financial Innovations, Money Demand, and the Welfare Cost of Inflation. *Journal of Money, Credit, and Banking* 47: 223–261.

Bernanke, B. S. and I. Mihov (1998) The Liquidity Effect and Long-Run Neutrality. *Carnegie-Rochester Conference Series on Public Policy* 49: 149–194.

Bernanke, B. S., V. R. Reinhart, and B. P. Sack (2004) Monetary Policy Alternatives at the Zero Bound: An Empirical Assessment. *Brookings Papers on Economic Activity* 2: 1–100.

Bernheim, B. D. (1987) Ricardian Equivalence: An Evaluation of Theory and Evidence. In: Fischer, S. (ed.), *NBER Macroeconomics Annual*, Vol. 2. Cambridge: MIT Press.

Bernheim, B. D. (2002) Taxation and Saving. In: Auerbach, A. J. and M. S. Feldstein (eds.), *Handbook of Public Economics*, Vol. 3, Chapter 18. Amsterdam: Elsevier.

Bewley, T. F. (1999) *Why Wages Don't Fall During a Recession.* Cambridge: Harvard University Press.

Beznoska, M. and R. Ochmann (2013) The Interest Elasticity of Household Savings: A Structural Approach with German Micro Data. *Empirical Economics* 45: 371–399.

Bils, M. and P. J. Klenow (2004) Some Evidence on the Importance of Sticky Prices. *Journal of Political Economy* 112: 947–985.

Bhattacharya, J., J. Haslag, and S. Russell (2005) The Role of Money in Two Alternative Models: When is the Friedman Rule Optimal, and Why? *Journal of Monetary Economics* 52: 1401–1433.

Blanchard, O. J. and C. M. Kahn (1980) The Solution of Linear Difference Models under Rational Expectations. *Econometrica* 48: 1305–1311.

Blanchard, O. J. and N. Kiyotaki (1987) Monopolistic Competition and the Effects of Aggregate Demand. *American Economic Review* 77: 647–666.

Board of Governors of the Federal Reserve System (1943) *Banking and Monetary Statistics 1914–1941*. Washington, D. C.

Board of Governors of the Federal Reserve System (1976) *Banking and Monetary Statistics 1941–1970*. Washington, D. C.

Board of Governors of the Federal Reserve System (1999) *86th Annual Report.* Washington, D. C.

Boel, P. and G. Camera (2011) The Welfare Cost of Inflation in OECD Countries. *Macroeconomic Dynamics* 15 (supplement 2): 217–251.

Boppart, T. and P. Krusell (2016) Labor Supply in the Past, Present, and Future: A Balanced-Growth Perspective. NBER Working Paper No. 22215.

Borio, C. (2014) The Financial Cycle and Macroeconomics: What Have We Learnt? *Journal of Banking and Finance* 45: 182–198.

Brealey, R. A., S. C. Myers, and F. Allen (2014) *Principles of Corporate Finance*. 11th edition, New York: McGraw-Hill.

Brennan, G. and J. M. Buchanan (1980) *The Power to Tax: Analytical Foundations of a Fiscal Constitution*. Cambridge: Cambridge University Press.

Brock, W. A. (1975) A Simple Perfect Foresight Monetary Model. *Journal of Monetary Economics* 1: 133–150.

Brunnermeier, M. K. (2009) Deciphering the Liquidity and Credit Crunch 2007–2008. *Journal of Economic Perspectives* 23: 77–100.

Brunnermeier, M. K. and Y. Sannikov (2016) On the Optimal Inflation Rate. *American Economic Review (PP)* 106: 484–489.

Buchanan, J. M. and R. E. Wagner (1977) *Democracy in Deficit: The Political Legacy of Lord Keynes*. New York: Academic Press.

Cagan, P. (1956) The Monetary Dynamics of Hyperinflation. In: Friedman, M. (ed.), *Studies in the Quantity Theory of Money*. Chicago: University of Chicago Press.

Calvo, G. A. (1983) Staggered Prices in a Utility Maximizing Framework. *Journal of Monetary Economics* 12: 383–398.

Camera, G. and Y. Chien (2013) Two Monetary Models with Alternating Markets. SAFE Working Paper Series, no. 33.

Campbell, J. Y. and J. F. Cocco (2007) How Do House Prices Affect Consumption? Evidence from Micro Data. *Journal of Monetary Economics* 54: 591–621.

Campbell, J. R., C. L. Evans, J. D. M. Fisher, and A. Justiniano (2012) Macroeconomic Effects of Federal Reserve Forward Guidance. *Brookings Papers on Economic Activity* 1: 1–80.

Carlstrom, C. T. and T. S. Fuerst (2001) Timing and Real Indeterminacy in Monetary Models. *Journal of Monetary Economics* 47: 285–298.

Case, K. E. (2000) Real Estate and the Macroeconomy. *Brookings Papers on Economic Activity* 1: 119–162.

Case, K. E., J. M. Quigley, and R. J. Shiller (2013) Wealth Effects Revisited: 1975–2012. NBER Working Paper 18667.

Chari, V. V., L. J. Christiano, and P. J. Kehoe (1996) Optimality of the Friedman Rule in Economies with Distorting Taxes. *Journal of Monetary Economics* 37: 203–223.

Chetty, R., A. Guren, D. Manoli, and A. Weber (2013) Does Indivisible Labor Explain the Difference between Micro and Macro Elasticities? A Meta-Analysis of Extensive Margin Elasticities. *NBER Macroeconomics Annual* 27: 1–56.

Christiano, L. J. and M. Eichenbaum (1992) Liquidity Effects and the Monetary Transmission Mechanism. *American Economic Review (PP)* 82: 346–353.

Christiano, L. J., M. Eichenbaum, and C. L. Evans (2005) Nominal Rigidities and the Dynamic Effects of a Shock to Monetary Policy. *Journal of Political Economy* 113: 1–45.

Clower, R. W. (1965) The Keynesian Counter-Revolution: A Theoretical Appraisal. In Hahn, F. H. and F. Brechling (eds.), *The Theory of Interest Rates.* London: Macmillan.

Clower, R. W. (1967) A Reconsideration of the Microfoundations of Monetary Theory. *Western Economic Journal* 6: 1–9.

Cochrane, J. H. (2011) Determinacy and Identification with Taylor Rules. *Journal of Political Economy* 119: 565–615.

Colander, D., P. Howitt, A. Kirman, A. Leijonhufvud, and P. Mehrling (2008) Beyond DSGE Models: Toward an Empirically Based Macroeconomics. *American Economic Review (PP)* 98: 236–240.

Constantinides, G. M., J. B. Donaldson, and R. Mehra (2002) Junior Can't Borrow: A New Perspective on the Equity Premium Puzzle. *Quarterly Journal of Economics* 117: 269–296.

Cooley, T. F. and S. F. LeRoy (1981) Identification and Estimation of Money Demand. *American Economic Review* 71: 825–844.

Copernicus, N. (1526) *Monetae Cudendae Ratio.* Cited from Taylor, J. (1955) Copernicus on the Evils of Inflation and the Establishment of a Sound Currency. *Journal of the History of Ideas* 16: 540–547 (544).

Crettez, B., P. Michel, and B. Wigniolle (1999) Cash-in-advance Constraints in the Diamond Overlapping Generations Model: Neutrality and Optimality of Monetary Policies. *Oxford Economic Papers* 51: 431–452.

Davis, M. A. and J. Heathcote (2007) The Price and Quantity of Residential Land in the United States. *Journal of Monetary Economics* 54: 2595–2620.

Deaton, A. and G. Laroque (2001) Housing, Land Prices, and Growth. *Journal of Economic Growth* 6: 87–105.

Degryse, H., M. Kim, and S. Ongena (2009) *Microeconomics of Banking.* Oxford: Oxford University Press.

Diamond, P. A. (1965) National Debt in a Neoclassical Growth Model. *American Economic Review* 55: 1126–1150.

Dixit, A. K. and J. E. Stiglitz (1977) Monopolistic Competition and Optimum Product Diversity. *American Economic Review* 67: 297–308.

Drazen, A. (1981) Inflation and Capital Accumulation under a Finite Horizon. *Journal of Monetary Economics* 8: 247–260.

Economides, G. and T. Moutos (2014) Minimum Wages, Capital Accumulation and Worker's Incomes. CesIfo Working Paper No. 4821.

Eggertsson, G. B. and P. Krugman (2012) Debt, Deleveraging, and the Liquidity Trap: A Fisher-Minsky-Koo Approach. *Quarterly Journal of Economics* 127: 1469–1513.

Eggertsson, G. B. and N. R. Mehrotra (2015) A Model of Secular Stagnation. Bank of Japan IMES discussion paper No. 2015–E–9.

Ennis, H. M. and T. Keister (2008) Understanding Monetary Policy Implementation. *Federal Reserve Bank of New York Research Paper.*

Estrella, A. and J. C. Fuhrer (2002) Dynamic Inconsistencies: Counterfactual Implications of a Class of Rational Expectations Models. *American Economic Review* 92: 1013–1028.

Evans, G. W. and G. Ramey (2006) Adaptive Expectations, Underparameterization and the Lucas Critique. *Journal of Monetary Economics* 53: 249–264.

Evans, G. W. and S. Honkapohja (2001) *Learning and Expectations in Macroeconomics.* Princeton and Oxford: Princeton University Press.

Falk, A. and E. Fehr (1999) Wage Rigidity in a Competitive Incomplete Contract Market. *Journal of Political Economy* 107: 106–134.

Fama, E. F. (1980) Banking in the Theory of Finance. *Journal of Monetary Economics* 6: 39–57.

Feavearyear, A. E. (1931) *The Pound Sterling. A History of English Money.* 2nd edition, Oxford (1963): Clarendon Press.

Feenstra, R. C. (1986) Functional Equivalence Between Liquidity Costs and the Utility of Money. *Journal of Monetary Economics* 17: 271–291.

Fergusson, A. (1975) *When Money Dies. The Nightmare of Deficit Spending, Devaluation and Hyperinflation in Weimar Germany.* London: William Kimber & Co.

Fischer, S. (1982) Seigniorage and the Case for a National Money. *Journal of Political Economy* 90: 295–313.

Fisher, I. (1896) Appreciation and Interest. *Publications of the American Economic Association* 11: 1–98.

Fisher, I. (1926) A Statistical Relation between Unemployment and Price Changes. *International Labour Review*, reprinted 1973 in *Journal of Political Economy* 81: 496–502.

Fisher, I. (1930) *The Theory of Interest.* New York: Augustus M. Kelley Publishers.

Fisher, I. (1933) The Debt-Deflation Theory of Great Depression. *Econometrica* 1: 337–357.

Freixas, X. and J.-C. Rochet (2008) *Microeconomics of Banking.* 2nd edition, Cambridge: MIT Press.

Friedman, M. (1957) *A Theory of the Consumption Function.* Princeton: Princeton University Press.

Friedman, M. (1968) The Role of Monetary Policy. *American Economic Review* 58: 1–17.

Friedman, M. (1969) Factors Affecting the Level of Interest Rates. In: *Proceedings of the 1968 Conference on Saving and Residential Financing.* Chicago: United States Saving and Loan League. Cited from the 1976 reprint in Havrilesky, Boorman, T. M. and J. T. Boorman (eds.), *Current Issues in Monetary Theory and Policy.* Arlington Heights 1976: AHM Publishing.

Friedman, M. (1969) The Optimum Quantity of Money and Other Essays. London: Macmillan.

Friedman, M. and A. J. Schwartz (1963) *A Monetary History of the United States*, 1867–1960. Princeton: Princeton University Press.

Gahvari, F. (1988) Lump-sum Taxation and the Superneutrality and Optimum Quantity of Money in Life Cycle Growth Models. *Journal of Public Economics* 36: 339–367.

Gahvari, F. (2007) The Friedman Rule: Old and New. *Journal of Monetary Economics* 54: 581–589.

Galí, J. (2015) *Monetary Policy, Inflation, and the Business Cycle*. 2nd edition, Princeton and Oxford: Princeton University Press.

Geanakoplos, J. (2009) End the Obsession with Interest. *Nature* 457: 963.

Gesell, S. (1916) *Die natürliche Wirtschaftsordnung*. Cited from the 9th edition, Nuremberg: Rudolf Zitzmann Verlag.

Geweke, J. (1986) The Superneutrality of Money in the United States: An Interpretation of the Evidence. *Econometrica* 54: 1–21.

Goldfeld, S. M. (1976) The Case of the Missing Money. *Brookings Papers on Economic Activity* 3: 683–730.

Gomme, P., B. Ravikumar, and P. Rupert (2011) The Return to Capital and the Business Cycle. *Review of Economic Dynamics* 14: 262–278.

Gordon, R. J. (2013) The Phillips Curve is Alive and Well: Inflation and the NAIRU during the Slow Recovery. NBER Working Paper 19390.

Grandmont, J.-M. (1983) *Money and Value: A Reconsideration of Classical and Neoclassical Monetary Theories*. Cambridge: Cambridge University Press.

Grandmont, J.-M. (1985) On Endogenous Competitive Business Cycles. *Econometrica* 53: 995–1045.

Grandmont, J.-M. (2008) Temporary Equilibrium. In: Durlauf, S. N. and L. E. Blume (eds.), *The New Palgrave Dictionary of Economics*, Vol. 8. 2nd edition, Basingstoke: Macmillan.

Gurley, J. G. and E. S. Shaw (1960) *Money in a Theory of Finance*. Washington: Brookings.

Hall, R. E. (2011) The Long Slump. *American Economic Review* 101: 431–469.

Hansen, A. H. (1951) Classical, Loanable Fund, and Keynesian Interest Theories. *Quarterly Journal of Economics* 65: 429–432.

Haug, A. A. and W. G. Dewald (2012) Money, Output, and Inflation in the Longer Term: Major Industrial Countries, 1880–2001. *Economic Inquiry* 50: 773–787.

Hayek, F. A. (1932) A Note on the Development of the Doctrine of "Forced Saving". *Quarterly Journal of Economics* 47: 123–133.

Heer, B. and A. Maussner (2009) *Dynamic General Equilibrium Modelling. Computational Methods and Applications*. 2nd edition, Berlin: Springer.

Hennessy, C. A. and T. M. Whited (2005) Debt Dynamics. *Journal of Finance* 60: 1129–1165.

Hicks, J. R. (1939) *Value and Capital*. Cited from the 2nd edition (1946), Oxford: Oxford University Press.

Homburg, S. (1991) Interest and Growth in an Economy with Land. *Canadian Journal of Economics* 24: 450–459.

Homburg, S. (2014) Overaccumulation, Public Debt, and the Importance of Land. *German Economic Review* 15: 411–435.

Homburg, S. (2015a) Superneutrality of Money under Open Market Operations. *Review of Economics* 66: 289–302.

Homburg, S. (2015b) Understanding Benign Liquidity Traps: The Case of Japan. Hannover Economic Papers (HEP) No. 557. Forthcoming in: *German Economic Review*.

Homburg, S. (2016) Pure Theory of the Federal Funds Rate. *Review of Economics* 67: 285–296.

Hornstein, A. (2010) Monetary Policy with Interest on Reserves. *Federal Reserve Bank of Richmond Economic Quarterly* 96: 153–177.

Howitt, P. (1992) Interest Rate Control and Nonconvergence to Rational Expectations. *Journal of Political Economy* 100: 776–800.

Huggett, M. (1993) The Risk-Free Rate in Heterogeneous-Agent Incomplete-Insurance Economies. *Journal of Economic Dynamics and Control* 17: 953–969.

Humphrey, T. M. (1986) Cumulative Process Models from Thornton to Wicksell. *Federal Reserve Bank of Richmond Economic Review*: 18–25.

Iacoviello, M. (2005) House Prices, Borrowing Constraints, and Monetary Policy in the Business Cycle. *American Economic Review* 95: 739–764.

Ihrig, J. E., E. E. Meade, and G. C. Weinbach (2015) Rewriting Monetary Policy 101: What's the Fed's Preferred Post-Crisis Approach to Raising Interest Rates? *Journal of Economic Perspectives* 29: 177–198.

Inada, K.-I. (1963) On a Two-Sector Model of Economic Growth: Comments and a Generalization. *Review of Economic Studies* 30: 119–127.

Ireland, P. N. (2005) The Liquidity Trap, the Real Balance Effect, and the Friedman Rule. *International Economic Review* 46: 1271–1301.

Ireland, P. N. (2014) The Macroeconomic Effects of Interest on Reserves. *Macroeconomic Dynamics* 18: 1271–1312.

Jordà, O., M. Schularick, and A. M. Taylor (2014) The Great Mortgaging: Housing Finance, Crises, and Business Cycles. NBER Working Paper No. 20501.

Kimbrough, K. P. (2006) Revenue Maximizing Inflation. *Journal of Monetary Economics* 53: 1967–1978.

Kindleberger, C. P. (1978) *Manias, Panics, and Crashes*. New York: Basic Books.

Kiyotaki, N. and J. Moore (1997) Credit Cycles. *Journal of Political Economy* 105: 211–248.

Knoll, K., M. Schularick, and T. M. Steger (2014) No Price Like Home: Global House Prices, 1870–2012. CesIfo Working Paper No. 5006.

Knolle, J. and K. Lehmann (2016) An Empirical Assessment of Global Capital Productivity. Hannover Economic Papers (HEP) No. 574.

Kocherlakota, N. R. (2000) Creating Business Cycles through Credit Constraints. *Federal Reserve Bank of Minneapolis Quarterly Review* 24: 2–10.

Kydland, F. E. and E. C. Prescott (1977) Rules Rather than Discretion: The Inconsistency of Optimal Plans. *Journal of Political Economy* 85: 473–492.

Lagos, R. and R. Wright (2005) A Unified Framework for Monetary Theory and Policy Analysis. *Journal of Political Economy* 113: 463–484.

Laidler, D. (1993) *The Demand for Money*. 4th edition, New York: HarperCollins.

Larson, W. (2015) New Estimates of Value of Land of the United States. Mimeo, Bureau of Economic Analysis.

Leijonhufvud, A. (1993) Towards a Not-Too-Rational Macroeconomics. *Southern Economic Journal* 60: 1–13.

Lintner, J. (1956) Distribution of Incomes of Corporations Among Dividends, Retained Earnings, and Taxes. *American Economic Review* 46: 97–113.

Liu, Z., P. Wang, and T. Zha (2013) Land-Price Dynamics and Macroeconomic Fluctuations. *Econometrica* 81: 1147–1184.

Ljungqvist, L. and T. J. Sargent (2012) *Recursive Macroeconomic Theory*. 3rd edition, Cambridge: MIT Press.

Lucas, R. E. Jr. (1976) Econometric Policy Evaluation: A Critique. In: Brunner, K. and A. H. Meltzer (eds.), *The Phillips Curve and Labor Markets*. Amsterdam: North Holland.

McCallum, B. T. (1983) The Role of Overlapping-Generations Models in Monetary Economics. *Carnegie-Rochester Conference Series on Public Policy* 18: 9–44.

McCandless, G. T. Jr. and W. E. Weber (1995) Some Monetary Facts. *Federal Reserve Bank of Minneapolis Quarterly Review* 19: 2–11.

Machlup, F. (1943) Forced or Induced Saving: An Exploration into Its Synonyms and Homonyms. *Review of Economics and Statistics* 25: 26–39.

Mankiw, N. G. (1985) Small Menu Costs and Large Business Cycles. *Quarterly Journal of Economics* 100: 529–537.

Mankiw, N. G. and R. Reis (2002) Sticky Information versus Sticky Prices: A Proposal to Replace the New Keynesian Phillips Curve. *Quarterly Journal of Economics* 117: 1295–1328.

Mankiw, N. G. and L. H. Summers (1986) Money Demand and the Effects of Fiscal Policy. *Journal of Money, Credit, and Banking* 18: 415–429.

Mas-Colell, A., M. D. Whinston, and J. R. Green (1995) *Microeconomic Theory*. New York: Oxford University Press.

Mehra, R. and E. C. Prescott (1985) The Equity Premium. A Puzzle. *Journal of Monetary Economics* 15: 145–161.

Mendoza, E. G. (2010) Sudden Stops, Financial Crises, and Leverage. *American Economic Review* 100: 1941–1966.

Metzler, L. A. (1951) Wealth, Saving, and the Rate of Interest. *Journal of Political Economy* 59: 93–116.

Milani, F. (2007) Expectations, Learning and Macroeconomic Persistence. *Journal of Monetary Economics* 54: 2065–2082.

Mill, J. S. (1848) *Principles of Political Economy.* Cited from the 1987 reprint, Fairfield: Augustus M. Kelley.

Minsky, H. P. (1986) *Stabilizing an Unstable Economy.* Cited from the 2008 reprint, New York: McGraw Hill.

Mulligan, C. B. and X. Sala-i-Martin (2000) Extensive Margins and the Demand for Money at Low Interest Rates. *Journal of Political Economy* 108: 961–991.

Muth, J. F. (1960) Optimal Properties of Exponentially Weighted Forecasts. *Journal of the American Statistical Association* 55: 299–306.

Nerlove, M. (1958) Adaptive Expectations and Cobweb Phenomena. *Quarterly Journal of Economics* 72: 227–240.

Noguchi, Y. (1991) Land Prices and House Prices in Japan. In: Noguchi, Y. and J. Poterba (eds.), *Housing Markets in the U.S. and Japan.* Chicago: University of Chicago Press.

Oates, W. E. (1969) The Effects of Property Taxes and Local Public Spending on Property Values: An Empirical Study of Tax Capitalization and the Tiebout Hypothesis. *Journal of Political Economy* 77: 957–971.

Obstfeld, M. and K. S. Rogoff (1983) Speculative Hyperinflations in Maximizing Models: Can we Rule them Out? *Journal of Political Economy* 91: 675–687.

O'Driscoll, G. P. (1977) The Ricardian Nonequivalance Theorem. *Journal of Political Economy* 85: 207–210.

Ohlin, B. (1937) Some Notes on the Stockholm Theory of Savings and Investment I. *Economic Journal* 47: 53–69.

Parkin, M. (1998) Unemployment, Inflation, and Monetary Policy. *Canadian Journal of Economics* 31: 1003–1032.

Patinkin, D. (1958) Liquidity Preference and Loanable Funds: Stock and Flow Analysis. *Economica* 25: 300–318.

Patinkin, D. (1965) *Money, Interest and Prices.* 2nd edition, New York: Harper & Row.

Phelps, E. S. (1968) Money-Wage Dynamics and Labor Market Equilibrium. *Journal of Political Economy* 76: 678–711.

Phillips, A. W. (1958) The Relation between Unemployment and the Rate of Change of Money Wage Rates in the United Kingdom, 1861–1957. *Economica* 25: 283–299.

Phillips, C. A. (1920) *Bank Credit.* New York: Macmillan.

Pigou, A. C. (1943) The Classical Stationary State. *Economic Journal* 53: 343–351.

Piketty, T. and G. Zucman (2014) Capital is Back: Wealth-Income Ratios in Rich Countries, 1700–2010. *Quarterly Journal of Economics* 129: 1255–1310.

Poole, W. (1968) Commercial Bank Reserve Management in a Stochastic Model: Implications for Monetary Policy. *Journal of Finance* 23: 769–791.

Puviani, A. (1903) *Teoria della illusione Finanziaria.* Palermo: Sandron.

Reichenstein, W. (1987) The Impact of Money on Short Term Interest Rates. *Economic Inquiry* 25: 67–82.

Reinhart, C. M. (2012) The Return of Financial Repression. *Banque de France Financial Stability Review* 16: 37–48.

Reinhart, C. M. and K. S. Rogoff (2009) *This Time is Different. Eight Centuries of Financial Folly.* Princeton: Princeton University Press.

Ricciuti, R. (2003) Assessing Ricardian Equivalence. *Journal of Economic Surveys* 17: 55–78.

Richter, W. F. (1993) Intergenerational Risk Sharing and Social Security in an Economy with Land. *Journal of Economics,* S7: 91–103.

Ríos-Rull, J.-V. (1996) Life-Cycle Economies and Aggregate Fluctuations. *Review of Economic Studies* 63: 465–489.

Robertson, D. H. (1937) Alternative Theories of the Rate of Interest: Three Rejoinders. *Economic Journal* 47: 428–436.

Romer, C. D. (1992) What Ended the Great Depression? *Journal of Economic History* 52: 757–784.

Romer, D. (2012) *Advanced Macroeconomics.* New York: McGraw Hill.

Samuelson, P. A. and R. M. Solow (1960) Analytical Aspects of Anti-Inflation Policy. *American Economic Review* 50: 177–194.

Sargent, T. J. and B. D. Smith (1987) Irrelevance of Open Market Operations in Some Economies with Government Currency Being Dominated in Rate of Return. *American Economic Review* 77: 78–92.

Sargent, T. J. and N. Wallace (1981) Some Unpleasant Monetarist Arithmetic. *Federal Reserve Bank of Minneapolis Quarterly Review* 5: 1–17.

Shepherd, B. (2012) When Are Adaptive Expectations Rational? *Economics Letters* 115: 4–6.

Shiller, R. J. (1978) Rational Expectations and the Dynamic Structure of Macroeconomic Models. *Journal of Monetary Economics* 4: 1–44.

Shiller, R. J. (1981) Do Stock Prices Move too Much to Be Justified by Subsequent Changes in Dividends? *American Economic Review* 71: 421–436.

Sidrauski, M. (1967) Rational Choice and Patterns of Growth in a Monetary Economy. *American Economic Review* 57: 534–544.

Siegel, J. J. (2014) *Stocks for the Long Run.* 5th edition, New York: McGraw Hill.

Sinai, T. and N. S. Souleles (2005) Owner-Occupied Housing as a Hedge against Rent Risk. *Quarterly Journal of Economics* 120: 763–789.

Sinn, H. W. (1980) *Ökonomische Entscheidungen bei Ungewißheit.* Tübingen: Mohr.

Slobodyan, S. and R. Wouters (2012) Learning in an Estimated Medium-Scale DSGE Model. *Journal of Economic Dynamics and Control* 36: 26–46.

Smets, F. and R. Wouters (2007) Shocks and Frictions in US Business Cycles: A Bayesian DSGE Approach. *American Economic Review* 97: 586–606.

SNA (2008) *System of National Accounts*. Published jointly by Commission of the European Communities, International Monetary Fund, Organisation for Economic Co-operation and Development, United Nations, and World Bank. Brussels, Luxembourg, New York, Paris, Washington.

Solon, G., R. Barsky, and J. A. Parker (1994) Measuring the Cyclicality of Real Wages: How Important is the Composition Bias? *Quarterly Journal of Economics* 109: 1–25.

Stadelmann, D. and R. Eichenberger (2009) Debt Capitalization: A New Perspective on Ricardian Equivalence. CREMA working paper.

Stiglitz, J. E. (1969) A Re-Examination of the Modigliani-Miller Theorem. *American Economic Review* 59: 784–793.

Stiglitz, J. E. and B. C. N. Greenwald (2003) *Toward a New Paradigm in Monetary Economics*. Cambridge: Cambridge University Press.

Stiglitz, J. E. and A. Weiss (1981) Credit Rationing in Markets with Imperfect Information. *American Economic Review* 71: 393–410.

Stone, D. and W. T. Ziemba (1993) Land and Stock Prices in Japan. *Journal of Economic Perspectives* 7: 149–165.

Strongin, S. (1995) The Identification of Monetary Policy Disturbances: Explaining the Liquidity Puzzle. *Journal of Monetary Economics* 35: 463–497.

Summers, L. H. (2014) <http//: www.aeaweb.org/webcasts/2014/Austerity>.

Taylor, J. B. (1979) Staggered Wage Setting in a Macro Model. *American Economic Review* 69: 108–113.

Thornton, H. (1802) *An Enquiry into the Nature and Effects of the Paper Credit of Great Britain*. London: Hatchard.

Tobin, J. (1965) Money and Economic Growth. *Econometrica* 33: 671–684.

Tsiang, S. C. (1956) Liquidity Preference and Loanable Funds Theories, Multiplier and Velocity Analysis: A Synthesis. *American Economic Review* 46: 539–564.

Turgot, A. R. J. (1766) *Réflexion sur la formation et la distribution des richesses*. Paris: Par. M. Y. Translated as *Reflections on the Formation and Distribution of Riches*. New York 1898: Macmillan.

Turner, A. (2016) *Between Debt and the Devil*. Princeton: Princeton University Press.

Velde, F. R. (2009) Chronicle of a Deflation Unforetold. *Journal of Political Economy* 117: 591–634.

Wallace, N. (1980) The Overlapping Generations Model of Fiat Money. In: Kareken, J. H. and N. Wallace (eds.), *Models of Monetary Economies*. Minneapolis: Federal Reserve Bank of Minneapolis.

Wallace, N. (1981) A Modigliani-Miller Theorem for Open-Market Operations. *American Economic Review* 71: 267–274.

Wallich, H. (1984) Recent Techniques of Monetary Policy. *Federal Reserve Bank of Kansas City Economic Review*, May: 21–30.

Walsh, C. E. (2010) *Monetary Theory and Policy*. 3rd edition, Cambridge: MIT Press.

Weiss, L. (1980) The Effects of Money Supply on Economic Welfare in the Steady State. *Econometrica* 48: 565–576.

Wessel, D. (2014) *Central Banking after the Great Recession*. Washington: Brookings.

Weizsäcker, C.-C. (2014) Public Debt and Price Stability. *German Economic Review* 15: 42–61.

Wicksell, K. (1898) *Geldzins und Güterpreise*. Jena: Gustav Fischer. Cited from the English translation by R. F. Kahn (1965) *Interest and Prices*. New York: Augustus M. Kelley.

Woodford, M. (2003) *Interest and Prices*. Princeton: Princeton University Press.

Index